DATE DUE

JE 3'99			

591
Il   The Illustrated
        encyclopedia of Wildlife

        Vol. 14

DEMCO

THE ILLUSTRATED ENCYCLOPEDIA OF WILDLIFE

VOLUME 14

The Invertebrates

Part IV

Wildlife Consultant

MARY CORLISS PEARL, Ph. D.

Distributed by Encyclopaedia Britannica
Educational Corporation

Grey Castle Press

Published by Grey Castle Press, 1991

Distributed by Encyclopaedia Britannica Educational Corporation, 1991

THE ILLUSTRATED ENCYCLOPEDIA OF WILDLIFE
Volume 14: THE INVERTEBRATES—Part IV

Library of Congress Cataloging-in-Publication Data

The Illustrated encyclopedia of wildlife.
     p.   cm.
        Contents: v. 1–5. The mammals—v. 6–8. The birds —
v. 9. Reptiles and amphibians — v. 10. The fishes —
v. 11–14. The invertebrates — v. 15. The invertebrates
and index.
        ISBN 1–55905–052–7
        1. Zoology.
     QL45.2.I44 1991   90–3750
     591—dc20   CIP

ISBN 1–55905–052–7 (complete set)
       1–55905–050–0 (Volume 14)

Printed in Spain

Photo Credits
Photographs were supplied by *Archivio IGDA*: 2787, 2791t, 2813; (Donnini) 2754b, 2798; (M. Giovanoli) 2818b, 2826l, 2822; (C. Rives) 2722t, 2766; *Ardea*: (R. & V. Taylor) 2788, 2789; *G. Barletta*: 2742, 2746t, 2749, 2760, 2761, 2791b, 2793t, 2795, 2797, 2801; *C. Bevilacqua*: 2853t; *H. Chaumeton*: 2697, 2698, 2699, 2700, 2701, 2702, 2706, 2712, 2714, 2715, 2718b, 2719b, 2720, 2722b, 2728, 2734, 2737, 2738–2740, 2746b, 2747, 2748, 2750, 2751, 2755, 2758, 2763, 2768, 2769, 2771, 2776, 2777, 2785, 2802, 2808, 2831, 2835, 2836, 2839, 2840, 2841, 2842, 2846, 2848, 2850, 2858, 2860, 2861, 2867; (Bassot) 2730b; (Lanceau) 2862r, 2843; *Bruce Coleman*: (J. Burton) 2709, 2710, 2711, 2717, 2732, 2733; (N. Coleman) 2741; (A. Davies) 2814; (J. Foott) 2868; (E. Pott) 2716; (A. Power) 2725; (F. Sauer) 2815; *Jacana*: (Carre) 2730t, 2784b; (F. Danrigal) 2693, 2713, 2718t, 2721, 2754t, 2770, 2775b, 2778, 2810, 2811, 2825, 2828t; (J.L. Dubois) 2703; (R. Dulhoste) 2803, 2828, 2820; (C. De Klemm) 2708; (Konig) 2830, 2857; (J.M. Labat) 2828; (P. Laboute) 2744, 2745, 2775t, 2781, 2853b, 2862; (L. Lacoste) 2828; (J. Munschy) 2743; (K. Ross) 2809, 2827; (Rouxaime) 2812; (F. Winner) 2719t, 2727, 2735, 2780b, 2790, 2794, 2863; (S. Yoff) 2806; *A. Margiocco*: 2870; *NHPA*: (A. Bannister) 2829; (J. Carmichael) 2838, 2839; (G.J. Cambridge) 2752, 2753; (E.A. James) 2830t; (S. Johnson) 2731, 2806b; *Oxford Scientific Films*: (K. Atkinson) 2773; (G.I. Bernard) 2707; (G. Douwma) 2783; (D.G. Fox) 2756, 2757; (C. Milkins) 2705; (D.M. Shale) 2782; (F. Wertheim) 2792; *Planet Earth Pictures*: (P. Atkinson) 2793b; (P. David) 2864, 2865; (D. George) 2724, 2845, 2852; (J. Greenfield) 2796t; (A. Kerstitch) 2780tm; 2786, 2800t; (K. King) 2851; (K. Lucas) 2847, 2869; (L. Madin) 2784t; (P. Oliveira) 2859; (P. Scoones) 2871; (K. Vaughan) 2696.

FRONT COVER: A nudibranch sea slug (NHPA/B. Wood)

CONTENTS

SHAPELY SHELLS

Gastropods constitute the largest group of mollusks and display a wealth of shell shapes and life-styles. They range from sea-living limpets, cowries and whelks to lung-breathing land snails and slugs

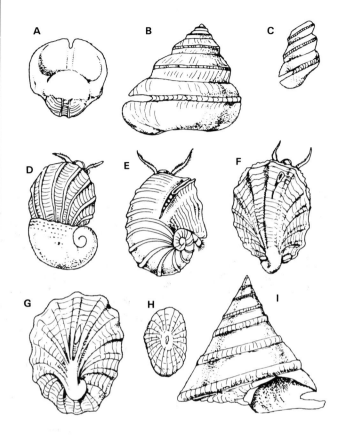

LEFT These drawings show the waste product outlets in both extinct and living species of prosobranchs (marine snails). In the shell of the now-extinct *Bellerophon bicarenus* (A), the snail's waste flowed out through a simple notch; in the fossil species *Pleurotomaria* (B) and *Murchisonia subsulcata* (C), waste passed out through a slit. The next series of drawings (D to H) follow the movement of a waste outlet in a keyhole limpet (genus *Fissurella*) as the animal ages. At first, the outlet slit is not visible (D). After the slit has emerged (E), it becomes a hole (F) that moves gradually (G) toward the center of the shell, so that the waste will pass out through the top (H). Living members of the prosobranch genus *Pleurotomaria* (I) either have a slit or a series of holes for removing waste. PAGE 2693 *Nassarius incrassatus* is a carnivorous marine snail (or prosobranch) that uses its tentacle-shaped siphon to sample the water in order to detect the presence of food.

The gastropods comprise the largest mollusk class, containing approximately 60,000 species. Gastropods are the most successful mollusk class, inhabiting a variety of environments in most regions of the world. They differ from other mollusks in two ways: their shells have evolved as spirals, and their bodies twist through 180 degrees. There are three subclasses of gastropods: the Prosobranchia (including marine snails); the Opisthobranchia (including sea slugs); and the Pulmonata (including land snails).

The subclass Prosobranchia has an ancient fossil history dating from the Cambrian period, 570 million years ago. It contains species of marine, freshwater and terrestrial gastropods and includes sea snails, limpets, winkles and cowries; aquatic species possess gills in their shell cavities. A greater abundance and variety of terrestrial prosobranchs occur in the tropical regions than in the temperate zones. Shells vary in shape and include the coiled forms of snails, the flattened cones of limpets and the tubular shells of certain warm-water species. All gastropod shell shapes evolved from the conical forms of the original, ancient prosobranch shell.

Mollusk shells: open, elongated or flat?

Through evolution, the prosobranchs adopted a flat, spiral shell that rests at right angles to the base of the foot. The modern shell is the result of thousands of years of evolution.

An open shell cone does not enable its owner to withdraw into it and therefore has only a limited protective function. On the other hand, a narrow, tall cone allows its owner to withdraw into it, but creates physiological problems; for example, it hinders water circulation within the shell, producing insufficient oxygen distribution through the body. Elongated shells make locomotion awkward, since they distance the center of gravity from the animal's foot. To circumvent such problems, prosobranchs' shells coiled into flat spirals, thereby avoiding the unsuitable open and elongated shells.

Twisted bodies

After the coiling of the shell, the second significant event in the evolutionary history of gastropods was a 180-degree twist of the body. The twisting caused part of the body, including the mantle and mantle cavity, the gills and the sexual and anal apertures to be carried at the front—the phenomenon occurs only during the larval phase of modern gastropods.

A twisted body has the following advantages for gastropods: since the shell cavity is at the front of the body, the mollusk can withdraw its head quickly when in danger; water circulation for respiration is greatly improved; after the respiratory organs moved (through evolution) from the back to the front end of the body, the prosobranch could directly "test" the oxygen content of water through its osphradium—a chemical receptive organ.

Serious functional problems, such as the expulsion of waste onto the head, offset the advantages of a twisted body. To avoid the discomfort of excrement on the head, mollusks of the superfamily Bellerophontaceae— the oldest-known gastropods—developed slits in the centers of their shells. The anus—located under the back edge of the slit—excretes waste matter, while water, entering on both sides of the head, washes through the slit, carrying excrement away.

Compact cones

The early spiral cones proved to be unsuited to prosobranchs since, as they grew with the mollusks, they became too large and cumbersome for easy locomotion. Consequently, prosobranchs developed the compact, conical spiral shells that characterize present-day gastropods. The new gastropod shells, however, unbalanced their owners and hindered mobility, since the entire weight of the shell had to be borne by one side of the body.

To compensate for the disadvantages of compact, conical shells, prosobranchs developed two adaptations—a partial untwisting of the body and an upward tilting of the shell to move the center of gravity over the middle line of the foot. As the shell evolved an upward tilt, its aperture modified so as to remain parallel to the foot, thereby enabling the prosobranchs to withdraw faster into their shells. The new position of the shell caused the first spiral of the shell to weigh heavily on the organs on the right side of the body, resulting in the disappearance of the right-hand gill, kidney and auricle of the heart; only prosobranchs of the order Archeogastropoda retained their right-hand organs. The new shell shape—a highly efficient product of centuries of evolution—allowed the class Gastropoda to expand, and this continues today.

The search for food

All prosobranchs have osphradiums—chemical receptive organs consisting of highly sensitive cells beside the gills. Osphradiums are highly developed in

BELOW The map shows the regions where aquatic mollusks are found, although they may occur over wider areas: Arctic (1); Labrador (2); Aleutian (3); Mediterranean (4); Boreal (5); Carolinian (6); Oregonian (7); Californian (8); Japanese (9); Indo-Pacific (10); Panamanian (11); Caribbean (12); West African (13); Magellanic (14); Australian (15); New Zealand (16); Peruvian (17); Argentinian (18).

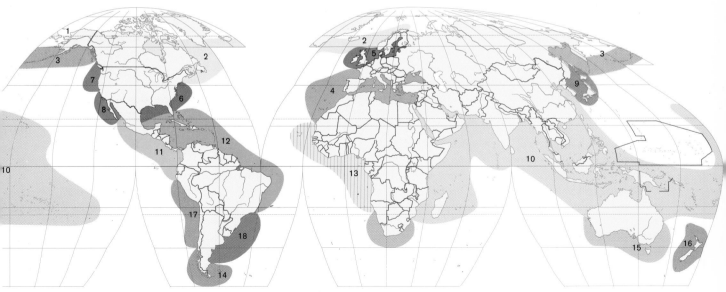

ABOVE A female common whelk may lay up to 2000 egg capsules, each measuring about an inch across. Every capsule contains a few hundred eggs, though only about 10-30 baby whelks finally emerge from their protective casing, having eaten the rest of the eggs.

prosobranch carnivores and scavengers, enabling them to locate carrion, organic chemicals and live prey from distances of up to 6 ft. 6 in.

Gastropods rely on their osphradiums to detect predators. Zoologists have demonstrated the use of the organs in experiments with gastropods of the herbivorous species *Strombus gigas*. In the presence of a predator, such as a whelk, gastropods in an aquarium react violently and attempt to flee from danger. In the absence of a predator, the experiment yields the same results if water that has merely been in contact with a predator is introduced into the aquarium.

Reproduction

Reproductive methods vary between prosobranch species. Although most prosobranchs have clearly differing sexes, several species are hermaphroditic, their members containing both male and female reproductive organs.

In some primitive groups, such as the limpets, fertilization takes place externally—the prosobranchs simply deposit their eggs and sperm in the water. External fertilization in mollusks is wasteful, since many eggs and sperm are lost without being fertilized. Consequently, it requires the production of huge quantities of eggs and sperm in order to ensure survival of the species. To allow the maximum chance of fertilization, many prosobranchs emit special chemical substances called pheromones that stimulate the simultaneous release of eggs or sperm in other members of their species.

Marine prosobranchs

Marine prosobranchs are distributed at certain levels within the sea. Each species inhabits a specific depth and only a few live equally well in both shallow and deep water.

The uppermost level of marine prosobranch habitation is the supralittoral level—a region above the high-water mark. The supralittoral level receives

MOLLUSKS CLASSIFICATION: 4

Slugs, snails and limpets (1)

The class Gastropoda is the largest class within the phylum Mollusca and consists of some 60,000 species of slugs, snails and limpets (broadly called gastropods). They usually have single, coiled shells and occur either on land or in sea or freshwater. The class Gastropoda is broken into three subclasses: the Prosobranchia (prosobranchs) containing mostly marine snails; the Opisthobranchia (opisthobranchs, such as sea slugs); and the Pulmonata (pulmonates, including land snails).

Prosobranchs

The prosobranchs of the subclass Prosobranchia are divided into three orders: the Archeogastropoda; the Mesogastropoda; and the Neogastropoda.

Within the order Archeogastropoda are six superfamilies. The Pleurotomariacea contains the families Pleurotomariidae with about 12 species of extremely primitive prosobranchs (the "slit shells") such as *Pleurotomaria africana*; and the Haliotidae (abalones) containing *Haliotis pourtalesii* of the North Atlantic coast of North America, and *H. tubercolata* of Europe's Atlantic coast. The superfamily Fissurellacea consists of the keyhole limpets, such as *Diodora graeca* of Portuguese waters, and *D. dysoni*, a shallow-water species from the Caribbean, Florida and Brazil.

The third superfamily in the order Archeogastropoda is the Patellacea, which contains five families of limpets, including the Acmaeidae (with about 100 species, such as *Lottia gigantea* of California); the Patellidae (true limpets) containing some 400 species, such as *Patella mexicana*, the Australian wide-ribbed limpet, *P. laticostata*, and the common European limpet, *P. vulgata*; and the Bathysciadiidae, which has only two species—*Bathysciadium costulatum* of the deep waters around the Azores in the Atlantic Ocean, and *Bonus petrochenkoi* occurring 30,000 ft. down in two Pacific Ocean trenches. (See the next classification box (5) for the remaining superfamilies.)

ABOVE Abalones, such as the species *Haliotis tuberculata* seen here, are mollusks famed for the smooth, iridescent substance known as mother-of-pearl that forms the shell's inner lining. The animal is a vegetarian, feeding on seaweed that it finds using the fringe of sensory tentacles running around its body. The oval holes on the outer edge of the shell are outlets for the water that has been drawn into the body in order to extract oxygen.

moisture from sea spray, but is reached by waves rarely and usually only during high tides at the equinoxes. Although the supralittoral level is a somewhat inhospitable environment for land organisms, it is home to several prosobranch species.

The littoral level lies between the high- and low-tide marks, while the sublittoral level begins below it and extends toward the edge of the continental shelf, to the limits of survival of algae. The deepest levels, where no light penetrates, are the bathyal level, between the surface and a depth of 6500 ft.; the abyssal level, between 6500 and 20,000 ft.; and the hadal level, in the furthest depths of the ocean.

Taxonomy

The prosobranchs are divided into three orders: the Archeogastropoda, the Mesogastropoda and the

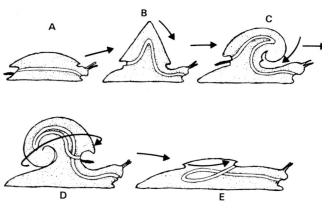

TOP The slit limpet of the genus *Emarginula* is one of the less advanced prosobranchs, having two gills like those of its ancient ancestors, rather than the single gill of more highly evolved gastropods such as whelks and winkles.
ABOVE The evolution of the mollusk shell from an ancestral gastropod. The shell began as a simple dorsal plate (A), then evolved into a cone (B), allowing the animal to withdraw inside to avoid predators. The spiraling of the shell allowed the snail to withdraw even further (C). The body then went through a 180-degree turn (D), after which the shell took on many shapes. Some advanced gastropods (the pulmonates) with absent or reduced shells are called slugs (E).

Neogastropoda. The archeogastropods derive their name from their primitive characteristics (from the Greek *arkhaois* meaning "ancient"). There are six superfamilies within the order. Members of the superfamily Pleurotomariacea have retained a pair of gills, two auricles of the heart and two kidneys—a condition that is characteristic of nearly all the archeogastropods. Only the more highly developed forms have lost their right gills and their right kidneys.

The slit shells

The superfamily Pleurotomariacea contains the most primitive of all the gastropods. The group was widely distributed during the Palaeozoic period (570-260 million years ago), but is now thought to be nearly extinct. There are only about 12 species in existence today. They live at great depths in the Caribbean, the Far East and in the seas around South Africa.

Pleurotomaria africana displays one of the characteristic features of the superfamily. It has a slit in its shell which begins at its peristoma (the entrance of the shell) and continues some distance into the shell. The slit serves to direct expelled waste material away from the gastropod's head. Its large, conical shell is wider at the base than at the tip. It is covered in thin growth lines that mark the stages of the animal's growth. It lives on soft seabeds in deep waters. The first specimen was fished in deep waters off the coast of South Africa in 1931. No more than 10 specimens of this living fossil have been discovered.

Abalones

The family Haliotidae in the superfamily Pleurotomariacea contains a group of mollusks known as abalones. Instead of a slit, their shells have a series of holes that serve the same purpose as the slit—discharging waste materials. The shells of members of the genus *Haliotis* form a flat helix or screw-shaped coil. The last five or six holes serve as a passageway for water to pass through, and the hole furthest from the abalone's head functions as the exhalant canal. Abalones' shells have a wide opening at the base, but the abalones are unable to hide themselves inside it to escape predators. The operculum (a lid that is located on the upper surface of the foot of many gastropods) disappears during their larval stage. Abalones live exclusively on hard substrates, where, if danger threatens, they attach themselves firmly to rocks.

The abalone, *Haliotis tubercolata*, which commonly occurs on the European Atlantic coast, and *H. lamellosa*, considered to be the Mediterranean variety of the former, shun the daylight. They hide in cracks in the rocks or under stones. At night, they leave their refuge and explore the rocks, using their sensory organs, which protrude from the edges of their shells and from the first four or five holes. They feed by scratching at the rocks with their toothed radulas. They remove both the algae that covers the surface of the rocks and the organic waste mixed in with it.

Keyhole limpets

The superfamily Fissurellacea, or keyhole limpets, contains a group of mollusks that have shells that resemble flattened shields. Their shell slits are reduced to a slight incision, known as an apical opening. At first, the apical opening is situated on the side of the keyhole limpet's shell, but it moves to a central position as the shell grows. The family Fissurellidae comprises three genera. Members of the genus *Emarginula* live in warm, temperate seas. The other two genera, *Diodora* and *Fissurella*, occur over a far wider area. However, all keyhole limpets have a similar way of life. They live in a rocky environment, and they all have a herbivorous diet.

ABOVE *Diodora apertura*, seen here creeping over seabed rocks on its large and muscular foot, is a species of keyhole limpet. Named for the keyhole-shaped opening at the top of its shell, it feeds on certain species of starfishes.

The shell of *Diodora graeca*, a Portuguese keyhole limpet, has 20 main ribs that run from its base to its tip. Other less prominent ribs, and 12 concentric rings, alternate among them. The inside of the shell is white, and the exterior is whitish, green or red, speckled with brown or white markings. *D. graeca* swims close to the surface of the water where the light encourages the growth of the algae and plants on which it feeds. It generally remains static and limits itself to short excursions, returning each time to its hiding place—usually a crevice in a rock or small, shallow hollow. The behavior of keyhole limpets is similar to that of the true limpets (to which they are closely related). Both occur in the same areas, but while the true limpet is able to live outside the water for fairly long periods of time, the keyhole limpet, *D. graeca*, cannot survive outside the water.

Although the apical opening (shell slit) expels waste, it does not provide sufficient protection to prevent the keyhole limpet from drying out once it is outside the water. Keyhole limpets are prey for starfishes, and *D.*

MOLLUSKS CLASSIFICATION: 5

Slugs, snails and limpets (2)

The final three superfamilies within the prosobranch order, Archeogastropoda, are the Cocculinacea; the Trochacea; and the Neritacea. The Trochacea contains seven families, including the Trochidae (top shells) with such species as the giant top shell, *Trochus niloticus*, the one-toothed top shell, *Monodonta turbinata*, and Gmelin's top shell, *Gibbula fanulum*, of European waters; and the Turbinidae (turban shells), which has the tapestry turban, *Turbo petholatus*, and the large green snail, *T. marmoratus*, of the Indian and Pacific oceans. The superfamily Neritacea has six families, including the Neritidae (species such as the green-tongued nerite, *Nerita textilis*, and the long-spined nerite, *Theodoxus longispina*, of freshwater rivers and lakes); and the Helicinidae whose members, such as the queen viana, *Viana regina*, of Cuba, have colonized dry land.

ABOVE In limpets of the family Patellidae, the embryonic shell is twisted into a clockwise spiral, but this is lost as the limpets mature. Only a few species, such as the blue peacock limpet, *Patina pellucida* (seen here), retain a slight spiral effect at the tops of their shells when mature. The coloring of this species, which measures just an inch long, is brightest when the limpet is young.

aspera, a species of the Pacific coast of North America, has a curious strategy for defending itself, which has not yet been properly analyzed. The keyhole limpet senses the approach of a starfish by recognizing certain substances emitted by the predator. It raises its shell as far as possible from the ground, and extends a fold of its mantle over itself until it is covered. The starfish, failing to recognize the prey, moves away.

Limpets

The superfamily Patellacea contains five families of limpets that live attached to rocks in shallow water, and on beaches up to the highest point reached by the spray. They attach themselves firmly to the substrate where they appear to be almost embedded. They create this effect by digging a niche for themselves, where they spend most of their time.

SHAPELY SHELLS

True limpets

The 400 or so species that belong to the true limpet family Patellidae occur in almost every sea. The largest living limpet, *Patella mexicana,* lives on the Pacific coast of North America, as far south as Patagonia in South America and the Caribbean. Other species are wide-ranging: the Australian wide-ribbed limpet inhabits the southwest coast of Australia; the snail limpet occurs in the seas south of Africa; the blue limpet lives in the waters around the Mediterranean and the subspecies *P. pontica* inhabits the Black sea.

Limpet species can be identified by the amount of time they spend underwater and by their position on the coastal rocks. In the temperate European regions, for example, the same coasts may contain specimens of the common European limpet, *Patella vulgata,* at upper levels, and *Patella aspera* at lower levels. Patellid limpets are able to withstand long exposure to the sun and rain. Species of the genus *Patella* have branchial filaments on the edges of their mantles, enabling them to breathe out of water.

The waterline is subject to constant environmental change, and only the most adaptable species can tolerate such conditions. Many patellid limpets move

ABOVE **Common limpets often fall prey to starfishes. Like all limpet species, the common limpet has powerful retractor muscles that pull its protective shell firmly against rock surfaces.**

Many starfishes, however, are strong enough to pry the shell open. Common limpets inhabit the seas of western Europe.
BELOW **The distribution of several limpet species of the family Patellidae.**

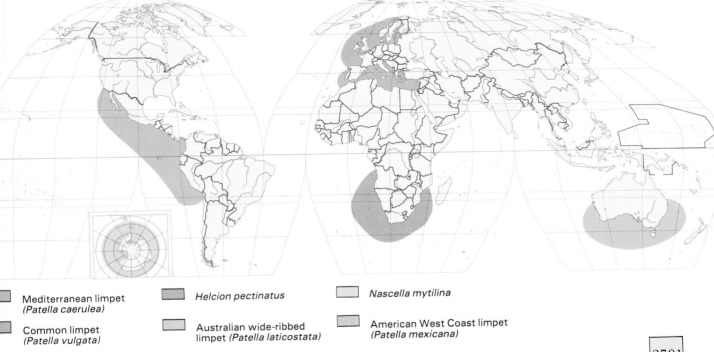

▨	Mediterranean limpet (Patella caerulea)
▨	Common limpet (Patella vulgata)
▨	Helcion pectinatus
▨	Australian wide-ribbed limpet (Patella laticostata)
▨	Nascella mytilina
▨	American West Coast limpet (Patella mexicana)

ABOVE The top shell limpet is a common inhabitant of the rocky coasts of northern and central Europe. Water—containing life-giving oxygen—enters the creature's shell cavity on the left side of its head.

reducing its chances of being eaten by a predator or of drying out.

Limpets of the family Lepetidae occur in the cold northern seas, and also in the Antarctic. They are hermaphroditic and occur both in the shallow coastal waters and at depths down to 4000 ft.

The family Bathysciadiidae of the superfamily Patellacea contains only two species of small, rare, deep-sea limpets: *Bathysciadium costulatum* occurs in the deep waters that surround the Azores in the Atlantic Ocean; and *Bonus petrochenkoi* lives in the Kuril-Kamchatka and Tonga trenches in the Pacific Ocean, at depths over 30,000 ft. Food is scarce at these depths and the limpets are thought to feed on the "beaks" of dead squids and other cephalopods.

Top shells

The superfamily Trochacea comprises seven families of marine snails, including the family Trochidae. Known as "spinning tops" or top shells, they have flat-bottomed, conical shells, containing a hole of varying dimensions, called the umbilicus. The hundred or so species within the superfamily occur in nearly every sea in the world. *Monodonta concamerata* populates the coasts of Australia, while the giant top shell, whose base may be as wide as 8 in., inhabits the waters of the Pacific. Because of their highly decorated shells, giant top shells have been ruthlessly hunted and made into bracelets or decorative ornaments.

European varieties

Many species of top shell, such as the one-toothed top shell, inhabit European waters. The one-toothed top shell has a small, robust shell with a flattened base and no umbilicus. Its shell has between six and nine wide, concentric lobes. The central axis, or columella, of its shell has a tooth in the center (a characteristic feature of top shells belonging to the genus *Monodonata*). The one-toothed top shell is yellow, gray or green in color and is decorated with red, violet, brown or black spots. It often climbs out of the water onto cement structures or rocks.

A daily migration

Daily migration frequently occurs among the animals of the waterline and shallow coastal waters. It enables the animals to reach food sources and to escape from predators such as birds. While the limpets

into estuaries, sometimes almost as far as freshwater. True limpets of the genus *Patella* dig a niche for themselves in the softer rocks by secreting chemicals and by rasping away the surface of the rocks. The dimensions of the niche match the contours of their shells, enabling the limpets to isolate themselves from the outside world.

Homing limpets

True limpets feed at night, traveling distances of up to 65 in. in search of food. They always leave a trail of mucus, enabling them to return before daylight to the same niche they left at nightfall. Some species are particularly sensitive to chemicals, enabling them to recognize their own trail of mucus. They are able to tell it apart from trails left by other members of the same species—a phenomenon known as "homing." The mucus trails of territorial species of homing limpet stimulate the growth of algae on which the limpets feed. By making its home near to a source of food, the limpet needs to move around less often,

are nocturnal, most top shells are active only in the daytime. But *Gibbula cineraria* passes the daylight hours hidden under stones and only becomes mobile at twilight, when it climbs to the top of a submerged rock in search of algae.

Although the intensity of the light serves as the animal's stimulus, top shells appear to use an "internal clock"—a mechanism that informs them when to start migrating without external stimuli. *Gibbula cineraria* is the only member of the genus to undertake these nightly migrations. The other species remain on the seabed or in the shelter of rocks, only venturing out to feed during the day.

Turban shells

The family Turbinidae contains the turban shells. The shells of the species belonging to the tropical genus *Turbo* are often used to make jewelry. They are hunted because of the brilliant shades of their shell lining. Known as mother-of-pearl, it is revealed by removing the outer layer or periostracum of the shells. Shells that are hunted for their mother-of-pearl include species from the Indian and Pacific oceans, such as the tapestry turban and the large green snail.

ABOVE **The one-toothed top shell, of the prosobranch species** *Monodonta lineata,* **lives inside cracks in rocks and coral reefs in the seas of Europe. It often climbs out of the water to rest on man-made structures or rock surfaces. When in danger,** *M. lineata* **withdraws completely inside its shell and closes the entrance with its** protective lid, or operculum. Unlike limpets, the one-toothed top shell is unable to attach itself to the substrate with enough force to prevent it from being washed away by the waves.
BELOW **The worldwide distribution of the major top shell species in the genus** *Calliostoma* **within the family Trochidae.**

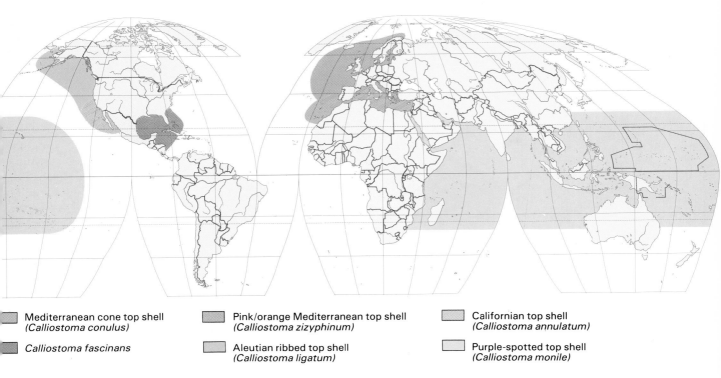

	Mediterranean cone top shell (*Calliostoma conulus*)		Pink/orange Mediterranean top shell (*Calliostoma zizyphinum*)		Californian top shell (*Calliostoma annulatum*)
	Calliostoma fascinans		Aleutian ribbed top shell (*Calliostoma ligatum*)		Purple-spotted top shell (*Calliostoma monile*)

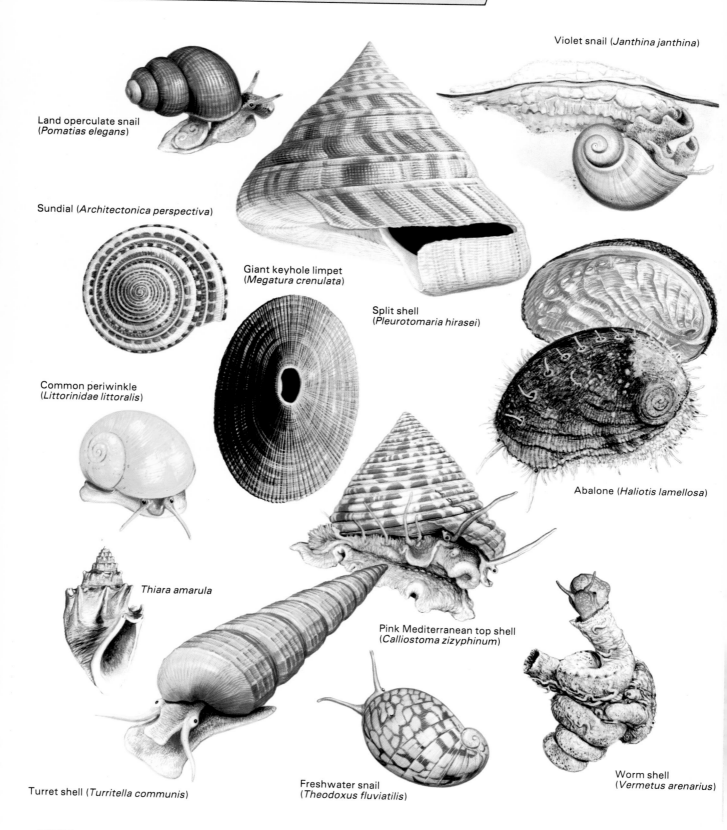

Land operculate snail
(*Pomatias elegans*)

Violet snail (*Janthina janthina*)

Sundial (*Architectonica perspectiva*)

Giant keyhole limpet
(*Megatura crenulata*)

Split shell
(*Pleurotomaria hirasei*)

Common periwinkle
(*Littorinidae littoralis*)

Abalone (*Haliotis lamellosa*)

Thiara amarula

Pink Mediterranean top shell
(*Calliostoma zizyphinum*)

Worm shell
(*Vermetus arenarius*)

Turret shell (*Turritella communis*)

Freshwater snail
(*Theodoxus fluviatilis*)

2704

Nerites

The superfamily Neritacea has six families including the family Neritidae, or nerites. They are of particular evolutionary and ecological significance because they are examples of the earliest species to have conquered land and freshwater environments. The nerites are able to retain the concentration of liquids in their bodies despite the environment, enabling them to venture out of the sea. The chameleon nerite spends long periods of time out of the water.

The green-tongued nerite and the South African coiled nerite occur widely in the Indo-Pacific and can even tolerate freshwater. The small, tessellate nerite reaches only an inch in diameter. Its spiral shell has wide, flat, ribbed markings. Its pear-shaped mantle opening widens at the bottom, but is small for a member of the family. Marked folds are present on its columella (central axis) and on the labial (lip) side of its shell. Its white lobes are covered with black dashes. Its mantle opening is also white, while the edge of its labia has a black-and-white chequered pattern.

Living in freshwater

Nerites of the genus *Theodoxus* (family Neritidae) are completely covered by the last coils of their shells, which are enormous when compared with the rest of the coils. They move slowly over the stones and submerged rocks of rivers and lakes, feeding on detritus and small organisms, and scraping the surface of aquatic vegetation.

In order to colonize freshwater, species of the genus *Theodoxus* have developed special adaptations, making them among the most highly evolved groups of archeogastropods. They have acquired new abilities or osmotic regulation (the control of internal body fluids), and have modified their reproductive behavior. *Theodoxus* species have adopted internal fertilization. They attach their fertilized eggs to the substrate, and the young emerge already able to crawl around and feed.

A terrestrial life-style

Members of the family Hydrocenidae have adapted to life on dry land. *Hydrocena cattaroensis* owes its name to an area of the Dalmatian coast called Cattaro, where it lives in great numbers. Members of the genus *Hydrocena* live in moist places, often in the cracks of rocks. They have lost their gills or branchiae, and are able to absorb oxygen directly from the air. Dense

ABOVE **A nerite winkle,**
Theodoxus fluviatilis,
crawls over a stone,
guided by its light-
sensitive tentacles
and eyes. The winkle
processes visual
information in several
masses of nerve tissue,
or ganglia.

networks of thin vessels have transformed their mantle cavities into lungs.

Like the hydrocenids, helicinids have also conquered dry land. They occur mainly in Central America, the West Indies, the Indo-Pacific islands, the East Indies and parts of eastern Asia and Australia. One species, the queen viana, lives in trees on the island of Cuba.

Adaptations to a life on land

Land-dwelling nerites, such as hydrocenids and helicinids, share their terrestrial environment with the much more numerous pulmonates, commonly called snails and slugs. Adapting to life on dry land has had a profound influence on the way their bodies work. The main changes have been in respiration, the maintenance of internal body fluids (in osmotic balance or osmolarity), metabolizing calcium and reproduction.

The evolution of a kind of lung (in place of their mantle cavities) has enabled terrestrial mollusks to breathe air directly. However, to prevent themselves from drying out, they have to make careful use of the water in their surroundings, or the water that they absorb from rain.

ABOVE A periwinkle feeds on algae and decaying matter on the seabed. It breaks down food with its muscular mouthparts and strong teeth; the radula — a long, rasping organ — contains the teeth. Periwinkles have long guts and spacious stomachs for storing bulky food substances.

A step forward in evolution

The order Mesogastropoda is the second order within the subclass Prosobranchia. It consists of 17 superfamilies and 10,000 species that are, in many respects, highly evolved. As a result of a twisting of their internal organs, their gills, chemoreceptors and kidneys on the right side have all disappeared, leaving only the corresponding organs on the left side. The right-hand chamber, or atrium, of the heart has also disappeared, leaving only one atrium and one ventricle. The nervous systems of all mollusks in the order have become concentrated in well-defined ganglia or nerve centers, connected by a few main nerves.

Most families in the order Mesogastropoda are marine, but there are many freshwater and some terrestrial species as well. The superfamily Viviparacea, which consists of three families, includes mainly freshwater species. They live in slow-moving water on the muddy bottoms of ponds and canals or among the vegetation along the banks. For example, Lister's river snail, which belongs to the family Viviparidae, lives along the banks of slow-moving streams and feeds on organic particles and other gastropods or immature bivalves in the water.

When there is insufficient oxygen in the deeper layers of the water, Lister's river snail is compelled to stay near the surface and supplement its diet with another feeding technique. It keeps its operculum — which normally covers the opening of the shell — slightly ajar, and remains on the same spot while water enters its mantle cavity. The mollusk moves its gill filaments, and they filter out and collect microorganisms from the water such as protozoans, unicellular algae and suspended particles of food. The collected material flows into an area inside the mollusk's mouth that is rich in mucus secretions.

The migrations of periwinkles

The superfamily Littorinacea includes three terrestrial families — the Pomatiasidae, Chondropomidae and Eatoniellidae — and two marine ones — the Lacunidae and Littorinidae. The periwinkles of the genus *Littorina* are some of the most common mollusks to be found on the shoreline on both sides of the Atlantic. In the United States the first specimen was discovered in 1868, and by 1880 periwinkles had

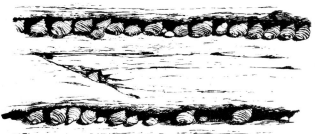

ABOVE **Common periwinkles,** *Littorina littorea,* **are a common sight on the Devon coast. The creatures inhabit rocky shores all over the world and feed on seaweed. Common periwinkles are edible and, consequently, many are** caught for sale to restaurants.
LEFT **At low tide, periwinkles crowd into every available crevice in the rocks to protect their bodies from dehydration and attack from predators.**

become the most common gastropods on the Massachusetts, New England, coast.

There are four main species of periwinkle on the rocky coasts of northern Europe—the British periwinkle, the northern rough periwinkle, the northwest European periwinkle and the common winkle. The British periwinkle is found on the inner shorelines and the others become gradually more prevalent—in the order listed—with increasing distance from the shore.

The British periwinkle is the species of periwinkle that most easily tolerates life out of the water—it can stay on dry land for several months. However, when the sun is at its hottest, it stops feeding on its diet of minute algae and diatoms and hides in cracks in the rocks. To reduce loss of water by evaporation, it attaches itself to the rock wall by means of a mucus secretion that solidifies upon contact with the air.

Cyclical migrations

The common winkle exhibits an interesting pattern of behavior known as a circadian migration—movements that vary according to time of day. During the hours of daylight, the mollusk stays on the seabed, hidden in the cracks of rocks or beneath stones and sheltered from possible predators. It moves only at nightfall, when it rises up to the surface of the water or comes onto dry land in search of food.

Researchers have attempted to reproduce the common winkle's migration cycles in laboratory conditions—putting them first in a darkened room and then in an environment that is constantly illuminated. Regardless of the amount of light in the laboratory, winkles continued to behave in the way that they would have done had they been at sea. It appears, therefore, that the common winkle possesses

ABOVE Most land mollusks travel by sending waves of muscle contractions along their feet. The land operculate snail, *Pomatia elegans*, however, is exceptional in that it "walks" with an almost bipedal gait. The snail sets up a crawling motion by moving the left side of its foot and immediately following the action through with its right side.
FAR RIGHT Rough periwinkles, *Littorina saxatilis*, feed on seaweed (channel wrack) attached to rock covered with black lichen. The species lives on both sides of the Atlantic.
PAGES 2710-2711 During daylight hours, yellow-shelled flat periwinkles, *Littorina littoralis*, hide beneath stones and in rock crevices on the seabed. At night, however, they venture onto the beach in search of food (this photograph was taken at night under artificial light).

periwinkles to avoid attacks by birds that are only active during the day.

Mucus trails

Many winkles and periwinkles follow trails of mucus left by other members of their species. The phenomenon has been closely studied in the marsh periwinkle, a common species on the coasts of Florida. There, processions of 15-20 individuals, perfectly aligned one behind the other, often move over the rocks.

Various theories have been put forward to explain their processional behavior. All crawling mollusks rely on a mucus secretion to move over the substrate. It takes energy to produce the secretion, so it is reasonable to suggest that winkles and periwinkles may prefer to follow the trail left by another mollusk in order to conserve some of their own energy.

Terrestrial tendency

Members of the superfamily Littorinacea have a tendency to leave the water and venture onto dry land. The British periwinkle could, indeed, be considered a terrestrial species. The only time that it must descend to the outer shoreline is during reproduction, so that it can give birth to its young.

The Mediterranean land winkle offers the best example of the terrestrial tendency. It requires soil with a fairly high calcium content, where it spends almost the entire day inside a small tunnel of soil that it digs under the shelter of a stone or tree trunk. Toward evening, when the temperature is lower and the air more humid, it emerges to search for food.

Being dependent on the climate, land-dwelling mollusks that inhabit temperate regions can only be active above ground at certain times of the year. Species of the genus *Pomatia*, for example, become inactive and bury themselves during particularly cold or dry spells. The mollusks considerably reduce their metabolism to survive, slowing down their heartbeats from a normal rate of 50 beats per minute to as little as two to four beats per minute.

The favorite habitat—and main diet—of the land-dwelling species of *Pomatia* consists of loose soil with plenty of decaying vegetation and dead leaves. The mollusks stay out of water even when they reproduce. On warm and humid days, the females deposit their eggs just below the surface, covering each one with a thin layer of earth.

an internal rhythm that works independently of external stimuli—a biological clock that tells the animal when to crawl out of the water and when to descend to the seabed.

The purpose of the common winkle's migratory behavior is not clear, but only strong selective pressure could have led to its evolution. In other words, in the course of evolution, natural selection must have favored a species that behaved in a specific way and selected it over others. It has been suggested that the migratory behavior allows winkles and

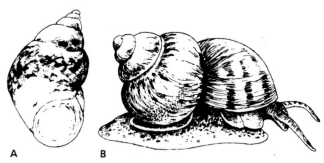

A   B

TOP Mesogastropods of the species *Hydrobia jenkisi* allow themselves to be swept to new feeding grounds with each tide. They feed on organic material deposited in muddy intertidal zones along the coasts of Europe. As many as 30,000 *Hydrobia* mollusks can occupy one square yard of beach.

ABOVE Two freshwater prosobranchs: *Bithynia tentaculata* (A) has a shell form typical of many immature gastropods, while half the mass of *Viviparus viviparus's* shell (B) consists of its last whorl.

Slugs, snails and limpets (3)

The order Mesogastropoda—the second order in the gastropod subclass Prosobranchia—contains 10,000 species in 17 superfamilies, of which 13 are dealt with in the chapter. The six superfamilies covered in this classification box are the Viviparacea, Littorinacea, Rissoacea, Heterogastropoda, Cerithiacea and Epitoniacea. The superfamily Viviparacea contains Lister's river snail, *Viviparus contectus*, in the family Viviparidae and the family Ampullariidae with the genus *Pila*. The superfamily Littorinacea includes the family Littorinidae (periwinkles), containing such species as the British periwinkle, *Littorina neritoides*, the northern rough periwinkle, *L. saxatilis,* the common winkle, *L. littorea,* and the Mediterranean land winkle, *Pomatias elegans*.

The superfamily Rissoacea has 25 families of small fresh and brackish water species. The families include the Hydrobiidae (spire snails, including Jenkins' spire shell, *Potamopyrgus jenkinsi,* and the faucet snail, *Bithynia tentaculata,* of Europe, Asia Minor and the southern USA); and the Truncatellidae which contains the subcylindrical truncatella, *Truncatella subscylindrica.* In the superfamily Heterogastropoda, the family Architectonicidae contains elegantly shelled species such as Reeve's sundial, *Architectonica reevi,* of Australia and New Zealand, the sundial, *A. perspectiva,* of Southeast Asia, and the beaded sundial, *A. nobilis,* of Caribbean waters; while the family Caecidae contains the 0.08-in.-long tusk-shelled caecid, *Caecum glabrum.*

The 15 families of the superfamily Cerithiacea include the Turritellidae (small turret shells) containing the gregarious turret shell, *Turritella communis,* of Europe; the Vermetidae (worm shells) with the Mediterranean worm shell, *Serpulorbis arenaria*; the Cerithiidae (horn shells) and the Triphoridae (sinistral miniature horn shells). The superfamily Epitoniacea includes the families Janthinidae (violet snails) and Epitoniidae (wentletraps, such as the precious wentletrap *Epitonium scalare.* (See classification boxes 7 and 8 for the remaining mesogastropodan superfamilies.)

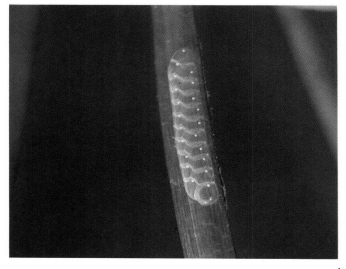

Spire shells

The superfamily Rissoacea comprises 25 families of minute mesogastropods that live in fresh or brackish waters, as well as on land. *Hydrobia ulvae,* a member of the family Hydrobiidae, or spire shells, has been studied at length, both because of its abundance (up to 60,000 individuals per square yard occur in some brackish lagoons) and because of its interesting behavioral patterns. Members of the genus *Hydrobia* form large populations on the mudbanks of brackish pools and estuaries, and are often the main diet of birds and fishes. When the high tide covers the mudbanks, hydrobiids allow themselves to be carried by the advancing water. Using mucous filaments, secreted by glands in their feet, they adhere themselves to the surface film of the water. The filaments also serve to capture the microorganisms on which the mollusks feed. When the tide goes out again, the hydrobiids remain on the mud, far away from their starting point.

By using this method of passive transport, hydrobiids are able to colonize vast areas in a short time. Wherever the ground is damp enough, they move around out of the water, feeding on the microorganisms and unicellular algae that they find in the mud or on green algae. When the mud dries out, the hydrobiids become less active. Burying themselves beneath the surface, they await the next high tide, which signals a new cycle of activity.

From salt- to freshwater

The small Jenkins' spire shell of the genus *Potamopyrgus* also belongs to the family Hydrobiidae. Originally from New Zealand, it was found for the first time in England in 1889, in a brackish marsh near the Thames, and in 1893 it appeared in freshwater. Within a few decades, this species had colonized large parts of Great Britain and other countries of northern Europe. It provides one of the few known examples of a saltwater species that has colonized freshwater. Spire shells of the genus *Potamopyrgus* reach new areas by clinging to the feet and beaks of birds that transport them great distances.

The Jenkins' spire shell species contains no males. All the individuals are female, and they reproduce by parthenogenesis. They incubate the eggs in pouches inside their mantle cavities until they develop into immature adults. The young Jenkins' spire shells

ABOVE The prosobranch species *Bithynia tentaculata* lays its eggs on the stems of water plants. Many mollusk species have completely lost their larval stage, since their large-yolked eggs provide enough nutrition to sustain the embryos until they reach adulthood.

reach full maturity in four to five months, when they measure about 0.16-0.2 in. in length. Apart from the species *Campeloma rufum* and members of the family Melanidae, there are no other known groups of parthenogenetic prosobranchs.

Jenkins' spire shells inhabit gently flowing streams where they may be found on stones, on algae or buried just under the surface of the mud. If environmental conditions are favorable for their development, they reproduce in large numbers, providing a plentiful source of food for various fishes.

The faucet snail

The faucet snail, *Bithynia tentaculata,* is a hydrobiid that occurs in the stagnant waters of Europe, the southern USA and Asia Minor. It has a smooth, conical, robust shell that reaches a maximum length of 0.6 in. Its oval-shaped shell opening can be closed by a tough calcareous operculum. The operculum is slightly larger than the opening itself, and even when the faucet snail has completely withdrawn into its shell, it cannot pull its operculum inside.

The faucet snail feeds on the detritus and plants that it gathers with its long proboscis. During the winter, when algae is scarce, the faucet snail withdraws to deeper waters. When there is a shortage of plants, it feeds on microorganisms such as protozoa, unicellular algae and other small particles of food that hang suspended in the water. The food enters the

MOLLUSK COMMUNICATION
— A CHEMICAL LANGUAGE —

In the higher primates, such as humans, the organs that detect chemical messages (taste and smell) are less well developed than the visual organs or eyes. In the mollusks, however, the organs that analyze chemical stimuli are more advanced than the eyes. Animals that live in the sediment-filled waters on the seabed would be at a disadvantage if they had to rely on their sight. By sensing the chemicals in their surroundings, they are aware of activity in their immediate area, no matter how murky the water.

The prosobranchs (limpets, winkles, cowries and whelks etc.) have developed their chemical receptivity to a high degree, and some, such as the conch of the family Strombidae, also have well-developed, sophisticated eyes.

Filtering chemical messages

The whole marine environment is continuously saturated with invisible chemical messages that are carried by the currents. Every marine species filters out the irrelevant stimuli and registers only the limited amount of information that affects it directly. In many ways, the process parallels the reception of radio waves that are continually passing through the air. A radio aerial can only decode the limited number of messages to which it is tuned.

Chemicals and reproduction

Many prosobranch species can distinguish between the thousands of chemical substances present in the water. They gather information only from those that have a direct bearing

on their survival. Slipper limpets of the genus Crepidula use certain chemicals in reproduction. Slipper limpet larvae do not have separate sexes when they are still immature. The females, which are sedentary, release substances into the water to attract the immature larvae to them. The larvae, drawn to the females by the chemical messages, attach themselves to her and then develop into males. The larvae only respond to substances emitted by females of the same species.

Searching for food

Chemoreceptivity plays a fundamental role in the search for food. Herbivorous, carnivorous and carrion-feeding prosobranchs all find food by detecting chemicals emitted by their food source. The periwinkle Littorina obtusata, for example, is able to detect the presence of algae belonging to the genus Fucus, on which it feeds. The algae produces a chemical substance, or group of chemical substances, exclusive to the species.

Predatory prosobranchs also locate their prey by chemoreceptivity—a phenomenon that has been observed many times in the laboratory. If the fish-eating mottled cone, Conus striatus, is placed in a tank with water that has been in contact with a fish, the

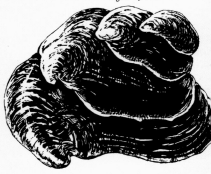

mollusk immediately exhibits its typical feeding response. It emerges from the sand and extends its long proboscis, trying to locate the source of the stimulus. The mottled cone is unable to distinguish a particular species of fish. The information it receives only informs it that a fish is present.

The common northern whelk, Buccinum undatum, is an example of a species that feeds on carrion. The information it receives does not indicate the presence of a single species or a specific group of animals. It simply tells it when organic matter of animal origin is present.

Recognizing predators

Chemoreceptivity plays an important part in the recognition of predators. In the laboratory, the Mediterranean beaded nassa, Nassarius reticulatus, flees when it detects a predatory starfish, but remains unmoved by the "smell" of a noncarnivorous asteroid, such as the American bat star, Patiria miniata. Many herbivorous prosobranchs flee every time they detect the chemical signature of a carnivorous gastropod.

FAR LEFT The slipper shell limpet, *Crepidula fornicata,* filters suspended organic particles through its mucus-covered gills. Usually, it holds its shell down against the seabed, leaving only two small openings to allow water and food to flow into its shell cavity.
LEFT Slipper shells lie on top of one another, forming "mating stacks" of several individuals. Each slipper shell is a hermaphrodite that acts as a female to the limpet above it and a fertilizing male to the one below.
TOP RIGHT Cone shells find food by following chemical trails left by predatory sea creatures.
RIGHT A *Nassarius* mollusk thrashes around with its shell in an attempt to frighten off predators such as starfishes (A). To kill its prey, a cone shell extends its proboscis and stabs the victim with its poisoned radula (B), using an obstacle to shield itself from view.

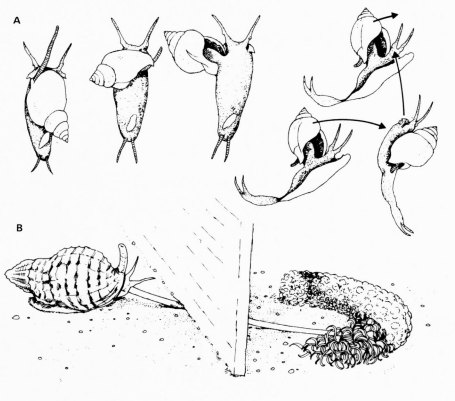

A

B

LEFT Large populations of turret shells live in the seas of Europe at depths of between 16 and 330 ft; they grow up to 2 in. in length. Young turret shells catch prey with their radulas, while the adults remain buried just beneath the substrate at some distance from the shore and filter food through their gills.

BELOW LEFT The newly hatched worm shell resembles most prosobranch larvae (A). As it matures, its shell grows into an irregular spiral shape, like that of the species *Serpulorbis arenaria* (B). An adult worm shell divides its greatly lengthened shell into segments as it matures (C).

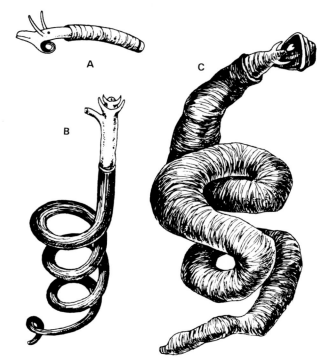

faucet snail's mantle cavity, and the long cilia direct it to a special area that is rich in mucus, where the collected particles are caught up and swallowed.

Cylindrical shells

The family Truncatellidae contains a species called the subcylindrical truncatella. A member of the genus *Truncatella*, it is only about 0.1 in. long and occurs on the shores of warm and temperate seas. It derives its name from its shell. When young it has a conical shell, but when it stops growing it breaks the rings at the tip of its shell and seals the opening with a wall of calcium. In this reduced form, its shell has an almost cylindrical appearance. The subcylindrical truncatella lives on the muddy or sandy bottom of the inner shoreline. It is able to spend long periods of time underwater because it has retained branchiae or gills; not all of its mantle cavity has adapted into lungs.

The subcylindrical truncatella feeds mainly on algae or disintegrated plants, which it seeks by moving in a curious fashion. First, it stretches its enormous proboscis forward and grips the ground with it. Then it moves its foot in the same direction, dragging its shell forward. Resting on its foot once more, the animal stretches out its proboscis and repeats the process.

Sundials

The superfamily Heterogastropoda contains the family Architectonicidae, a group of mollusks with beautiful shells. Reeve's sundial from Australia and New Zealand, the Partridge sundial from the Malay coast and the sundial *Architectonica perspectiva* from the Indo-Pacific all have highly decorated shells. Their shells are shaped like flattened or discoid cones. They have a wide, deep umbilicus (the depression at the base of the shell) that provides a glimpse of their

internal shell curves. However, the beaded sundial of the Caribbean has a rather small umbilicus that is outlined with a prominent, rope-like twist. Its shell has a yellowish background with reddish brown spots and it can grow up to 2 in. in diameter.

The species *Torinia variegata* inhabits the Indian Ocean. Reaching 0.4-0.6 in. in diameter, it is one of the smallest of the sundials. It has a conical shell, and each coil has four spiral rope patterns that intersect with radial coils, forming a wedge-shaped structure. The lower part of its shell reveals a flat umbilicus. *Torina variegata* is white with reddish brown lines arranged irregularly on each curve.

Caecids

The family Caecidae contains mollusks that are only about 0.1 in. long. They have unusual shells in which the first spirals have been completely lost. At first, the shell winds itself into a flat spiral, then it straightens into a slightly arched tube. The small dimensions of the tusk-shelled caecid, which is barely 0.08 in. long, enable it to live among the coarse grains of sand in the outer coastal shelf. (The movement of the waves prevents finer sediments, such as clay, from being deposited.)

Turret shells

The superfamily Cerithiacea comprises 15 families and hundreds of species, most of them marine. Their shells vary in shape, but are generally curved. The turret shells of the genus *Turritella* are probably the most well known and widespread. The gregarious turret shell often occurs in great numbers on muddy seabeds around the coasts of Europe. Some areas have so many turret shells that they are defined as "*Turritella* seabeds."

Mature turret shells are filter feeders, but their young collect particles of food with their radulas or toothed tongues. Filter feeding ensures that mature turret shells do not have to move around much when feeding. At a certain distance from the coast, a turret shell will bury itself just below the muddy seabed and gather food out of sight of possible predators.

It digs a channel to connect its mantle cavity with the water above. It remains buried, while it moves the mud with its foot. The turret shell produces a second opening near the first and reinforces both of them with mucus secreted from its foot. The two channels

ABOVE **A beaded sundial shell of the Caribbean rests on the seabed among coral pebbles and mollusk shells.**

Beaded sundials have slightly depressed shells that grow up to 2 in. in diameter.

act as inhalant and exhalant siphons. Cilia on its long branchial filaments create a continuous current of water through its mantle cavity. Plankton and particles of detritus floating in the water are collected and swallowed. A row of tentacles in front of its mantle opening prevents fine particles of clay from blocking up the turret shell's branchiae. The fringed borders of its operculum perform a similar filtering function.

Worm shells

The family Vermetidae comprises a group of mollusks that possess some of the most distinctive shells of all the prosobranchs. The vermetids, or worm shells, have shells in which only the first curves have the regular spiral shape. The rest of the shell looks like a contorted, irregular, calcareous tube, which the

worm shell attaches to coral, rocks or the shells of other mollusks. Many individuals grow together into a fused mass. At first glance, they resemble sedentary annelids, but closer examination of their soft parts reveals the basic mollusk structure.

The Mediterranean worm shell has unusual feeding habits. It captures the microorganisms on which it feeds by excreting long mucous filaments (produced by glands in the foot). The filaments act like a net in the water, catching algae, protozoa and other small animals. In some species, the radulas carry the filaments and the collected matter to their mouths.

Horn shells

The family Cerithiidae, or horn shells, are marine mollusks. *Bittium reticulatum* gathers in large groups under stones or in cracks in the rocks, along the shores of Europe and America. Horn shells belonging to the genus *Cerithium* occur in warm and temperate seas around the world. Horn shells of the family Cerithiopsidae, and the sinistral miniature horn shells of the family Triphoridae, feed in a similar way: they both feed on porifera (sponges). Once one of these small mollusks has located its prey, it inserts its long, narrow proboscis through the exhalant aperture (osculum) of the sponge until it reaches the sponge's softer inner parts. The mollusk tears the tissue and organs out with its jaws. It transports the food to its mouth using the numerous small teeth on its radula. Horn shells do not attack the outer part of the sponge because it is reinforced by a sharp-spined, calcareous skeleton and is particularly tough.

All the members of these two families have small, conical shells that vary in shape. Some species live in continuous association with their prey. Others are highly specialized and deposit their egg capsules

ABOVE LEFT The Cerithiid species *Bittium reticulatum* inhabits the warm and temperate coasts of Europe and America. It usually lives in large colonies among algae, beneath stones and in rock crevices. The males fertilize the females with sperm packets, since they lack copulatory organs.
LEFT The species of the superfamily Cerithiacea include sea and freshwater dwellers, inhabitants of mangrove swamps and mud deltas, and breathers of both air and water. Tanzania's Lake Tanganyika contains over 84 species that resemble marine-dwelling mollusks, despite the fact that their ancestors were cut off from the Indian Ocean over 180 million years ago.

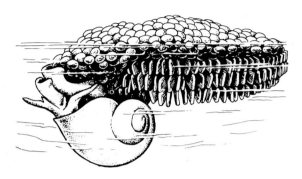

inside the sponges: *Cerithiopsis barleei,* for example, is associated with the sponge *Suberites domuncula,* and *Cerithiopsis tubercolaris* is associated with the sponge *Hymeniacidon sanguinea.*

Violet snails and wentletraps

The superfamily Epitoniacea includes two families of carnivorous mollusks: the family Janthinidae, or violet snails, and the family Epitoniidae, or wentletraps. Members of these two families are anatomically similar although different in their behavior patterns and choice of habitats.

The violet snails of the genus *Janthina* occur in most seas throughout the world, apart from the coldest zones. Some of their habits are unique among the prosobranchs. Voracious, pelagic carnivores, they float near the surface of the water with the help of air bubbles.

Floating on air

The violet snails have bright red bodies with thin, fragile, lightweight, violet-colored shells that reach no more than an inch in height. They sustain themselves at the surface of the water by constructing a mucous float, containing air bubbles. The float can withstand even the strongest waves, and the violet snails remain submerged in an upside-down position.

The violet snails are incapable of locomotion on their own, and their movements are controlled more by the wind than by ocean currents. (The beaches are often littered with thousands of the violet shells of these delicate mollusks, which have been driven there by strong winds.) They feed on hydroids of the genus *Velella,* which also live at the surface of the sea.

Violet snails lack eyes and appear to locate their prey by chemical stimuli. When they find a hydroid, they emit a purplish secretion—produced by glands in their mantle cavities—that spreads through the water and

TOP Mollusks of the genus *Clathrus* have long-spired shells with narrow mantle cavities.

ABOVE The violet snail, *Janthina janthina*, hangs upside-down from its "raft"—a floating structure of bubbles and mucus secretion. Vast numbers of violet snails can be found washed up on beaches after storms.

TOP LEFT Some raft-building species of sea snails attach their eggs to their rafts so that they are not swept away by the waves.

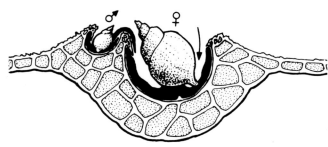

MOLLUSKS CLASSIFICATION: 7

Slugs, snails and limpets (4)

The next four superfamilies in the order Mesogastropoda—the second order of the subclass Prosobranchia—are the Eulimacea, Strombacea, Calyptraeacea and Cypraeacea.

The superfamily Eulimacea includes snails of the families Eulimidae (free-living and parasitic species); the Stiliferidae (containing parasites of genera *Mucronalia* and *Stilifer*); and the Pyramidellidae (pyramid shells, such as the parasitic *Odostomia scalaris*). The superfamily Strombacea includes the families Aporrhaidae (pelican foot shells) of Atlantic and Mediterranean waters; and the Strombidae (conchs) of warm seas, which includes the spider shells (genus *Lambis*) and the 50 species of sea snails of the genus *Strombus* (such as the 15-in.-long *S. goliath* of Brazil).

The superfamily Calyptraeacea contains four families, including the Capulidae (hoof snails); the Calyptraeidae (slipper limpets, such as *Crepidula fornicata*); and the Xenophoridae (with carrier shells, genus *Xenophora*). The cowrie shells of the superfamily Cypraeacea occur in subtropical and tropical seas, and are divided into six families, including the Triviidae (with genera *Trivia* and *Erato*); the Ovulidae (containing the species *Calpurnus verrucosus*); and the Cypraeidae (true cowries), which contains the tiger cowrie, *Cypraea tigris*, and the money cowrie, *Cypraea moneta*, of the Indian Ocean. (See classification box 8 for the remaining three superfamilies.)

ABOVE LEFT Gastropods of the species *Balcis devians* — of the family Eulimidae — are parasitic on echinoderms such as the European sea lily, *Antedon bifida*. An evolutionary history of dependence upon lilies has caused the species to develop a body shape uncharacteristic of mollusks.
ABOVE The gastropod species *Megadenus arrhynchus* lives parasitically in the plates that grow on an echinoderm's skin.

seems to have anesthetizing properties. Once they have captured their prey, the violet snails leave their "raft" and consume their prey. When they have finished eating, the construct another float. The ventral surface of the float serves as a surface on which the snails attach their egg masses.

Decorative ornaments

Wentletraps of the family Epitoniidae have roughly conical shells that are noted for their beauty. They are usually white in color and are sometimes banded or mottled in brownish hues. Unfortunately, because of their highly decorative shells, wentletraps have been overcollected and used as decoration by many people throughout the world. In the 19th century, Chinese merchants are believed to have made copies of the shell of the precious wentletrap from rice-flour putty to satisfy the demands of European collectors.

Small, spiral shells

The shells of wentletraps generally measure less than an inch in height. They are roughly spiral and have axial ribbing, often formed of thin plates. These thin plates protect the wentletrap from predators, particularly from mollusks that penetrate the shells of their prey.

Some of the most beautiful species of wentletraps, such as the lamellose wentletrap, the magnificent wentletrap and the precious wentletrap of the genus *Epitonium,* inhabit the Indo-Pacific. The lamellose wentletrap measures between 0.8 and 1.2 in. and has a very long shell. Its coils are convex, and each has 12 axial, plate-like ridges. The ridges of each coil combine with those from the preceding coil, so that the ribs appear to run in an unbroken line from the top to the bottom of its nut-brown shell.

Wentletraps live from shallow intertidal waters to great depths in seas throughout the world, but mostly in the tropical regions. Members of the genera *Clathrus* and *Opalia* appear in more northerly waters, and the species *Arcisa borealis* lives in the Arctic Ocean.

Predatory carnivores

The wentletraps and the graceful violet snails, which live at the surface of the sea, are linked by their feeding habits. Like the violet snails, the wentletraps are carnivorous. They feed predaciously on various species of coelenterates, especially sea anemones. Though little is known about the life of wentletraps, it is thought that they secrete a reddish substance from their salivary glands that probably anesthetizes their victims.

Primitive parasites

The archaeogastropods and the more primitive groups of the mesogastropods generally have a microscopic and herbivorous diet, feeding on algae or microorganisms. However, some prosobranchs eat larger items of food, and this presupposes a greater degree of evolution since it requires highly specialized structures. Parasitic mollusks, in contrast, often have simplified body structures that are not the sign of a primitive development, but the result of a long period of evolution.

Eulimid sea snails

The superfamily Eulimacea in the order Mesogastropoda includes the families Eulimidae, Stiliferidae and Entoconchidae. The family Eulimidae contains sea snails with small, smooth, glossy, spiral shells; most species are parasitic.

Parasitic eulimid snails live on echinoderm hosts such as starfishes, keeping a grip on the echinoderms' skins with mucus strands secreted by their feet. They feed by inserting their long, piercing mouthparts into

TOP Predatory sea snails of the genus *Odostomia* feed on the blood of mussels and other bivalves. When an opening appears in the host's shell, the snail inserts its long, tubular mouthpart into the shell cavity, pierces the host's tissues and sucks its blood.
ABOVE Since sea snails of the species *Odostomia scalaris* are small, more than one individual may parasitize a single mussel.

their hosts and sucking out body juices while leaving the solid tissues intact. Many species of eulimid snails, such as *Balcis devians,* parasitize only one specific host species; host specificity indicates a high degree of evolutionary specialization.

Stiliferids

Sea snails of the family Stiliferidae parasitize echinoderms, but unlike eulimids they exhibit a range of parasitic habits: some live freely on their host's surface, while others embed themselves in the body wall.

Stiliferids of the genus *Mucronalia,* for example, live on the surface of animals such as sea urchins, starfishes, sea cucumbers and brittle stars. Before feeding, they secrete corrosive digestive juices onto the skins of their hosts and "burn" holes in the body walls.

ABOVE The silver conch, *Strombus lentiginosus*, has a pair of movable eyestalks that bear two large, orange-ringed eyes. The mollusk also has slender, sensory tentacles that it projects from the base of each eyestalk.

BELOW Spikes project from the shell lip of the bird's-foot shell, *Aporrhais serresianus*, giving it a strong resemblance to a bird's claw when seen from above. Most species feed on organic particles suspended in the water.

The snails feed by sucking body fluids through the holes with their long mouthparts.

Parasitic pyramid shells

Parasitic pyramid shells belong to the family Pyramidellidae, which was once closely related to the families Eulimidae and Stiliferidae. However, some zoologists now consider that the pyramidellids belong to a separate order as they have evolved unique life-styles.

Pyramidellid snails inhabit all the world's seas and oceans. They live parasitically on invertebrates such as bivalve mollusks, worms and coelenterates (sea anemones and corals). Pyramidellids have patterned shells that are conical in shape and often ribbed; many grow up to 0.7 in. in length. They possess specialized piercing mouthparts that contain pairs of long, slender jaws for puncturing the skin of their hosts.

Members of the species *Odostomia scalaris* often choose mussels and other bivalves as prey. The pyramidellid positions itself on the shell of a mussel and, when the shell opens, cautiously inserts its long mouthpart into the host's mantle cavity. The snail sticks to soft mollusk tissue with a strong, muscular sucker at the end of its mouthpart, cutting through the tissue with its slender jaws. After withdrawing its jaws, the snail sucks up its host's blood.

Pelican's-foot shells

The superfamily Strombacea contains several dozen mesogastropod species in three families. The pelican's-foot shell, *Aporrhais pespelecani*, lives in the Atlantic and Mediterranean and is particularly widespread around the coasts of Portugal, northern Spain and France.

The shell of the pelican's foot is an elongated spiral, decorated with protuberances on each whorl. In fully grown and sexually mature individuals, the outer edge of the shell-opening widens into four digits similar to those of a bird's foot—hence the name "pelican's foot."

Conchs

Conchs, or trumpet shells, live in warm seas, in temperatures of not less than 68°F. They prefer shallow water and are often found on coral reefs. The shell openings of mature conchs have thickened, curling edges, and some species, such as the spider shells, have thorn-like projections on their shell openings. The species *Strombus goliath* shows a further adapation: its opening expands into a plate-like structure that prevents the shell from rolling over. Members of all conch species have pairs of colored eyes that project from their heads on stout eyestalks. When conchs withdraw into their shells, they close the openings with horny pads on their feet. In conchs, however, the horny pads are modified to form claws for self-defense and locomotion.

Slow gaits, fast getaways

The unusual locomotion methods of conchs have been the subject of much zoological research. The two most studied genera are *Strombus* and *Lambis*—both of which supplement their slow, everyday movements with rapid escape movements in times of danger.

Ordinary *Strombus* locomotion consists of a slow "hopping." The conch anchors its foot to the seabed with its horny claw and raises its shell by stretching upward on its foot. The movement—coupled with the use of the claw as a lever—pushes the shell forward, until it falls down into a position slightly in front of its starting point. After it has pushed its shell forward, the conch withdraws its foot, anchors it in the seabed as far forward as possible and repeats the cycle. In normal circumstances, the *Strombus* conch moves forward at a rate of only about an inch per minute. In the period between two successive hops, it grazes on algae and other vegetable matter on the seabed.

Spider shell conchs (*Lambis*) move more quickly than *Strombus* conchs since they possess two long spikes—one at the front and one at the back end of their shells. Once the spider shell has anchored its claw in the seabed, it raises its shell until the weight of its front spike causes it to fall forward. After "falling," it lifts its foot completely off the seabed, advances it by about an inch and reanchors its claw to begin a new movement.

Certain predatory gastropods—such as cone shells— hunt conchs for their flesh; cone shells kill their victims by piercing them with a poison dart. Consequently,

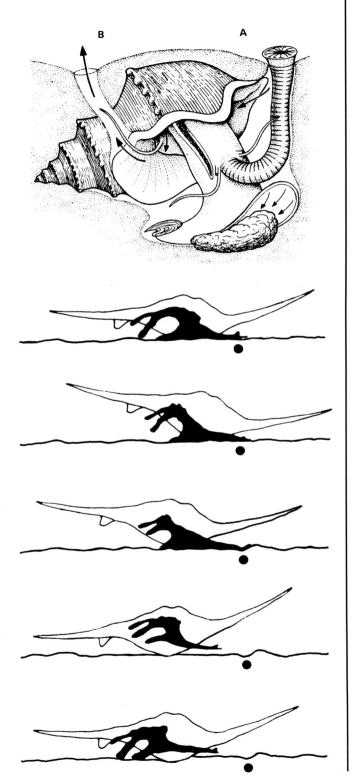

ABOVE RIGHT Ostrich-foot shells filter food particles from water that enters the gill cavity through a siphon (A). The water is then expelled through an opening at the rear of the animal (B).

RIGHT The spider shell moves by anchoring its foot in the seabed and lifting and extending its body as far forward as possible. The black dot marks the mollusk's starting point.

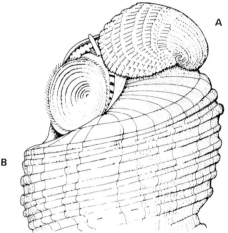

conchs have developed a fast type of movement for fleeing hunting cone shells. Their sense of smell—after detecting an approaching predator—automatically triggers an escape response: a threatened conch extends its stalked eyes and, while waving its tentacles, digs its claw into the seabed. Using the claw as a lever, it jumps backward, landing far away from danger. Several jumps take the conch a safe distance from its predator, at which point it resumes its normal movements. During its escape movement, the conch does not leave its usual trail of mucus and therefore cannot be detected by predators.

The related families of the ostrich-foot shells and pelican-foot shells resort to similar escape strategies in times of danger.

Slipper limpets

The superfamily Calyptraeacea contains four families, including the Calyptraeidae (slipper limpets); the Capulidae (hoof snails); and the Xenophoridae (carrier shells etc.). For much of their lives, slipper limpets remain attached to stones, rocks or the shells of other mollusks. They feed on suspended food particles that enter their mantle cavities with incoming water. Within the cavity, strings of mucus on the surfaces of the gills trap the food particles and carry them to the limpets' tubular mouthparts.

Slipper limpets are hermaphrodites—creatures with both male and female characteristics, capable of producing both sperm and eggs. Slipper limpets, such as the species *Crepidula fornicata,* change sex during their development: all young limpets are males that develop into females as they grow older. The oldest—the females—lose the ability to crawl and attach themselves to rocks, stones or shells. The younger limpets—the males—rest on top of the females, fertilizing them from above. Often, slipper limpets form "mating stacks" of 10 or more individuals, with the females beneath and the males on top.

In 1872, slipper limpets were accidentally introduced into European waters from America, on the shells of bivalve mollusks that had been imported for human consumption. Once introduced, the limpets began to invade the seabed in areas inhabited by oysters, thus depriving the oysters of their natural habitat and causing many to die out. The fast-growing numbers of slipper limpets formed layers on the seabed 4-6 in. thick.

TOP Slipper limpets, *Crepidula fornicata,* resemble stumpy, clawed hands with clenched fingers. Although they are underwater feeders, they may spend hours exposed to the air at low tide. ABOVE A hoof snail (A) attaches itself near the shell opening of a turret shell (B). It feeds parasitically by sucking food from the gill cavity of its host. Hoof snails often live in close association with other mollusks. FAR RIGHT The tiger cowrie, *Cyprea tigris,* lives on the seabed where its mottled skin coloration provides camouflage against predators. When threatened, it attempts to startle its enemy by drawing its skin back to reveal the bright shell colors beneath.

2725

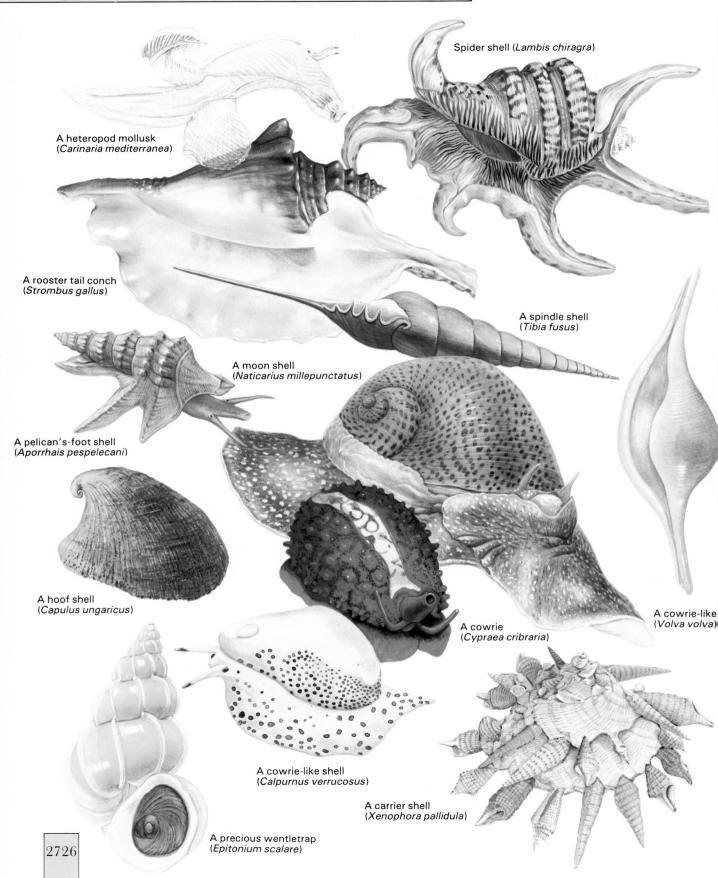

Spider shell (*Lambis chiragra*)

A heteropod mollusk
(*Carinaria mediterranea*)

A rooster tail conch
(*Strombus gallus*)

A spindle shell
(*Tibia fusus*)

A moon shell
(*Naticarius millepunctatus*)

A pelican's-foot shell
(*Aporrhais pespelecani*)

A hoof shell
(*Capulus ungaricus*)

A cowrie-like
(*Volva volva*)

A cowrie
(*Cypraea cribraria*)

A cowrie-like shell
(*Calpurnus verrucosus*)

A carrier shell
(*Xenophora pallidula*)

A precious wentletrap
(*Epitonium scalare*)

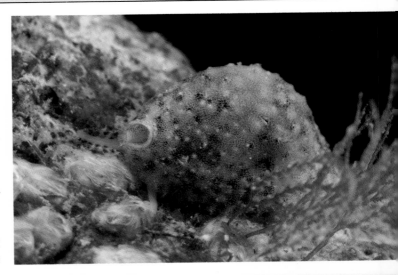

Carrier shells

Carrier shells are sea snails of the genus *Xenophora* within the family Xenophoridae. They live in warm seas at depths of between 130 and 10,000 ft., where they feed by trapping tiny organic particles with the cilia on their gills.

Carrier shells derive their name from their unique practice of camouflaging their shells with coverings of empty mollusk shells, pebbles and other hard objects— holding all in place with sticky secretions from their feet. As a carrier shell grows, it adds larger pebbles and broken coils of shells to its camouflage, arranging the materials so that they do not impede its movement. Encrusting animals, such as species of bristle worms, acorn barnacles and corals, sometimes attach themselves to the shell, rendering it almost indistinguishable from the surrounding environment. As well as providing camouflage protection from predators, the encrustations serve as heavy armor.

The carrier shell species *Xenophora exustus*—an inhabitant of the western Pacific—differs from the other members of its genus in that it camouflages its shell with only a few grains of sand.

Cowries

Cowries—large sea snails of the tropical and subtropical seas—comprise the six families of the superfamily Cypraeacea. They have smooth, shiny oval shells with slit-like openings on the undersides; the edges of the openings roll inward and often possess grooves or teeth. The skin of all cowries extends through the shell opening to cover most of the outside of the shell. Although cowrie shells grow spirally, the last shell whorl usually hides the spiral patterns. Shell shapes vary among species: some (such as those of velvet shells) are rounded and ear-shaped in structure while others are regular ovals. Cowries of the family Pseudosacculidae remain shell-less throughout their lives. Unlike many gastropod species, cowries cannot completely close their shell openings, since their feet do not possess horny pads.

Hunters of sea squirts

Cowries of the genus *Trivia* have colorful outer skins that cover most of their shell surfaces, leaving only single cracks along the centers of the tops of the shells. The skin at the front end of a *Trivia* cowrie forms two lobes that merge into a tube for the intake

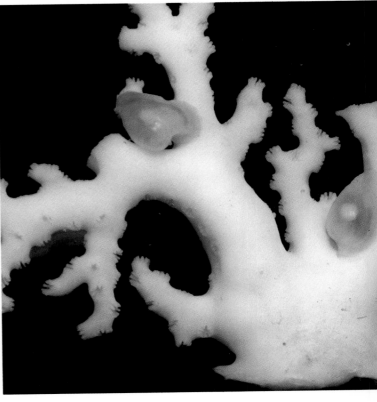

TOP The shells of the cowrie species *Lamellaria perspicua* grow up to 6 in. in length. Each shell is completely covered with a warty skin. Skin coloration varies between individuals: some have red, violet or yellow skins with red or white spots, while others, such as the one shown, have white-spotted, mottled gray skins. *Lamellaria perspicua* feeds on sea squirts and soft corals.
ABOVE Small, smooth-shelled cowrie-like snails of the species *Pedicularia sicula* feed on coral in the Mediterranean.

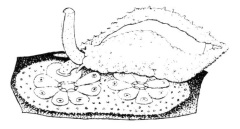

ABOVE The skin of the *Trivia arctica* cowrie covers most of its shell surface and forms a tubular siphon at the front of the animal. Water—needed for respiration—enters the siphon and passes into the gill cavity.

LEFT The *Erato voluta* cowrie feeds on the flesh of a sea squirt by inserting its long, piercing mouthpart through the mouth of its victim. The cowrie tears at the sea squirt's flesh with its toothed radula or tongue.

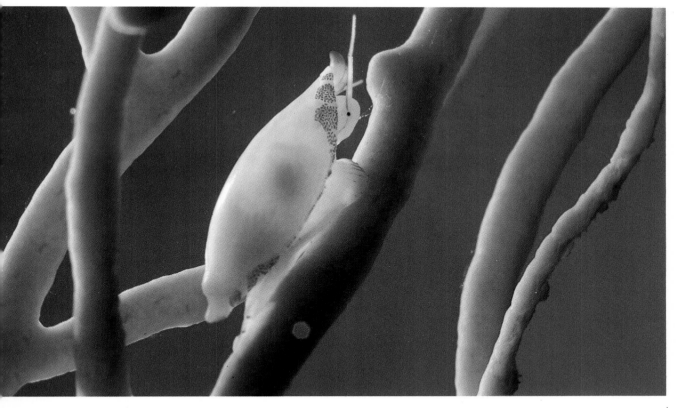

ABOVE Sea snails of the genus *Simnia* usually have coloration similar to that of the coral on which they live and feed. A snail takes on a pure coral color if the skin covering of its shell absorbs pigments from digested coral. *Simnia* snails feed on individual coral polyps one at a time, tearing at the polyp flesh with their strong paired jaws and toothed tongues.

and expulsion of water. *Trivia* cowries are carnivorous animals that usually feed on sea squirts, which they detect by smell. They use their jaws to remove and eat the outer skins of their victims.

Cowries of the genus *Erato* do not eat the outer coverings of sea squirts. Instead, they insert their long mouthparts through the mouths of their prey and bite off flesh with their jaws. The *Erato* cowrie uses its toothed tongue to convey pieces of flesh to its inner mouth. The skin covering its shell has ornamental finger-like projections, the color and shape of which imitate the exteriors of sea squirts.

The family Lamellariidae contains cowries that prey on sea squirts. Members of the species *Lamellaria perspicua* have either violet skin with white spots or yellow skin with red and white spots. Their shells—which grow up to 6 in. in length—consist mainly of the final whorl of the spiral, the rest of the coil being

very small. The general shape of the shell is spherical and slightly flattened, and its walls are semitransparent with thin, barely visible growth lines. Cowries of the species *Lamellaria perspicua* live outside the low-tide mark in the European coastal waters of the Atlantic, moving to shallower waters during the egg-laying season (February to March). The cowries deposit their eggs in flask-shaped capsules that they lodge in the body walls of sea squirts.

Masters of camouflage

The shells of the family Ovulidae are lipless and uniformly colored, but otherwise similar in shape to those of the sea squirt hunters. Many species of ovulid cowries adopt—for camouflage purposes—the colors of the corals on which they feed. The shell of the European species *Simnia spelta,* for example, has a coral-like pink skin covering with red spots.

Shell shapes vary within the family Ovulidae: in the species *Volva volva,* for example, the ends of the shell protrude to form narrow canals that give the shell a characteristic spindle shape. In the Caribbean species *Cyphoma gibbosum,* however, the shell is oval with a wide, slit-shaped mouth. The shell has a humped appearance since a pronounced ridge extends across its top from one side to the other. During periods of

ABOVE True cowries have glossy, oval shells with single slit-like openings on their undersides. Their heads bear slender tentacles and a single pair of eyes. Most species graze on tiny plants in shallow seawater.
FAR RIGHT A groove-toothed cowrie (*Cypraea sulcidentata*) rests in a cave filled with tube coral. The species inhabits the coasts of Hawaii.
PAGES 2732-2733 Many conch species, such as the pink conch, *Strombus gigas*, pull themselves along the seabed or beach with serrated, claw-like appendages.

activity, the skin of the *Cyphoma gibbosum* cowrie becomes colored with brown-edged yellow spots, like those on a giraffe's coat.

True cowries

The so-called "true cowries" (family Cypraeidae) have been caught and admired throughout the world for thousands of years, because of their glass-like brilliance, gaudy colors and unusual patterns. Even in modern times, it is not unusual to find the spotted shell of the tiger cowrie, *Cypraea tigris*, as a household ornament. Cowries have assumed cultural significance in certain parts of the world: in ancient Egypt, for example, they were often buried with the dead; in some parts of Thailand, China, and Africa certain species of cowrie are exchanged as money.

The young cowrie has an elongated, spirally coiled shell; a single, large coil takes up much of the shell area while the tip contains several small coils. As the cowrie develops, its shell expands in width, rather than height, as new calcium deposits collect at the edges of the shell opening. When the animal reaches maximum size, its shell opening thickens and rolls inward, acquiring tiny teeth and ridges along its length. If the

cowrie requires further space inside its shell, it dissolves away the innermost layers with acidic secretions. Adult cowries vary in length from 0.4 in.—as in species such as the money cowrie, *Cypraea moneta*—to 6 in. in the deer cowrie, *Cypraea cervus*.

Skin defense

When a true cowrie emerges from its shell, its skin completely covers the shell's surface. The protective skin covering is often covered with fine, finger-like projections, which are thought to have a sensory function. Skin protects the cowrie in two ways: if the cowrie is disturbed, its skin may secrete an acidic substance as a means of defense; if it withdraws quickly into its shell, the sudden change from skin color to shell color may startle a predator. In species such as the mole cowrie, *Cypraea talpa*, the color and ornamentation of the skin resemble those of the sea cucumber, which many predatory fishes find distasteful. Predators of the cowries include large crabs, some species of cone shells and fishes.

Most cowrie species live in shallow seawater in the tropics, although some—such as *Cypraea midwayensis*—inhabit depths down to 1600 ft. Cowries prefer hard substrates, in particular coral reefs, where they graze on encrusting algae and sponges, usually at night. They move by creeping over the seabed on their muscular feet; only part of the foot moves at any one time—the rest keeps a tight grip on the substrate until the foot is safely anchored in its new position. The cowries' careful method of locomotion helps them avoid being dislodged by powerful waves.

Mating and fertilization

Cowries have separate sexes and reproduce by mating. The male has a penis with which he deposits sperm inside the reproductive opening of the female. After mating, the female stores sperm inside a special chamber within her body until her eggs are ready for fertilization (sometimes up to 11 days later). Inside the female's body, the eggs collect in flask-shaped capsules—each capsule contains several hundred eggs. A single female usually lays a number of egg capsules and attaches each firmly to the substrate. The eggs of most species develop into free-swimming planktonic larvae over a period of about three weeks. The female guards the egg capsules and keeps them clean during her larvae's development.

TOP A cowrie of the species *Cypraea zonaria* withdraws into its shell for protection, leaving only its tentacles protruding.
ABOVE A cowrie's outer skin deters predators since it resembles a poisonous sea cucumber.

BELOW A *Simnia patula* cowrie grazes on corals in the warm waters in which it lives, detecting its food with its short snout. Its broad, flattened foot provides a large surface area with which to grip the substrate.

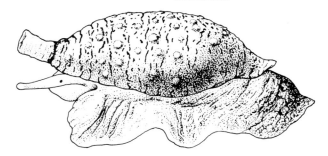

After hatching, the larvae escape from the egg capsules through small openings at the capsules' tops. They swim around freely for a while before settling on the seabed, where they produce a shell. Cowries of some Australian species have no free-swimming larval stage—the young cowries emerge from the eggs completely formed.

Heteropodans

The superfamily Heteropoda contains 30 species of sea snails in three families: the Atlantidae, the Carinariidae and the Pterotracheidae. Heteropodans are free-swimming (they swim on their backs), carnivorous creatures that usually live in the surface waters of warm seas. The shells of Atlantids and carinariids are greatly diminished, while those of the family Pterotracheidae are entirely absent.

Shell loss through evolution, while allowing easy movement, deprived heteropodans of a valuable means of protection. The complete or partial loss of the shell allowed heteropodans to float and was therefore a necessary stage in their adaptation to life in the open sea. Where a shell does remain, it is thin and fragile, with only one layer of spirals. The front parts of the heteropodans' transparent bodies are modified to form swimming organs.

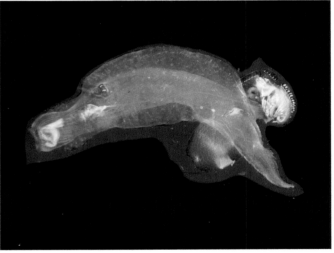

TOP *Atlanta peroni* is a species of tiny sea snail that lives in the open sea. It seizes minute organic prey with its tubular mouthpart and toothed tongue, and swims using its fin-like foot.

ABOVE Sea snails of the genus *Carinaria* swim on their backs, propelling themselves with their modified feet. In the picture, the snail's small, cap-like shell appears on the "underside" of its body (to the right), opposite the whitish fin. The mollusk's mouth is sited at the far left.

Adult heteropodans are unusual creatures, since they are one of the few mollusk groups to have adapted to life in the open sea. Among the prosobranchs, only the violet sea snails and members of the heteropoda superfamily have abandoned the seabed. However, while violet sea snails (genus *Janthina*) float on the surface of the sea and move with the wind, heteropodans are capable swimmers that inhabit several depths.

See-through predators

Heteropodans of the family Atlantidae have compressed swimming feet and wide, thin, transparent shells that resemble those of limpets. Members of the Atlantid genus *Carinaria* prey on fast-moving marine creatures such as small fishes. They swim upside-down, with their feet uppermost and their shells hanging beneath.

The *Carinaria* heteropodan has a flattened head and foot that cannot be withdrawn inside the shell (which contains the body's organs). The head contains the mouth—a structure surrounded by muscles that enable it to stretch outward; and a pair of touch-sensitive tentacles. The eyes—which rest at the base of the tentacles—rotate in all directions, providing the heteropodan with a wide field of vision. On top of the animal the foot expands into a "rudder" for steering; it contains a sucker to keep the heteropodan firmly attached to its partner during mating. *Carinaria* heteropodans have separate sexes—the males fertilize the females internally with their well-developed penises.

The transparency of the *Carinaria* heteropodans lends them a partial invisibility, compensating for their inability to withdraw into their shells when threatened by predators. It is possible to see a *Carinaria* heteropodan's internal organs and even the structure of its nervous system.

Carinarians usually swallow their prey whole, although they do have long-toothed tongues for tearing flesh into small pieces before ingestion. Their diet includes other open-sea mollusks, planktonic bristle worms and small fishes.

Moon shells

Moon shells are highly evolved sea snails with globe-shaped shells and strong, piercing mouthparts; approximately 150 species comprise the superfamily

BELOW The worldwide distribution of various species of cowrie. Cowries generally inhabit the tropical and subtropical regions between latitudes of 40 degrees north and 40 degrees south.

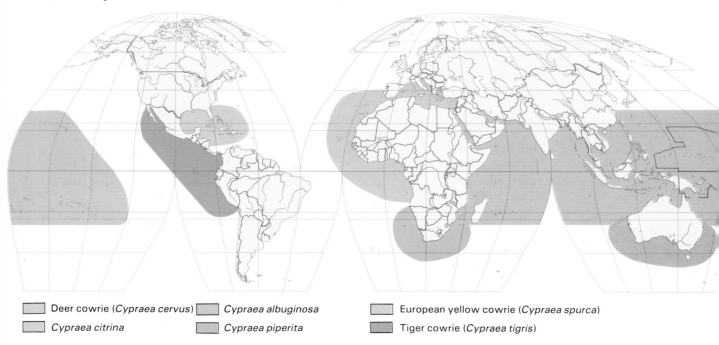

☐ Deer cowrie (*Cypraea cervus*)   ☐ *Cypraea albuginosa*   ☐ European yellow cowrie (*Cypraea spurca*)

☐ *Cypraea citrina*   ☐ *Cypraea piperita*   ☐ Tiger cowrie (*Cypraea tigris*)

MOLLUSKS CLASSIFICATION: 8

Slugs, snails and limpets (5)

The final three superfamilies dealt with in the order Mesogastropoda (subclass Prosobranchia) are the Heteropoda, Naticacea and Tonnacea. The superfamily Heteropoda contains 30 species of free-swimming, carnivorous gastropods divided into three families, including the Carinariidae (with the genus *Carinaria*). The superfamily Naticacea (moon shells) contains 150 species in a single family, the Naticidae.

The superfamily Tonnacea contains about 270 species of marine carnivores found throughout the world, especially in warm temperate and tropical seas. They are divided into five families: the Cassidae (helmet shells); the Cymatiidae (triton shells, such as Triton's trumpet, *Charonia tritonis*, of the Indian and Pacific oceans) with about 130 species; the Bursidae (frog shells) of warm, tropical seas; the Tonnidae (tun shells, such as the giant tun *Tonna galea*); and the Ficidae (fig shells, such as the common fig shell, *Ficus communis*).

ABOVE Sea snails of the genus *Natica* have large feet that enable them to dig their way under the seabed without trapping sand inside their gill cavities.
BELOW When feeding on a bivalve mollusk, the naticid snail bores a hole through its shell and sucks out the soft tissues with its long, piercing mouthparts (A). After it has fed, it leaves behind an empty shell with a hole (B). PAGES 2738-2739 The triton shell, *Tritonalia nodifer*, searches the Mediterranean seabed for food.

Naticacea's only family—the Naticidae. Moon shells inhabit many areas of the world, living in loose sediment on sandy or muddy areas of the seabed. The behavior, methods of locomotion and physical characteristics of all species show a high degree of adaptation to the typical naticid diet of bivalve mollusks.

The moon shell has a smooth shell consisting of one large, and several small, coils. The structure of the foot allows the snail to "plow" through the surface of the seabed in search of prey: when the animal moves, its foot stretches to form a flattened disk. The propodium, or front part of the foot, extends forward and upward, forming a fleshy shield that covers much of the head and protects the entrance to the gill cavity. The rear part of the foot has side flaps that extend upward to cover the sides of the shell.

Specialized predators

The moon shell detects the presence of bivalves from distances of up to 12 in. After locating a suitable prey, it seizes it and wraps it in mucus strands secreted by the foot. Once it has subdued its victim,

ABOVE The naticid snail frequently buries itself in the seabed, obtaining oxygen through a channel formed by extensions of its skin. When buried, it "plows" through the bottom with its foot. The front part of the foot acts as a head shield, protecting the eyes and gill cavity from sand.

the moon shell drags it below the surface of the seabed to eat in safety. Before eating, it uses its toothed tongue to form a circular abrasion on the bivalve's shell, making the task easier by softening the shell surface with an acidic secretion from a gland at the tip of its mouthpart. The moon shell inserts its mouthpart through the resulting hole and tears at the meaty inner flesh with its tongue.

Helmet shells

The 270 or so species of the superfamily Tonnacea are carnivorous mesogastropods that feed on a variety of marine invertebrates, including bivalves, echinoderms and snails. All species are sea-dwelling, and most inhabit the seas of the tropics, subtropics and warm temperate regions.

The family Cassidae contains the helmet shells (also known as bonnet shells)—so called because of their large, strong, heavy shells. The helmet shell's long, thin and often toothed shell-opening narrows into a frontal groove that protects its water siphon. The snail has a well-balanced body structure: the axis of its shell runs parallel to the axis of its foot, and is positioned directly above the foot's mid-line so that the shell remains in a symmetrical position over the body. The symmetrical arrangement suits the helmet shell's predatory life-style, since it allows for speed of movement.

Helmet shells of the species *Cassidaria echinophora* inhabit the coastal regions of the Mediterranean Sea, where they are fished commercially from the muddy seabed. Their white and pale brown shells—which grow up to 3 in. in length—are somewhat thinner than those of tropical helmet shells. The main shell whorl has five or six spiral ridges, each of which bears numerous knob-like bumps.

Gaudy Caribbean giants

Helmet shells of the Caribbean species *Cassis tuberosa* grow up to 9 in. in length. Most of the *Cassis tuberosa*'s shell consists of its last coil (a usual helmet shell characteristic) and is covered with crosswise rows of bumps—the size of the bumps varies between individual shells. The outer shell lip has black and white stripes and half a dozen large white teeth on its inner surface. The grooved, black inner lip extends

ABOVE **A banded helmet sea snail,** *Phalium bandatum*, **35 ft. below the sea's surface. It has a symmetrically arranged body structure to allow for speed of movement. The banded helmet feeds on marine invertebrates such as bivalves, echinoderms and snails.**

RIGHT **A helmet shell snail of the species** *Cypraecassis rufa* **immobilizes a sea urchin with nerve poison and removes its protective spines (A). The snail turns the defenseless sea urchin upside-down, inserts its mouthpart into the urchin's anus and sucks out the body tissues (B).**

into a gaudy shield-like flap that covers large areas of the shell surface. The shell's gray back bears zigzag rows of decorative red spots.

The *Cassis tuberosa* helmet shell usually hunts nocturnally, preying on sea urchins. With tentacles outstretched, the snail bears down on its prey, smothers it from above with its foot and paralyzes it with nerve poison. The helmet shell extends its piercing mouthpart under its foot and bites a hole (about 0.2 in. wide) into its immobilized

ABOVE Helmet shells of the species *Cassidaria echinophora* are common inhabitants of the Mediterranean, where fishermen catch them on muddy, coastal seabeds. Like other helmet shells, the snails hold their shells symmetrically over their bodies to enable easy, well-balanced movement.

BELOW Helmet shells of the tropical species *Cassis tuberosa* grow up to 9 in. in length and hunt nocturnally. A snail holds its foot over an urchin (A) and kills it with a paralyzing secretion (B).

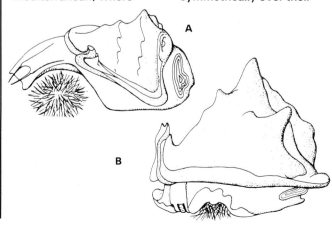

victim's tough skin; an acidic secretion from the mouth helps to soften the skin. When the hole is wide enough, the snail inserts its piercing mouthpart into the sea urchin and eats the soft body tissues, including the stomach, which usually contains semidigested vegetable matter. Although the helmet shell sometimes eats its victim's spines, it excretes them whole without absorbing their nutrients.

Triton shells

The triton shells of the family Cymatiidae cling to rocks and coral on the seabeds of warm seas throughout the world. They are predatory carnivores

that feed on other snails, clams, starfishes and sea urchins. A triton shell attacks its victim by expelling a secretion of sulfuric acid that it produces in its salivary glands. Using its piercing mouthparts, it bores through its victim's shell and eats its flesh with its jaws and toothed tongue (located inside its piercing mouthparts).

Triton shells have strong, spiral shells, usually elongated and made up of about six whorls—the main body whorl being much larger than the others. The shells are often decorated with spiral ridges and knobs that may be hairy or fibrous. The shells range in size from 0.4 to 20 in. in height.

The larger species of triton shells, especially those of the genus *Charonia,* have been used by man since ancient times as containers or primitive wind instruments. For example, specimens of *Charonia,* dating from the Stone Age show evidence of having been used as horns.

Indiscriminate collection

The family Cymatiidae includes several gigantic species. The best known is Triton's trumpet, which grows to 18 in. long. It preys on the crown-of-thorns starfish—a major destroyer of the coral reefs of the Indo-Pacific. Because of its large size and the beauty of its shell, Triton's trumpet has been overhunted and is now a threatened species on the coral reefs. Since the Triton's decline in numbers, the crown-of-thorns starfish has become such a serious threat to the survival of the reefs that the indiscriminate collection of Triton's trumpets is now illegal.

Of the members of the genus *Cymatium,* the species *C. parthenopaeum* has a particularly unusual shell. Reddish brown in color, it bears thick hairs measuring up to 0.8 in. long. The last whorl of its shell has two seams and a series of ribs that spiral from its opening to its base. The shell opening is wide and has a notched, inward-curling lip.

Frog shells

The frog shells of the family Bursidae occur in warm, tropical seas. Most of them prey on bristle worms, which they paralyze with secretions from their salivary glands and then swallow whole. *Bursa scrobiculator,* which measures 1.5 to 3 in. long, is probably the only species of the family to occur in the Mediterranean. It has a strong, elongated, cone-shaped shell with spiraling seams. It is decorated

ABOVE Triton shells are among the largest of marine snails (gastropods), measuring up to 20 in. in length. They live in warm seas, where they feed on clams, starfishes, sea urchins and other sea snails, attacking their victims by paralyzing their nervous systems with secretions of sulfuric acid. The triton shell takes its name from Triton, a minor sea god of ancient Greek mythology, who used just such a twisted shell as a trumpet to calm the seas or call up rough waves.

with broad, round protuberances, each of which lies between two deep pits. The shell thickens considerably toward the shell opening.

Tun shells

The tun shells of the family Tonnidae are the most sophisticated predators among the mesogastropods. They feed mainly on sea cucumbers and other echinoderms. They kill their prey by injecting it with a salivary secretion, containing 2-4 percent sulfuric acid. Their powerful jaws act like hooks, tearing the prey into small pieces, enabling the tun shells to swallow the pieces. Although their shells are usually large (sometimes over 12 in. long), tun shells cannot withdraw their bodies completely into their shells. One of the most common species is the giant tun, which occurs in all except the coldest seas.

ABOVE Triton's trumpet is one of the largest triton shells, growing up to 18 in. long. It is a major predator of the crown-of-thorns starfish, which is largely responsible for destroying the coral reefs in the Indian and Pacific oceans.

The fig shells of the family Ficidae derive their name from their fig or pear-shaped shells, which are decorated with many fine, spiral ribs. Their long, wide shell openings are drawn out at the front end to form canals that hold the water siphons (the fleshy tubes through which they draw water into their gill chambers).

The members of the genus *Ficus* (the only genus in the family) occur throughout the tropics. The fossil record shows that fig shells occurred widely throughout the Mediterranean during the Pliocene era (between 2 and 10 million years ago) until the Ice Ages confined them to more southerly regions.

In appearance, the common fig shell resembles a fig. The tip of its spiral barely rises above its main body whorl. Its siphon canal is wide, deep and elongated. The surface of its shell is covered in a series of fine spiral ribs (some more prominent than others) that intersect with narrower crossways ribs, resulting in a pattern of little squares. The outside of its shell is yellowish white in color, while the inner surface of the shell opening is reddish brown.

Neogastropoda

The third order of prosobranch mollusks is the order Neogastropoda. As their name suggests, these creatures are of more recent origin than the archeogastropods and the mesogastropods (*neos* meaning "new" in Greek). Neogastropods first appeared in the upper Cretaceous period 130 million years ago.

The neogastropods are all sea-dwelling creatures, and most species are either predators or scavengers. Their shells usually have siphon canals, through which water enters their gill chambers. They each have a chemical-sensitive patch of skin (called the osphradium) within their gill cavities, which maximizes their ability to detect smells in the water. Their rasping tongues, if present, are made up of successive rows of teeth with a maximum of only three teeth to each row. There are three superfamilies within the order Neogastropoda, containing about 5000 different species.

Muricacea

The superfamily Muricacea contains a large number of mollusks of varying shapes and sizes. Members of the family Muricidae, known as murexes or rock shells, display an infinite range of decorative ridges, spines and knob-like projections. All species have a water siphon, which is sensitive to the water around them. Although they occur in a range of shapes, all murexes have similar habits. They live in shallow waters to depths of 650 ft., and are all predators. They feed on acorn shells, bivalve mollusks and, occasionally, chitons. When feeding, a murex covers its prey with its foot and slowly cuts through the shell of its victim with a rotating movement of its tongue. A glandular

ABOVE **The tun shell, *Tonna perdrix*, kills its prey by injecting acid into the body of its victim. The snail then tears it into** small pieces with its hook-like jaws.
BELOW **The map shows the distribution of various murex species.**

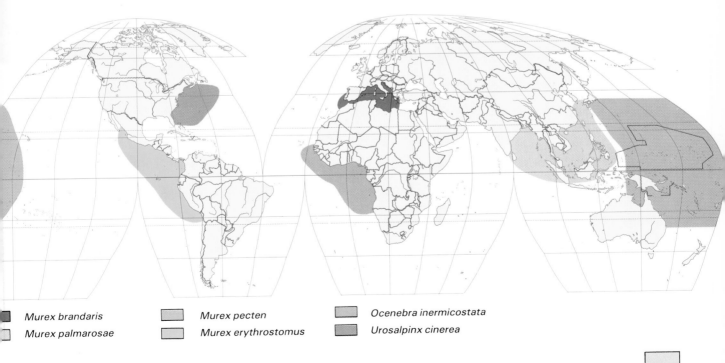

	Murex brandaris		Murex pecten		Ocenebra inermicostata
	Murex palmarosae		Murex erythrostomus		Urosalpinx cinerea

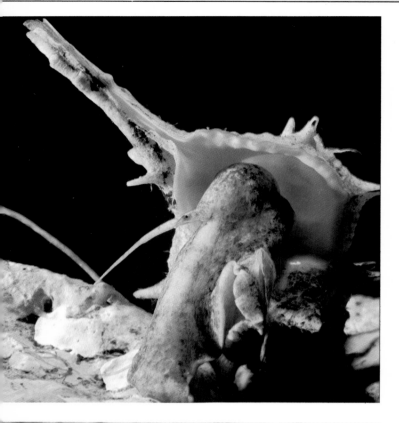

MOLLUSKS CLASSIFICATION: 9

Slugs, snails and limpets (6)

The third order of mollusks in the subclass Prosobranchia is the Neogastropoda—about 5000 species of sea-dwelling snails that are divided into three superfamilies and 21 families. The first superfamily, the Muricacea, contains 17 families. These include the Muricidae (murexes or rock shells, containing the giant eastern murex, *Muricanthus fulvescens,* the common dog whelk, *Nucella lapillus*, and the oyster drill, *Urosalpinx cinerea*); the Columbariidae (pagoda shells); the Coralliophilidae (coral-feeding snails); the Buccinidae (whelks, such as the common whelk, *Buccinum undatum*, of North Atlantic and Arctic waters, and the Neptune shell, *Neptunea contraria*); the Columbellidae (dove shells); and the Nassariidae (dog whelks, such as the thick-lipped dog whelk, *Nassarius incrassatus*, and netted dog whelk, *N. reticulatus*, as well as mud snails and basket shells).

Further families in the superfamily Muricacea are the Melongenidae (crown conchs and whelks, such as the channeled whelk, *Busycon canaliculatum*, of the west coast USA; the Vasidae (vase shells, such as the Indian chank, *Turbinella pyrum*, found off southern India and Sri Lanka); the Volutidae (volutes or bailer shells, such as the music volute, *Voluta musica*); and the Mitridae (miter shells).

The second superfamily of the order Neogastropoda contains about 150 species of snails in just one family, the Cancellariidae (which includes the cancellated nutmeg shell, *Cancellaria cancellata*).

The final superfamily, Conacea, contains the Conidae (cone shells, such as the sand-dusted cone, *Conus arenatus*, the marble cone, *C. marmoreus*, and the Mediterranean cone, *C. mediterraneus*); the Turridae (turret shells); and the Terebridae (auger shells).

TOP LEFT Most murexes feed on acorn barnacles and bivalve mollusks. They attack their prey by covering it with their feet, and then rotating their toothed tongues so as to cut through the shells.

LEFT The shells of murexes are frequently covered with tunnel-dwelling bristle worms. The worms give the snails the protective, camouflaged look of underwater rocks.

secretion from its foot softens the chalky layer of the victim's shell, enabling the murex to cut through more easily. Once it has completed the hole, the snail inserts its piercing mouthparts and feeds on the tissues within.

Although this is the most common predatory technique in the Muricidae family, some species behave differently. For example, the giant eastern murex levers oysters open with the edges of its shell. Many murexes have spines on the inside edges of their shells, which they force between the valves of their prey. The spine makes an opening just large enough for a murex to insert its mouthparts.

Mysterious dyes

For hundreds of years, murexes were hunted and gathered extensively in order to obtain the substance secreted by glands at the base of their gills. The secretion turns from red to purple when it comes into contact with light and air, and was used as a purple dye. Its properties, known to the ancient Phoenicians, were later exploited on a large scale by the Romans, who used it to dye cloth for high-ranking personnel and for ritual purposes. How this secretion benefits the snail is not fully understood. However, it is thought that it has an anesthetizing effect on the prey.

ABOVE Murexes were once much sought after for the secretion produced by glands at the base of their gills. The secretion turns purple when it comes into contact with light and air, and was consequently highly valued as a dye for clothing.

Spiky shells

Murex palmarosae, which inhabits the waters around India and Indonesia, owes much of its beauty to the striking spiny projections on its surface. Arranged in three rows around its shell, the spines continue up both sides of its siphon canal. The siphon canal is completely enclosed by a tubular extension of its shell that protects it from predators. The long siphons of many prosobranch mollusks are easy prey for fishes that live at the bottom of the sea.

Murex shells are decorated with tiny, beaded ribs that resemble minute strings of pearls. Their basic color varies from yellow to brown. The tips of their projections are pink, while the insides of the lip projections and the inner surfaces of their shell openings are whitish in color.

Accumulating color

One of the most common prosobranch mollusks of the Atlantic shores of Europe is the common dog whelk of the family Muricidae. Common dog whelks

ABOVE **The common dog whelk is one of the commonest murexes to be found on European Atlantic shores. It feeds on common mussels, but will also eat other bivalves and acorn barnacles. These whelks may be white or yellow (seen here), orange, or black with white and yellow stripes.**

have always aroused interest because of the great variety in the colors of their shells. The colors vary from white, yellow and orange to black with white or yellow stripes. Common dog whelks feed mainly on common mussels, although they also prey on other bivalve mollusks and on acorn barnacles. In order to feed on a bivalve mollusk, a common dog whelk drills through the bivalve's shell using its toothed tongue— an operation that can take as long as two days. With barnacles, however, it does not drill through the shells. Instead, it smothers them with its foot until the barnacles open their valves.

The diet of the common dog whelk greatly influences the color of its shell. Those individuals that feed on acorn shells are pale in color, while those that prey mostly on mussels are more brightly colored. Common dog whelks accumulate pigments from their prey during feeding and transfer them to their own shells as they grow.

Genetic influences

Along the French coast of the English Channel, many varieties of common dog whelk occur. The different varieties have varying numbers of chromosomes (threads of genetic material found in the nucleus of every cell in the body), ranging from 13 to 18 pairs. The number of chromosomes appears to have a bearing on the shape, thickness and color of their shells. The outward appearance of the common dog whelk is greatly influenced by both genetic and environmental factors.

Another member of the family Muricidae, the oyster drill, causes great damage to oyster beds. Widespread in North America and along the Atlantic coasts of Europe, it feeds almost exclusively on oysters, which it attacks by boring through their shells.

Pagoda shells

The pagoda shells of the family Columbariidae have spindle-shaped shells with few whorls. They generally measure less than 2 in. long and are unusual in that their siphon canals are longer than their shell spires. Each of the coils has a ridge adorned with strong, thick spines. The final coil also has a second, smaller ridge.

Coral-feeding snails

Coral-feeding snails of the family Coralliophilidae are similar in appearance to the murexes, but they have different feeding habits. They are parasitic on corals and inhabit only warm seas. They have no tongues and feed by sucking in the tiny coral polyps. Some live on the surface of the coral, while others burrow into it.

Coralliophila lamellosa, which is quite common in the Mediterranean, is perfectly adapted to a parasitic life-style. It enters madrepore corals while still immature, and remains there for life. Its shell transforms into a long, winding, chalky tube that grows at the same pace as the coral. The snail lives at the open end of its shell, and is separated from the rest of it by an internal shell partition.

Members of the genus *Latiaxis* occur only in the Indo-Pacific. They are particularly common in the waters around Japan, where they live at depths of 330 to 500 ft. Their shells are often decorated with a profusion of spiral ridges and thin, upturned spines. *L. mawae* has a particularly characteristic shell. Each coil juts out beyond the previous one and flattens out on top. The upper edge of each coil has a crest of broad, knob-like projections. Its shell opening is large and oval-shaped, and extends into a deep, narrow siphon canal.

Whelks

The family Buccinidae contains a group of sea snails known as whelks. They occur all over the world, from

ABOVE **Although members of the mollusk family Coralliophilidae resemble the murexes, their feeding habits are quite different. Unlike the murexes, which bore into the shells of other invertebrates such as barnacles, the coralliophilids are parasitic snails, living and feeding on coral in tropical and subtropical seas.**

LEFT **The oyster drill produces many egg capsules that it attaches to the surface of its shell. Each capsule contains between 4 and 11 eggs, depending on the size of the parent. The eggs develop on the shell of the parent and hatch into fully developed young snails that do not undergo a free-swimming larval stage.**

the tropical seas to the seas of northern Europe. Most species of whelk inhabit the cooler, temperate seas rather than those of the tropics, although about 30 species occur in the Mediterranean. Most whelks live on hard substrates—only a few species live on soft parts of the seabed. They are carnivorous, and many species are scavengers, feeding on dead or dying creatures such as fishes, other mollusks and invertebrates. Whelks drill through the shells of bivalve mollusks with their toothed tongues and some species, such as the Japanese species *Siphonalia signum,* cause serious damage to oyster beds.

Whelks of the genus *Buccinum* occur in temperate or cold seas, including the Arctic. The common whelk lives in both the North Atlantic and Arctic waters, and is often fished by man for food. It ranges from intertidal zones to depths of 350 ft. or more. A predatory species, the common whelk attacks various kinds of bivalve mollusk such as mussels, oysters and large species of scallop. It also attacks fishes that have been entangled in fishing nets. Its mouthparts, which include a rasping tongue, are twice the length of its body, enabling it to reach the inner organs of its victim.

A common whelk can detect the scent of dead or wounded creatures from a considerable distance. Fishermen have exploited this feeding behavior and catch large numbers of whelks by placing wicker baskets, baited with fish and freshly killed crabs, on the seabed.

Surprise attack

Unlike other members of its genus, the common whelk does not bore through the shell of its prey. Instead, it forces its victim's shell open using its strong foot. Having jumped on its prey in a surprise attack, the common whelk thrusts the outer edge of its shell between the two valves of its prey to prevent them from closing. It then inserts its mouthparts through the crack and cuts through the muscles that hold the two valves of the shell together. Once it has overcome its victim's defenses, the whelk devours the soft tissues of its prey.

Shell variety

Whelk shells vary in shape from rounded to elongate spirals with smooth or ridged surfaces. Usually thick and strong, they have wide shell openings that extend at the front, serving as siphon

ABOVE The common whelk lives in North Atlantic and Arctic waters, where it preys on bivalve mollusks and fishes caught up in nets.
BELOW The American whelk locates its prey—a clam or oyster—by smelling the water (A) with special cells inside its gill chamber. It approaches its victim and holds it firmly with its foot (B) in order to pry it apart or crack its shell. After sucking out the flesh (C), it moves off (D), leaving the empty shell behind.

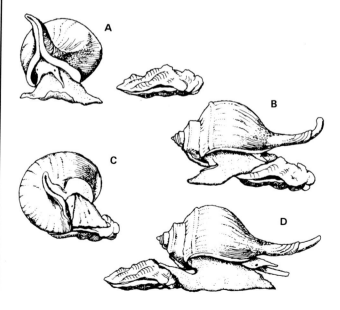

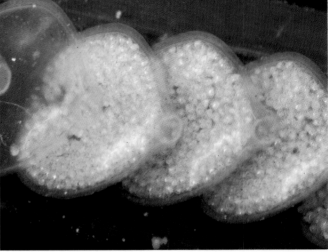

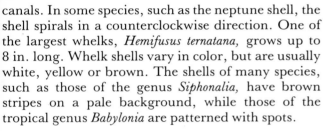

canals. In some species, such as the neptune shell, the shell spirals in a counterclockwise direction. One of the largest whelks, *Hemifusus ternatana,* grows up to 8 in. long. Whelk shells vary in color, but are usually white, yellow or brown. The shells of many species, such as those of the genus *Siphonalia,* have brown stripes on a pale background, while those of the tropical genus *Babylonia* are patterned with spots.

Dove shells

The small dove shells of the family Columbellidae occur in coastal waters all over the world. Their shells, which are usually shiny and highly colored, have long, straight openings with toothed edges. Most species are carnivorous and live as parasites on sponges.

Dog whelks

The dog whelks, or mud snails, of the family Nassariidae occur in the shallow or coastal waters of warm seas. They live on soft areas of the seabed, such as sand or mud. They have conical shells with spiraling, decorative projections and short siphon canals.

Dog whelks are mostly scavengers, and can scent dead or wounded creatures from up to several yards away. Dog whelks are stimulated to go in search of food by chemicals that are released from the torn tissues of injured prey. For example, the netted dog whelk will live peacefully in an aquarium alongside other fishes and mollusks, without attacking even the smallest of creatures. But as soon as one of its companions cuts itself, the dog whelk attacks the injured animal. Piercing the victim with its mouthparts, the dog whelk tears away at its flesh.

Most dog whelks are nocturnal creatures. During the day they lie buried in the sediment, with only their

ABOVE LEFT The thick-lipped dog whelk lives in rocky or stony areas of the sea- shore. It is a nocturnal scavenger and is attracted to dead or wounded creatures, which it can detect by smell from a distance of several yards. ABOVE The eggs and larvae of the netted dog whelk develop within jelly-like, **flask-shaped containers, from which they emerge as young whelks rather than larvae. PAGES 2752-2753 Dog whelks, *Nucella lapillus,* with their yellow egg capsules cling to a rocky outcrop. Each capsule contains hundreds of eggs from which small individuals will emerge after about four months.**

siphons aboveground. As it grows dark, they emerge and go in search of carrion. When looking for food, they exert as little energy as possible. By using the weak currents on the seabed, they are able to explore the largest possible area with the minimum of effort.

An escape reaction

A number of dog whelk species, such as *Cyclope neritea* and the netted dog whelk, have special chemicals in their tissues that serve to warn other members of their species that they are being attacked. If a crab, for example, attacks a dog whelk and breaks its shell, chemicals are released, signaling to the other members of its species that danger is nearby. The dog whelks bury themselves in the seabed to escape from the predator.

Crown conchs, whelks and false trumpets

The family Melongenidae, which contains the crown conchs, whelks and false trumpets, includes some of the largest whelks.

The American whelk of the genus *Busycon* preys on bivalve mollusks, such as clams. When attacking its prey, the whelk opens the shell valves of its victim by

ABOVE The tulip shell is a carnivorous snail that feeds on clams and worms. The head bears a pair of short tentacles, each with an eye near its base, while the front of the shell is extended to form a protective canal for the water siphon.

BELOW The red coloring of tulip shells' bodies is their most characteristic feature. The shell's coils are usually sculptured, and the shell opening can be sealed off when the snail withdraws its body, using a brown, horny pad on the foot.

pulling on them with its foot, sometimes splintering the outside edges in the process. As soon as it has made a small opening in the valves, the whelk slides the lip of its shell into the gap and wedges them apart. Some species chip away at the shell of their victims by battering them with the lips of their own shells. Once they have made a hole that is large enough for them to feed through, the whelks insert their mouthparts and eat the flesh of their victims.

The channeled whelk occurs around the west coast of America. Each coil of its shell has a ridge around the top third, giving it the appearance of a turret. Its shell opening forms a long, deep groove which extends into a deep siphon canal, the edges of which fold inward to form tooth-like ridges. The surface of its shell has longitudinal ribs intersected with fine, spiral stripes. It is light brown in color with dark brown crossways stripes.

Horse conchs and tulip shells

Most horse conchs and tulip shells of the family Fasciolariidae live in warm seas. They have elongate, spindle-shaped shells that are 1-24 in. in length. The tips of their shells form pointed, whorled spires that are often decorated with spiral and longitudinal ridges. Their shell openings are usually oval and extend to form long siphon canals at the front end. Snails of the genus *Fusinus* often have extremely long siphons. The water that enters their siphons passes into their gill chambers where a patch of sensory cells detects the scent of predators or prey.

Tulip shells prey on worms and clams. Like whelks of the genus *Busycon,* they force the clam shells open with their feet, wedging them open either with their siphon canal, or with the lips of their shells. Like the majority of predatory snails, tulip shells can identify their prey either by detecting their scent in the water or by following the mucous trails they leave on the ground.

Avoiding attack

Although it is a predator, the tulip shell *Fasciolaria tulipa* often falls victim to other mollusks such as the Eastern nassa and the queen conch. When faced with one of these predators, the tulip shell, using its foot to lift itself, retreats in a series of rapid, convulsive leaps like somersaults. The leaping movement enables the creature to move over an inch at a time and confuses the predator.

Courtship or cannibalism?

Tulip shells sometimes react in this way to other members of its species. When it encounters another tulip shell, it reacts in one of two ways, depending on the size and sex of the approaching mollusk. If the second tulip shell is larger, the first snail retreats; if it is smaller, the first tulip shell pursues and often catches it. If the prisoner is of the same sex as its attacker, it is usually eaten, but if it is of the opposite sex, they may mate.

Beautiful shells

Six families in the superfamily Muricacae contain snails that are reputed to have some of the most beautiful shells in the world. They range in color from pink to golden-yellow or reddish brown, often with colored spots, stripes or spiral lines and delicate folds along the rim. Most species are tropical, living in the shallow waters of warm seas.

The olive shells, members of the family Olividae, are mostly tropical snails with rounded, squat shells that rarely exceed 4 in. in length. Each shell has a short spire, and the last coil almost completely envelops the preceding ones. The shell opening is long and narrow, forming a deep siphon canal at its front end. The shell surface is smooth and glossy and has an extremely varied range of colors.

There are nearly 200 species of olive shell, and even within a species they often vary in color from white or brown to orange. When an olive shell's foot is fully extended, its shell is almost completely covered by side flaps of skin—a feature also seen in the cowries. At the front, its foot forms a triangular, or shield-like, flap that protects the creature's head when it burrows and is used by some species for swimming.

Members of the genus *Oliva* are nocturnal carnivores. During the day, they lie buried in the sand with only their long water siphons peeking out of the seabed. At night, however, they emerge to search for prey— usually small mollusks. Their shells are perfectly balanced so they can move rapidly. The Caribbean species *Ancilla glabrata* has the unusual habit of producing large quantities of sticky mucus to protect itself from attack by fish and crab predators. Its shell varies in color from cream to a rich golden-yellow. It is oval in shape with a pointed tip. The last coil of the shell is divided from the rest by a deep groove that is partly hidden by a thickening of the surface.

ABOVE The olive shells occur in a wide range of colors; white, brown or orange specimens can be found among members of the same species. The shell is held horizontal to the foot, enabling the snail to move along extremely quickly. PAGES 2756-2757 On a beach in Lincolnshire, England, the yellow egg cases of a common whelk cluster together on a rock.

The vase shells, members of the same family Vasidae, live in tropical and subtropical seas in the Indo-Pacific, where they prey on bivalve mollusks and bristle worms. Undoubtedly the best known of the vase shells is the Indian chank, which is considered to be sacred by one of the Hindu sects. It lives in the sea to the south of India and around Sri Lanka, and is collected and made into bracelets that are believed to increase fertility. The coils of some Indian shank shells have developed in a counterclockwise direction, and they are worshiped in Hindu temples. The shells measure 4-6 in. long, and are thick and heavy. They are white in color, with scattered brown spots and a dark, fibrous outer covering. The shell opening is white, except for the edge of the outer lip, which is pink.

Self-defense

The harp shells consist of 14 tropical species in the family Harpidae. The snails are easily distinguished by their rounded shells, which are decorated with pronounced longitudinal ridges and beautiful patterns of color. The shells have a glossy surface, and are usually cream-colored with brown, orange and pink patterns.

The genus *Harpa* consists entirely of nocturnal species that feed on prawns and crabs, both alive and dead. Although the snails have large shells, their

PROSOBRANCHS
— METHODS OF SELF-DEFENSE —

Prosobranchs, gastropods that include the marine snails, have evolved various methods of self-defense. The simplest is the possession of a thick, heavy shell that may bristle with spikes, such as the type belonging to the pelican's-foot shell. Although armor of this sort provides good protection for the snail, it often slows the animal down.

Defensive camouflage

Camouflage provides another form of defense. Prosobranch shells often become encrusted with algae and other marine invertebrates, such as corals, enabling the prosobranchs to blend in with their seaweed or coral surroundings. Some species exploit color camouflage still further. The shell of the

cowrie, Calpurnus verrucosus, is covered with a layer of skin that is the same color as the corals on which it feeds. When the snail extends its foot in order to move forward, the cowrie's body remains camouflaged against the coral, since the foot and shell bear the same coloring. Similarly, the cowries that feed on sea squirts disguise their shells with layers of skin that have both the texture and color of their prey. Not all snails rely on imitative coloring for disguise, however. The small-shelled heteropods, for example, live in the open sea and rely on the transparency of their bodies for protection.

Instead of concealing themselves, poisonous snails, such as the cone shells, usually advertise their presence

with brightly colored shells. These warn predators to keep their distance. The most important defensive adaptations are often behavioral. Many snails stay buried in the sand throughout the day, only moving at night. In this way, the snails avoid most of their potential predators, such as fishes, that feed mainly by day.

Secretive life-styles

Some prosobranchs have adopted a secretive way of life, living in cracks in rocks, or hiding beneath them. Some even dig themselves a shelter inside their own prey; members of the genus Stilifer live embedded in the body walls of sea urchins on which they feed.

Highly evolved prosobranchs have developed more specialized defensive strategies. In these animals, the most immediate response is usually that of escape. The conchs, for example, have developed a rapid escape technique, enabling them to take short leaps that quickly carry them out of the path of danger.

Prosobranchs are not always fast enough to escape danger, and sometimes have to confront their enemies. They have developed a number of strategies in order to survive. Mud snails either shake their shells violently from side to side, or else somersault out of the way. The harp shell, on the other hand, gains time to escape by cutting off the rear end of its foot with the edge of its shell, leaving it behind for the attacker to eat.

The most highly developed prosobranchs, the neogastropods, emit toxic substances or acids that not only stun and kill their prey but also deter attacks by larger mollusks and fishes. The violet snail of the genus Janthina

has a special method of protecting itself from predators. Since it lives at the surface of the sea, suspended from a raft of gas bubbles, it is particularly exposed to predation by fishes and birds. In times of danger, it produces a purple liquid that quickly spreads out in the water to form a dark cloud that engulfs and hides it.

Poisonous darts

Cone shells use the poisonous darts with which they kill their prey to attack predators. Indeed, human collectors of cone shells frequently fall victim to these poison darts, and in some instances they have died as a result of their encounters.

A chemical warning

Some species of prosobranchs defend themselves when they detect certain chemical substances in the water. Mud snails and dog whelks, for example, are stimulated by chemicals released by an injured member of the same species. If a crab crushes a small dog whelk with its nippers, all the other members of the same dog whelk species in the area quickly dig themselves into the sand. Their defense reaction is a little delayed, but it is activated even before they have identified the predator. Obviously, this strategy only works when many of these snails are living in close proximity to each other, where the death of one ensures the survival of the others.

FAR LEFT The tiny parasitic snails of the genus *Stylifer* live embedded in the body wall of the sea urchins on which they feed.
RIGHT The harp shells have an unusual method of self-defense. When approached by a crab (A), the snail cuts off part of its own foot (B). While the crab feeds on this, the snail either makes its escape, or else it turns around and covers the crab with a sticky secretion and sand (C). When the crab is immobilized, the snail kills and eats it (D).

ABOVE The cancellated nutmeg shell does not have a horny pad on its foot with which to seal its shell after withdrawing into it. Instead, it forms a temporary door by sticking grains of sand together, giving predators the impression that it is merely an empty shell.

bodies are too bulky to withdraw completely into them. Consequently, harp shells remain vulnerable and are often attacked by large crabs. When this happens, the snails defend themselves in an elaborate and unusual manner.

If a harp snail is attacked by a large crab, it is able to cut off the back part of its own foot—a process known as autotomy. The crab immediately devours the severed flesh, thus giving the snail a chance to escape. The missing part of the foot soon grows again. On the other hand, if the crab is not too large, the snail fights back by squirting large quantities of sticky saliva at its attacker. At the same time, the snail throws up jets of sand. The unfortunate crab is soon immobilized and eated by the snail. In order to eat its meal, the snail digs its mouthparts into the flesh and rasps at it with its tongue.

There are about 200 species of volutes, or bailer shells, in the family Volutidae. They have beautiful shells that vary from elegant and tall-spired to rounded and low-spired. The shells are usually glossy and highly colored, and many have a sculptured surface.

The volutes have a totally carnivorous diet, feeding on other mollusks and small invertebrates. They are largely distributed throughout the tropics, and three-quarters of all known species live in the Indo-Pacific Ocean. On the whole, the volutes prefer to live in shallow waters on sandy seabeds. However, specimens have been brought to the surface from depths as great as 10,000 ft.

Small and elegant

There are about 400 species of miter shells, members of the family Mitridae. Their shells are elongated and coiled, usually with sculptured surfaces of spiral or longitudinal ridges. The shells rarely exceed 6 in. in length, and they are decorated with colored bands, generally in brown, black, white, red or orange.

Miter shells live at depths of up to 5000 ft. The most characteristic genus is *Mitra*. The largest species living in the Mediterranean Sea is *Mitra zonata*, which is especially prolific in the Adriatic Sea. Until a few years ago, it was considered to be a rare species. It has an elegant, slender, spindle-shaped shell that forms a sharp point at the apex. A deep groove separates its coils. The exit of its water siphon is lodged within the wedge-shaped shell opening. Its shell is reddish brown in color, with yellowish patches and faint longitudinal stripes.

Cancellariacea

The superfamily Cancellariacea consists of a small group of about 150 species of snail within a single family—the Cancellariidae. They have small, conical shells that are between 0.8 and 2 in. in length and a short siphon canal. The surface of their shells consists of sharp spiral and longitudinal ribs that intersect to form a pattern of rectangles. The inner edge of the shell opening has two to four folds, while the inner surface of the shell lip bears ridges.

Snails in the family Cancellariidae usually live in deep water. They have no horny pads on their feet with which to close their shells when they withdraw inside them. Instead, they close their shells by covering them with grains of sand that they press together. Their "doors" of sand are probably also a means of self-defense—predators easily mistake them for empty shells.

SHAPELY SHELLS

The episcopal miter *Mitra mitra* is one of the largest species of miter shells (family Mitridae in the gastropod subclass Prosobranchia). It grows up to 4 in. in length, and occurs in many regions of the Indian and Pacific oceans. The name "episcopal" comes from the Latin *episcopus,* meaning "bishop," since the shell is said to resemble the tall headdress (miter) worn by bishops. Other miter shells have names that are associated with the pope for the same reason: the papal miter and the pontifical miter. Miter shells continue to be popular among collectors because of their bright colors and patterns; the shell of *M. mitra,* for example, is attractively covered with orange checks. Miter shells live in warm and shallow seas, where they lead carnivorous lives, using their long, tentacle-like proboscises to attack and feed on bivalves and worms.

Ridges and patterns

The margin shells are members of the gastropod family Marginellidae. Most of the 30 genera are tropical, found in shallow seawater to depths of at least 650 ft. The majority of these genera live off the coasts of western Africa (one subfamily, the Marginelloninae,

ABOVE The miter shell is a tropical sea snail that spends much of its time buried in the sands of coral reefs. It kills prey, such as worms and echinoderms, with its poisonous toothed tongue.
BELOW The distribution of certain species of the family Volutidae.

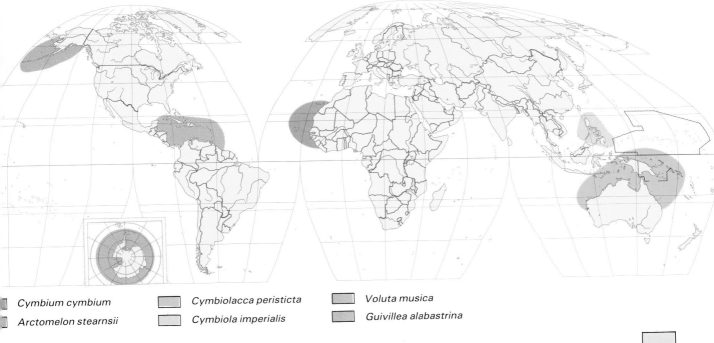

- Cymbium cymbium
- Arctomelon stearnsii
- Cymbiolacca peristicta
- Cymbiola imperialis
- Voluta musica
- Guivillea alabastrina

2761

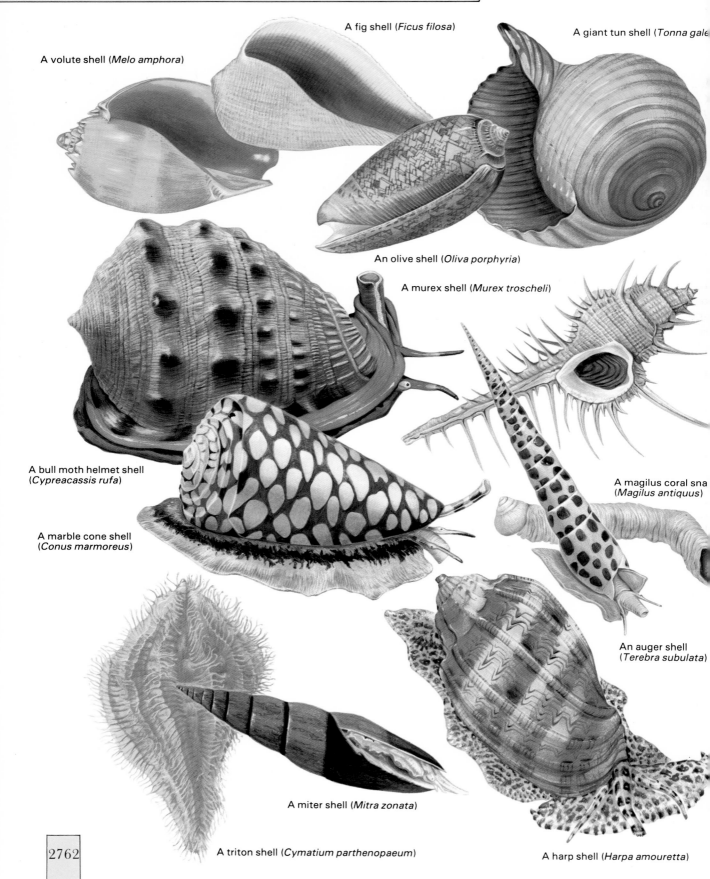

A volute shell (*Melo amphora*)

A fig shell (*Ficus filosa*)

A giant tun shell (*Tonna gale*

An olive shell (*Oliva porphyria*)

A murex shell (*Murex troscheli*)

A bull moth helmet shell
(*Cypreacassis rufa*)

A marble cone shell
(*Conus marmoreus*)

A magilus coral sna
(*Magilus antiquus*)

An auger shell
(*Terebra subulata*)

A miter shell (*Mitra zonata*)

A triton shell (*Cymatium parthenopaeum*)

A harp shell (*Harpa amouretta*)

has been found off South Africa and in the Indian Ocean) and Australia; there is one freshwater genus, *Rivomarginella*, that occurs in Thailand.

Margin shells are similar to cowries in appearance, with oval-shaped, glossy shells that have a long, narrow, slit-like opening. They are 0.4-0.8 in. long, and when the snail extends its foot, it covers most of the shell with a protective layer of skin. The margin shell's head bears long, thin tentacles at the bases of which are the eyes.

The outer edge (or margin) of the shell opening is thickened to form a distinct rim that is often finely ridged on its inner surface—hence the name, margin shell. The inner edge of the shell opening has a number of decorative folds that are very pronounced in some species. Unlike cowrie shells, margin shells usually have short spires. They are frequently patterned with a series of colored spots, stripes or spiral lines.

Cone shells

Cone shells hunt at night, preying on bristle worms, mollusks and fishes. Most species inhabit shallow waters at depths down to 150 ft., although a few species venture into deeper water. Cone shells are distributed throughout the tropical seas, being particularly common in the Indo-Pacific. Some species inhabit coral-covered seabeds, hiding in cracks in the rock or beneath stones during the day. Others live on muddy or sandy areas of the seabed, remaining in burrows beneath the surface during periods of inactivity.

Nature's harpooners

It is popularly believed, although not scientifically proven, that the cone shell immobilizes its prey with its hollow, lance-like poisoned teeth or darts. The teeth are produced by the tongue and stored in a bag-like structure at the base of the mobile tubular mouthpart (proboscis) within the mouth opening. A poison-filled duct that opens into the proboscis connects at its far end with a muscular bulb, which contracts to force the poison out when the cone shell attacks its prey. The proboscis itself is a muscular extension of the gut that can be retracted or thrust forward through the mouth.

Since the cone shell is a rather sedentary creature, it does not pursue its prey, but waits until it comes within striking distance. The snail prepares for attack by releasing poisoned teeth from its tongue into the tip of the proboscis. When hunting other mollusks, it

TOP Most margin shells are colorful sea snails of the tropical regions. Their smooth, glossy shells often extend into short spires. In most species, lateral folds of skin partly cover the shell during movement.
ABOVE Some species of margin shells resemble cowries.

uses its proboscis as a harpoon to "shoot" one or more teeth at its prey, following the harpoon attack with a secretion of noxious chemicals. The secretion forms a cloud of nerve gas that, when combined with the action of the poisoned teeth, instantly paralyzes its victim. After immobilizing its mollusk victim, the cone shell pulls it from its shell and swallows it whole.

Buried predators

Fish-eating cone shells lie buried in the sand where they use their extended water siphons to smell the

ABOVE The cone shell, *Conus mercator*, is a West African sea snail that inhabits the soft, sandy or muddy seabeds of shallow waters. It is a small snail, barely 0.8 in. long. The markings on its shell are distinctive, consisting of two dark bands with whitish markings, which stand out against the yellow background. Like all cone shells, it is a predatory species and feeds at night.

water for the scent of prey. When a suitable victim comes within striking distance, the cone shell extends its proboscis—which contains a poisoned tooth—and strikes the side or belly of the fish; poison enters the fish through the tooth's hollow center. If the attack successfully immobilizes the prey, the cone shell rears up out of the sand, withdraws its proboscis and swallows the fish whole, complete with the embedded tooth. If the attack is unsuccessful, however, the cone shell abandons its prey along with its tooth. All species of cone shells use each of their poison teeth on one occasion only. Fish-eating cone shells are very particular about their choice of prey: many species eat only one or two species of fish.

Fish eaters, such as the Mediterranean cone, *Conus mediterraneus,* have distinctive, round shells with slightly swollen body whorls. The Mediterranean cone has a thin, fragile shell that varies in color between yellow, brownish purple and green.

Worm eaters

Most species of cone shells prey on bristle worms, paralyzing them with single poisoned teeth in their proboscises. The worm eaters include the sand-dusted cone, *Conus arenatus*—a creamy-white cone shell with an irregular pattern of chestnut dots scattered over its surface—and *C. planorbis,* a rough-shelled snail with spirally ribbed shell coils. Both species have heavy shells with flattened spires. The first few coils of the *C. planorbis* cone shell are flat or concave with three to six raised spirals intersected by narrow, longitudinal stripes. Its shell is yellow or white and marked with spiral lines broken up into short, thin, brown dashes (occasionally these fuse to form a continuous stripe). The base of the shell is brown with a reddish tinge, and has two pronounced yellow, spiral bands. The shell opening is narrow and straight, while the inside of the shell is a creamy-white decorated with a purple band at its front.

The marble cone shell

The marble cone shell, *C. marmoreus,* is one of a number of mollusk-feeding species. Its thick, robust

shell is about 4 in. in length with a flattened spire. The first few coils are flattened and decorated with a row of small bumps. The shell bears a striking pattern of regularly arranged white, triangular scales on a black or dark brown background. The white, inner surface of the shell opens into a long slit with a thin, sharp outer edge.

Turret shells

The turret shells comprise the family Turridae—one of the largest of the superfamily Conacea. The Turridae, with its numerous subfamilies, presents problems of taxonomic classification, since its different species vary greatly in size, deceiving the casual observer into believing that they belong to separate families.

Their spindle-shaped shells have spiral and crosswise moldings while the openings extend into long siphons. Like all Conacea, turret shells kill or stun their prey with poisonous secretions.

The turret shell species *Mangelia powisiana* lives on muddy and sandy parts of the seabed, where it preys mainly on the bristle worms that are abundant in such areas. Sometimes, members of the species hold onto their prey with their mouthparts, spear them with poison teeth and inject paralyzing poison. However, since many individuals do not have the strength to

ABOVE Cone shells lay their eggs in pouch-like capsules that they either attach to a rock, using their sticky basal disks, or deposit on the sand. The free-swimming larvae hatch after about 10 days. **BELOW** Cone shells immobilize their prey using a poisoned dart. The cone shell lies buried in the sand and senses the approaching prey with its water siphon, which protrudes above the surface (A). It then extends its proboscis, holding its poisoned dart firmly in place (B). When the cone's probing, extended proboscis touches the fish, it embeds the dart into the side of the fish. The poison is injected into the prey through the hollow center of the dart (C). The cone shell engulfs its prey and swallows it whole. It is unable to withdraw its proboscis until the prey has been digested (D).

A

B

C

D

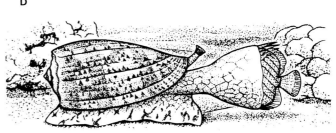

hold onto their prey for more than a few seconds, they drag their bodies through the seabed and scoop up buried bristle worms as they travel.

Auger shells

Auger shells (family Terebridae) inhabit coral sands in shallow, tropical waters; only a few species venture into deeper water. All species have tower-shaped shells of great weight and size. The shell of the rare species *Terebra triseriata,* for example, contains more than 50 coils and measures about 3 in. in length. Since many auger species cannot balance the weight of their thick, heavy shells above their bodies, they lay them on their sides and drag them along the seabed. As members of some species, such as the Mozambican *T. staminea,* move through sediment, the tips of their shells leave characteristic trails in the sand.

The opisthobranchs

The subclass Opisthobranchia within the order Neogastropoda contains both shell-less mollusks and

ABOVE Auger shells have tower-like shells composed of a number of coils. They inhabit the seabeds of warm, shallow waters, and feed on bristle worms. Their shells are too heavy to carry, so they bury themselves in the seabed and leave their shells resting on the surface while they hunt.
BELOW Cone shells are found in many regions of the world, extending as far north as Portugal and as far south as the southern African coastline.

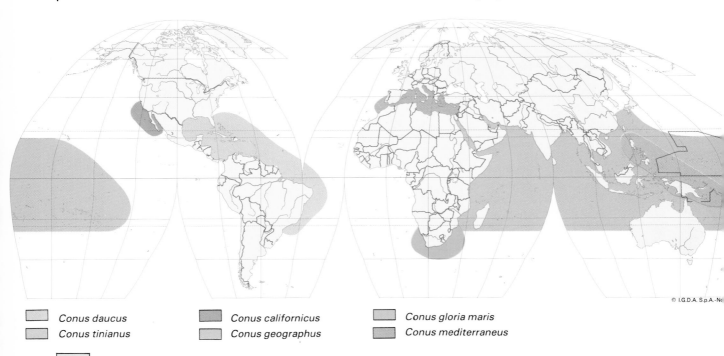

© I.G.D.A. S.p.A.-Ne

| | Conus daucus | | Conus californicus | | Conus gloria maris |
| | Conus tinianus | | Conus geographus | | Conus mediterraneus |

mollusks with coil-less shells. In some opisthobranch orders, the absence of coils has led to a gradual evolutionary disappearance of the mantle (the skin layer that secretes the shell). The loss of the mantle has thus led to the disappearance of the shell, the external gill chamber formed by the overhang of the shell and the gills. Evolution has also given the opisthobranchs a bilateral symmetry—that is, the two halves of the body are mirror images of each other.

The formation and development of the opisthobranchs' larvae provide a clue to the evolution of the subclass. The typical opisthobranch larva is a planktonic creature known as a veliger larva. During its early development, it becomes twisted, as do many prosobranch larvae, and, like adult prosobranchs, it has a shell that can be sealed with a horny pad on its foot (an operculum). However, during metamorphosis the larva straightens out, and, in many cases, its shell disappears. The Opisthobranchia probably broke away (in evolutionary terms) from the Prosobranchia about 340 million years ago, during the Carboniferous era.

Bubble shells comprise 13 families within the order Cephalaspidea—the largest of the opisthobranch orders. Zoologists consider bubble shells of the family Acteonidae to be the most primitive opisthobranch mollusks, since they have many of the structural characteristics of the lowest prosobranchs. The shell of the acteonid bubble shell has gentle spirals and an operculum; its opening to the gill cavity is on the right-hand side of the body and contains only one gill. The body organs have the coiled arrangement typical of prosobranchs; the nerve connections cross each other in pairs and do not form the symmetrical system characteristic of the higher opisthobranchs. The other opisthobranch families are distinct from the family Acteonidae in that their internal organs have developed symmetrically around a central body axis.

Physical differences

The different species of opisthobranchs vary greatly in appearance, since the total or partial loss of their shells has allowed their body shapes to evolve with a

---

MOLLUSKS
CLASSIFICATION: 10

Opisthobranchs (1)

The subclass Opisthobranchia is the second major subclass within the class Gastropoda (the first was the subclass Prosobranchia). Opisthobranchs consist of some 2000 species of largely shell-less marine slugs that are distributed throughout the world's seas, including Arctic and Antarctic waters. They are divided into 109 families and nine orders. The orders are Cephalaspidea, Runcinoidea, Acochlidioidea, Sacoglossa, Anaspidea, Notaspidea, Thecosomata, Gymnosomata and Nudibranchia. (The last 3 are dealt with in mollusks classification box 11.)

The largest opisthobranch order is the Cephalaspidea (bubble shells). It contains 13 families, including the Acteonidae; the Ringiculidae; the Bullidae, which contains the common Atlantic bubble, *Bulla striata*; the Gastropteridae, whose members can swim; the Philinidae (lobe shells); and the Scaphandridae (canoe shells). Opisthobranchs of the order Runcinoidea include the species *Runcina coronata*; the order Acochlidioidea contains the *Acochlidium amboinence,* which can tolerate freshwater. Opisthobranchs of the order Sacoglossa are herbivores and are grouped into seven families, such as the Juliidae (the only bivalve gastropods) and the Elysiidae of European waters.

The opisthobranch order Anaspidea contains five families of slug-like, seaweed-feeding animals called sea hares. They include the European family Akeridae, and the Aplysiidae (containing the genus *Aplysia,* used for research work). The order Notaspidea contains three families of bottom-dwelling, carnivorous, slug-like animals: the Umbraculidae (umbrella shells) containing the Mediterranean umbrella shell, *Umbraculum mediterraneum*; the Tylodidinae, containing the genus *Tylodina* of warm temperate and tropical seas, and the genus *Tylodinella* of the eastern Atlantic Ocean; and the Pleurobranchidae, whose members feed on sea squirts and sponges.

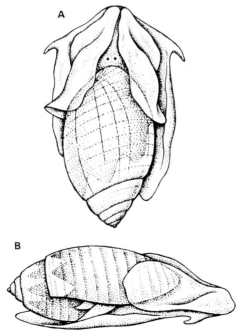

minimum of physical restriction. The more advanced species have developed differentiated feet, additional swim lobes, and bilateral symmetry of the external body. Primitive orders (such as the bubble shells and sea hares) have prosobranch-like gill chambers and gills on the right-hand sides of their bodies, but the most advanced groups (such as the true sea slugs) breathe through secondary gills on their backs. When an opisthobranch species loses the gill cavity through evolution, the osphradium (the sensory organ for receiving chemical stimuli) also disappears.

Vegetarians and cannibals

The feeding habits of opisthobranchs vary greatly among species: many are herbivores that feed mainly on the chlorophyll-rich seaweed that grows abundantly in shallow waters at depths of about 100 ft.; most others are predators that hunt sponges, sea anemones, crustaceans and mollusks. Some species eat fish eggs; the sea slug, *Calma glaucoides,* for example, feeds on the eggs of gudgeon and pout (two small varieties of fish that live close to the seabed in coastal waters). Cannibalism occurs in a few species.

The great variety of feeding habits among the different opisthobranch species implies that there have been many evolutionary modifications to their digestive systems. The typical opisthobranch has a mouth that contains a horny "tongue" and the type of jaw structure characteristic of all mollusks. The pharynx leads into the first part of the gut (the esophagus), which in turn leads to the stomach, the intestine and the anus. Unlike all other families in the animal kingdom, most opisthobranch families have gizzard plates—hard, plate-like structures that crush semidigested food as it reaches the lower part of the esophagus. Bubble shells of the genus *Philine* (lobe shells) swallow bivalve mollusks whole, and use their

ABOVE LEFT The bubble shell, *Acteon tornatilis*, is considered to be the most primitive of all the opisthobranch mollusks, having retained a twisted nervous system as well as having a shell that it can close with a horny pad on its foot. It lays hundreds of tiny white eggs inside a tall, flask-like capsule that it attaches to the seabed by its base.
LEFT The bubble shell, *Japonacteon nipponensis*, seen from above (A) and from the side (B). Its head is protected by two lobes that fold across it to form a shield, enabling the animal to burrow. Its eyes are visible on the back of its head.

gizzard plates to break up the shells. In some opisthobranch species, the pharynx (throat) expands to swallow large prey by turning inside-out.

Nerve rewiring

Unlike the prosobranchs and primitive opisthobranchs, most opisthobranch species have symmetrical nervous systems with relatively high concentrations of nerve centers in their heads. The sophistication of their nervous systems arose with the uncoiling of their body masses through evolution. In the highest opisthobranch orders, the nerve centers form primitive brains.

Mating chains

Most opisthobranch species are hermaphrodites, containing both male and female reproductive organs. Hermaphroditism occurs in most groups of stationary and semimobile animals, since it increases their otherwise small capacity for reproduction. During mating, opisthobranchs act as both males and females: each partner may transmit sperm and each is capable of being fertilized. Members of some species inject sperm directly through the skins of their partners. During the mating season, opisthobranchs of the sea hare genus *Aplysia* form long chains of up to

ABOVE Some species of true sea slugs, such as *Calma glaucoides*, feed on the eggs of small fishes that live near the seabed in shallow waters, reducing their numbers.

The body of *C. glaucoides* lacks both a shell and a gill chamber, and is covered with long, fleshy projections through which the sea slug absorbs oxygen from the water.

10 individuals: each acts as a male to the individual in front of it, and a female to the one behind.

Locomotion

Locomotion methods vary among the different opisthobranch species. Some "glide" over the seabed using cilia on their feet, while others crawl on their feet by setting up waves of muscle contractions. However, evolution has modified the feet of most species into large swimming lobes that enable them to move through the water by flapping their bodies.

The swimming lobes of certain advanced genera fuse into funnels through which they squirt jets of water—providing enough force to propel their bodies forward. As they weave about on the seabed in a series of slow movements, "funneled" opisthobranchs resemble large, colorful butterflies.

Although most opisthobranchs are marine creatures, a few, such as *Acochlidium amboinensis,* live in brackish

ABOVE Canoe shells of the family Scaphandridae rarely exceed 2 in. in length and have conical or cylindrical shells into which they can withdraw. They live on muddy or sandy parts of the seabed, where they feed on tusk shells that live buried in the sediment. Cilia on the surface of their bodies keep their gill chambers and sensory organs free from debris, while they dig for their prey.

water or freshwater. In general, opisthobranchs are confined to shallow waters, but live on any type of substrate, from mud or sand to seaweed or rocks.

Methods of self-defense

Many of the 2000 species of opisthobranchs are formidable hunters, and they are rarely troubled by predators because they have developed a variety of effective defense mechanisms. Many species have developed numerous glands on the surface of their bodies that secrete evil-smelling or acidic substances to repel enemies.

Sea slugs have a unique form of self-defense. They have fleshy projections all over their backs, and in the tips of the projections they store the stinging cells of sea anemones and other coelenterates on which they feed. If an intruder such as a fish attacks them, they respond by holding their fleshy projections erect or directing them toward the attacker, thus drawing attention away from their heads. Only when an intruder touches their skin do the sea slugs fire their stinging cells—and in most cases that rapidly repels the offender.

Opisthobranchs have evolved so successfully without shells not only because they have developed sophisticated defense mechanisms. They have also developed a remarkable capacity for mimicry. There are many instances of imitative coloring. For example, the slug-like species *Elysia viridis* is the same color as the green seaweed on which it feeds. Many sea slugs have taken mimicry one step further with their capacity to imitate the shape of their food. *Duvaucelia odhneri,* which lives on the branches of sea fans, has a number of appendages that closely resemble sea-fan polyps in both shape and color. *Guyonia flava,* a species that feeds on sponges, also mimics its host in appearance.

Bubble shells

The order Cephalaspidea is the largest order within the subclass Opisthobranchia. It contains marine slugs that are commonly known as bubble shells. There are 13 families of bubble shells, including the most primitive members of the subclass. Most species live in shallow waters, where they frequent soft areas of the seabed. The majority are carnivorous, feeding on protozoa, bristle worms and bivalve mollusks.

All bubble shells have shells, although they are frequently small or internal. They also have gills that are often no more than folds on the inside of their mantles. Their heads often form flattened shields for burrowing, and are sometimes equipped with sensory tentacles for feeling and smelling their surroundings. Some species have a second pair of tentacles, called rhinophores, with plate-like folds on the upper half. The increased surface area of skin gives bubble shells a greater capacity to detect scents. On their right-hand side, between their feet and their heads, bubble shells have an organ of taste and smell called Hancock's organ.

Sealed-in

The most primitive opisthobranchs are bubble shells of the family Acteonidae. Unlike most other opisthobranchs, these creatures have a complete covering of shell into which they can withdraw totally. They can also seal the shell openings with the horny pads, or operculums, on their feet.

The genus *Acteon* is typical of the family Acteonidae. It is represented in Europe by *Acteon tornatilis,* a marine slug with a robust, oval shell. The shell's spire is pronounced, even though its final coil envelops most of the early whorls. Its lip is sharp, and the inner edge of its opening has a raised fold. The surface of the shell tends to be pink, with between one and three yellowish white spiral bands, regular spiral stripes and a fragile, amber-colored operculum.

The diet of *Acteon tornatilis* consists of bristle worms that live buried in sandy areas of the seabed. To reach them, the bubble shell burrows into the substrate. Sometimes it moves along under the surface of the seabed as well, using its shield-like head to plow through the sand. Unlike prosobranch mollusks, the opisthobranchs do not have siphons with which to maintain contact with the water. Instead, the upper edge of an opisthobranch's head extends to form a breathing tube through which it draws water into its gill chamber. The water passes out of the gill chamber through a channel on the right-hand edge of the creature's foot.

From robust to fragile

Other families of bubble shell have a variety of external shells into which they can withdraw completely, but none can seal themselves off once inside. For example, members of the family Ringiculidae, in a single genus consisting of about 12 tropical and subtropical species, have robust and prominent shells that are usually less than 0.4 in. in length. The shells have a thickening around their outer lips and pronounced folds around the inner edges of their

ABOVE Sea hares are hermaphrodites, having both male and female reproductive organs. However, they are not self-fertilizing. When mating, one of the pair acts as a female, the other as a male. Sea hares do not only mate in pairs; sometimes seven or eight individuals mate in a circle, or in a long chain as they swim along.
BELOW The geographical distribution of certain species of bubble shell belonging to the family Acteonidae.

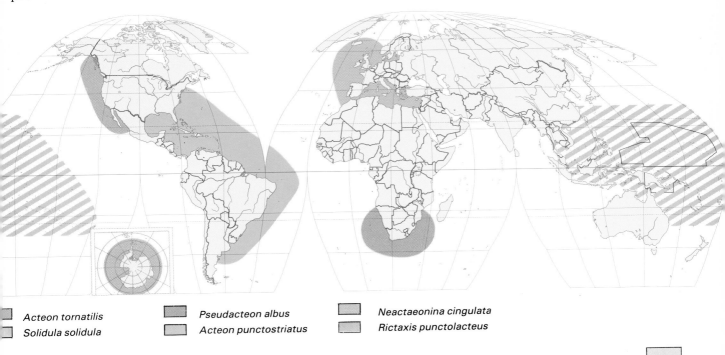

	Acteon tornatilis		Pseudacteon albus		Neactaeonina cingulata
	Solidula solidula		Acteon punctostriatus		Rictaxis punctolacteus

openings. By contrast, shells of the family Diaphanidae, consisting of species that live mostly in cold waters, are fragile, white, almost transparent and less than 0.2 in. long.

Species in the family Bullidae, inhabitants of warm tropical or temperate seas, have egg-shaped shells that are over an inch long. In the common Atlantic bubble, the shell's final whorl conceals its preceding whorls, and its spire is hidden. The shell's opening is narrow and extends its whole length, widening at the front to allow the animal to protrude. The shell is chestnut colored, with irregular light or dark patches. Most members of the family are nocturnal and feed on plants.

Members of the family Retusidae are barely 0.1 in. in length and have tiny, delicate, almost transparent white shells. They are inhabitants of temperate and cold seas, living in muddy seabeds or areas where mud and sand are mixed. Members of the genus *Retusa* are ferocious predators of small marine snails, even though they have neither jaws nor tongue. They swallow their prey whole and crush it with three horny plates in their stomachs.

Splendid coloring

Members of the family Hydatinidae exemplify the splended coloring sometimes present among the opisthobranchs. They have colorful bodies and thin, egg-shaped shells adorned with brightly colored spiral bands. The family consists of two genera that inhabit warm, temperate seas and live in sandy areas of the seabed where they feed on bristle worms.

Most members of the family Hydatinidae can withdraw completely into their shells. They each have a large, muscular foot, with lobes on either side that can cover their entire shells. Their heads bear a single pair of strong, backward-pointing lobes and two pairs of forward-pointing lobes. Bubble shells in the genus *Hydatina* have shells that are mostly cream colored, with a pattern of brown spiral bands. Their body lobes and feet are an almost transparent, flesh pink color with a vivid blue border.

Butterfly bubble shells

Members of the family Gastropteridae are the only bubble shells that can swim. Their feet have two large swimming lobes, one on either side of their bodies, and they each have a tail lobe. They move by beating their swimming lobes up and down, producing jerky, imprecise movements. They have an internal coiled shell that is less 0.04 in. in length and is mostly membranous. There are less than 10 species in the family Gastropteridae, and they are distributed worldwide. A common species in many seas, including the Mediterranean, is *Gastropteron meckeli,* which has a bright red body with darker markings and blue-edged swim lobes.

Slug-like creatures

There are nearly 50 species in the family Aglajidae. They are plain, slug-like creatures with two furrows across their backs. The skin on their backs is drawn out into two backward-pointing lobes, and they each have a tiny, flat, open coil of shell on the back half of their bodies. None of them have jaws, tongues or horny stomach plates. However, they are still capable of actively preying on worms, mollusks and fishes. They swallow their prey whole and excrete any indigestible material, such as mollusk shells, in their feces.

One member of the family Aglajidae, the American species *Navanax inermis,* lives in sandy and muddy areas of the seabed at depths of about 65 ft. Like all opisthobranch mollusks, its vision is poorly developed, so it locates its prey by means of chemical stimuli rather than by sight. If it is disturbed or attacked, *N. inermis* emits a yellow fluid that repels potential predators. Its body is brown with prominent yellow bands, and its eyes are black. The skin on its back expands into two lobes at the rear and is orange with yellow and blue markings.

Miniature suction pumps

The family Philinidae contains the single genus *Philine,* or lobe shells. Distributed worldwide, lobe shells are frequently found in shallow waters, where they form clusters on the seabed. They have white, fleshy bodies divided into four lobes and shells that are reduced to thin, chalky and completely internal shields.

The best-known species of lobe shell is *Philine quadripartita.* Since it preys mainly on immature bivalve mollusks, it gathers in large numbers where there is a

RIGHT The bubble shell, *Hydatina physis*, can cover the whole of its shell with its large body lobes. Its body lobes and large muscular foot are flesh pink with a vivid blue border. It inhabits the waters off southeast Australia.

A European bubble shell
(*Acteon tornatilis*)

A thecosome mollusk
(*Cymbulia peroni*)

A sea butterfly
(*Hylocylis striata*)

A thecosome mollusk
(*Cavolinia tridentata*)

A true sea slug
(*Glossodoris valenciennesi*)

A true sea slug
(*Coryphella verrucosa*)

A gymnosome moll
(*Clione limacina*)

A sea hare
(*Aplysia punctata*)

A true sea slug
(*Aeolis papillosa*)

A true sea slug
(*Flabellina affinis*)

A true sea slug
(*Chromodoris quadricolor*)

A true sea slug
(*Dendronotus arborescens*)

dense population of the mollusks. It swallows them whole, relying on the horny plates in its stomach to break them down. It also feeds on large bristle worms, using the hooked teeth on its tongue to pull the worms out of their tubes that lie buried in the sediment.

Philine quadripartita cannot always find an abundance of prey, especially at 16,500 ft., the maximum depth at which the species can live. Conseqently, it has developed a mechanism that enables it to feed on microscopic organisms. Sand and mud are always rich in protozoa, and the lobe shell can, by extending its mouthpart, suck these tiny creatures out of the sediment. Lying exposed on the seabed it, too, might be easy prey if not for the fact that it can expel poisonous substances such as sulfuric acid, from glands in its skin.

The order Runcinoidea

The tiny slug-like members of the order Runcinoidea are represented in Britain by the species *Runcina coronata,* which lives in rock pools and crevices that remain filled with water when the tide goes out. It feeds on seaweed and, like all the other members of the order, it has no head shield for digging, no tentacles, and no side lobes extending from its foot. *R. coronata* is a uniform dark brown color, with two clearly visible eyes and a gill protruding from the gill chamber on the right side of its body.

The order Acochlidioidea

The order Acochlidioidea consists of a small number of worm-like species that are never more than 1.2 in. in length and often barely 0.04 in. long. Their general shape reflects their adaptation to life in coarse-grained sand, where they move about in the gaps between the sand grains and feed on debris and microscopic algae.

Acochlidioideans do not have gills, but because they are small, they are able to obtain sufficient oxygen by breathing through their skins. Most species lack shells. Instead, they have transparent outer coverings containing chalky needles. A few species can tolerate water with a low salt content, and one species, *Acochlidium amboinense,* can live in freshwater.

The order Sacoglossa

The order Sacoglossa in the subclass Opisthobranchia consists of seven families of small, slug-like mollusks

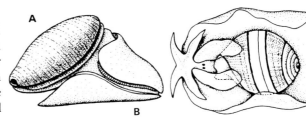

TOP Bubble shells of the family Hydatinidae have thin, egg-shaped shells that are decorated with spiral bands. They have brightly colored bodies that they can withdraw into their shells.
CENTRE The white, fleshy bubble shells of the genus *Philine* have thin, plate-like shells that they enclose with their mantles.

ABOVE The side view of the bubble shell, *Scaphander lignarius,* (A) shows the organ of Hancock (B), which is a region of sensory cells that it uses in food detection. The bubble shell, *Hydatina velum,* (C) has a protective head shield with a single pair of backward-facing lobes and two pairs of forward-facing lobes.

ABOVE **The European sea hare, *Akera bullata*, has a small, fragile shell at the rear of its body that protects its major body organs. The sides of its foot form broad swimming lobes. When resting, the sea hare folds them over its back.**

Alderia modesta lives on a particular type of green seaweed that grows in lagoons and bays situated near estuaries, where the water is fresh rather than brackish. Like certain other members of the family, such as *A. nuda* and *Stiliger talis,* which live in mangrove swamps, it can survive for short periods out of water. However, it lacks a protective shell, so its body is prone to drying up if it stays out of the water for long.

When feeding, *A. modesta* secretes a sticky mucus that enables it to fix its mouth firmly to the seaweed. Then, using its rasping tongue like a saw, it makes an incision in the surface of the weed. It sucks out the plant's juices with the help of its muscular throat. *S. vesciculosus* adopts a similar technique to feed on the eggs of sea slugs.

Flipper-like swimming lobes

The most common member of the family Elysiidae is *Elysia viridis*, a species that ranges from Norway to the Mediterranean. Its smooth, slug-like body is about 1.6-2 in. long. It has no gills or cerata, but possesses two long swimming lobes. The mollusk keeps its lobes folded on its back while it is moving on the surface, but spreads them out on either side of its body when it is motionless. It can also use the lobes to propel itself through the water for short distances, undulating them like flippers.

Like some other members of the order Sacoglossa, *E. viridis* feeds on green seaweed, cutting into the surface of the plant with its tongue and sucking out the fluids. Its body is normally the same color as the substrate upon which it lives, and its imitative coloring is accentuated by the fact that single-celled algae live in the surface cells of its body. *E. viridis* varies in color from green to red according to the pigments in its diet, and it has numerous red, blue and white markings.

Mimicry is only one of the techniques that *E. viridis* uses against predators. When danger strikes, it also emits a secretion that acts as a repellent. The secretion is produced by special cells situated on the underside of its swimming lobes—the area probably most exposed in the event of an attack.

Sea hares

In the order Anaspidea the subclass Opisthobranchia contains the sea hares. It consists of five families of slug-like mollusks that live in water and feed on seaweed. Species in the order have two pairs of tentacles on their heads, small internal shells and one foot each with broad side lobes that extend upward and across the backs of their bodies.

The family Akeridae is represented in Europe by the single species *Akera bullata,* which lives at the bottom of the sea among fields of sea grass. It has a thin, semitransparent, oval-shaped shell at the rear end of its body, protecting its major organs. It can measure up to 2.4 in. in length, and its body varies in color from gray to orange. It is marked with small flecks of white or a dark color, and dark red lines at the front.

The sides of *A. bullata's* body extend outward to form broad swimming lobes. The mollusk beats the lobes up and down in synchrony to propel itself forward through the water for short distances. The weight of its shell and the position of its internal organs at the rear of its body keep the animal in an upright position while it is swimming.

If it is attacked, *A. bullata* repels its enemy by releasing a nauseating red liquid from single-celled glands in the lining of its gill chamber. At the same time, it releases a certain amount of water in order to form a red cloud. While the predator is confused by the smell and the sudden appearance of the red cloud, *A. bullata* escapes.

Experimental research

The genus *Aplysia* belongs to the family Aplysiidae and is one of the best-known genera in the subclass

Opisthobranchia. Members of the genus are commonly used for experimental research purposes. They have transparent bodies and unusually large nerves and nerve centers, so they are used particularly in neurophysiology—the study of nerves and how they work.

The behavior of the various species in the genus *Aplysia*—particularly their feeding habits—has been observed extensively in laboratories. If they have not eaten for several days, species of *Aplysia* dig themselves into the substrate. When they detect food, they emerge from the sediment, stretch out their heads and oral tentacles and "sniff" the water. They soon locate the source of the smell and head off in that direction.

Aplysians have sensory cells on both their mouths and oral tentacles, and they use them to detect the scent of seaweed—the diet of all sea hares. The sides of their bodies are enlarged, forming swimming lobes that undulate with the rest of their bodies and enable them to swim. Once the aplysian has located a patch of seaweed, it circles over it, looking for the youngest and most tender shoots. It grasps the weed firmly with its foot and guides the tip of the selected shoot into its mouth. With its tongue, it draws in about 0.8 in. of the weed and then cuts it off. Once swallowed, the seaweed passes into the mollusk's stomach, where it is broken up by its horny teeth and then digested.

Water in a sac

Two other genera of sea hares are *Dolabella* and *Notarchus.* To move, they join their swimming lobes together to form a kind of sac, gather water into the sac and then expel it backward with great force.

Sea hares are usually a dull color. The three European species—*Aplysia punctata, A. depilans* and *A. fasciata*—are greenish or dark brown. More striking is *A. dactylomela,* a species found off the coasts of Africa and America. It has a yellowish body with bright purple rings. One of the largest species is *A. vaccaria,* which lives along the Pacific coast of America. It grows up to 22 in. long, and can easily be recognized by the long anal siphon protruding from its back between its two swimming lobes.

All sea hares have a completely internal shell that is so thin and fragile that it is hardly more than a scale. It offers little protection, but when danger strikes, sea hares can defend themselves extremely well. They emit a white or reddish substance made up of plant pigments mixed with proteins. The substance serves two purposes.

ABOVE When swimming, the swimming lobes of *Akera bullata* spread out sideways and beat gracefully up and down, rather like the wings of a butterfly. The downward beat of the swimming lobes pushes the animal upward through the water, and the rear end of the body hangs down resembling the clapper of a bell.

It sets up a smoke screen between predator and prey, and it upsets the predator's sense of smell so that it cannot locate the prey. As soon as the sea hare has emitted its liquid, it swims away rapidly.

Order Notaspidea

Within the subclass Opisthobranchia, the order Notaspidea consists of less than 150 species of marine, bottom-dwelling mollusks. Carnivorous and slug-like, they are divided into three families, with many species living in warm temperate and tropical seas.

Umbrella shells

Members of the family Umbraculidae are known as umbrella shells because their shells resemble small umbrellas perched on top of their bodies. The Mediterranean umbrella shell, *Umbraculum mediterraneum,* which feeds on sponges, is a typical species. It grows up to 8 in. in length and has a foot that is both broad and tall. Its body is brown and has a dense covering of whitish, finger-like projections.

Umbraculum mediterraneum's shell resembles that of a limpet. Its apex is brownish yellow, and it is often

generally less than 0.4 in. in length. Umbrella shells have a wide range of shapes, with or without shells, which makes it difficult to generalize about the different species. However, members of the order do possess some common characteristics. They are all herbivores, and since they lack jaws they all tear at plant tissues with their rasping tongues and suck out the fluids. Indeed, they often assume the color of the food on which they feed. Members of the order have a single row of teeth running down the middle of their tongues. When their teeth wear out, they replace them and store the old ones in a sac in their throats. Sometimes, they have fleshy projections known as cerata covering their backs.

Bivalve mollusks

Within the order Sacoglossa, the family Juliidae consists of tropical and subtropical species with slug-like, green bodies. They measure less than 0.4 in. in length and are flattened inside their bivalve shells, which resemble those of clams. At one time, their fossilized shells were thought to belong to the class Bivalvia. However, the discovery in 1959 of the first living specimens of the species *Berthelinia limax* enabled scientists to classify the group correctly as the only known bivalves in the class Gastropoda. Its body has the characteristic creeping foot common to all gastropods.

The two valves of the shells of mollusks in the family Juliidae are joined internally by a muscle. When the animal contracts the muscle, the valves come together to form a tight seal. There is a weak hinge at the apex of the shell, and when the animal moves, the hinge stays vertically over its body. The larvae usually have spiral shells with an operculum. As they grow, their embryonic shells remain permanent features at the apex of their left valves.

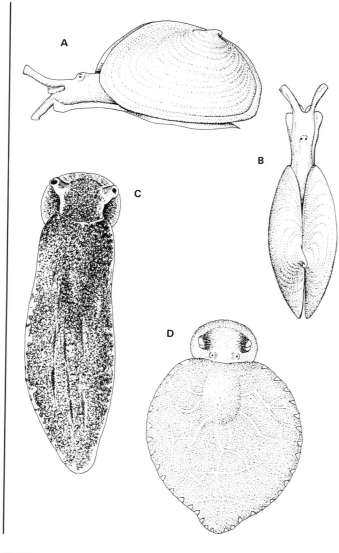

ABOVE LEFT **The shell-less mollusk, *Bosellia mimetica*, is green in color from eating seaweed. It pierces the seaweed fronds with its toothed tongue and sucks the juices.**
LEFT ***Berthelinia limax* is the only gastropod that has a bivalve shell. It has a creeping foot, and it holds its shell over its body as it** moves (A). **The bivalve shell (B) forms as the animal grows older. *Bosellia mimetica* changes its shape to suit its needs. When moving, its body is long and streamlined like the stems of seaweed (C). During feeding, its body assumes a flattened shape, similar to that of the seaweed fronds (D).**

As the mollusk moves, the front part of its body protrudes from the front of its shell. It reveals its head, which has a pair of ordinary tentacles and a pair of modified tentacles, or rhinophores, for tasting the water. Its eyes are situated on bumps on the back of its neck. Water flows into gill chambers on either side of its foot toward the front end of its body. After it has removed oxygen from the water at the gill surface, the water flows out toward the rear of its body through the half-closed valves. All members of the family Juliidae feed on plants, and they are often restricted to a single type of seaweed.

Distracting attackers

Mollusks in the family Oxynoidae characteristically have two modified tentacles each, which lie coiled on their heads in the form of outward-pointing cones. The species *Lobiger sowerbii* lives in the Indo-Pacific and Pacific Ocean off the coast of North America, where it feeds on seaweed. It has a green, slug-like body covered with pronounced, pale fleshy bumps. The rear end of its body extends into a pointed "tail." Its fragile shell has a large opening. The shell only partially covers the creature's back, so it cannot withdraw into it completely. *Lobiger sowerbii* has two swimming lobes that jut out from the sides of its body like long, narrow wings, enabling it to swim for short distances. If provoked, it sheds the back part of its foot to distract its attacker.

Dispensing with shells and gills

Members of the family Caliphyllidae, inhabitants of warm temperate and tropical seas, have dispensed completely with shells and true gills. Instead, they breathe entirely through their skins. The mollusks have a number of leaf-like, fleshy projections that act as external secondary gills. Called cerata, they increase the surface area of their bodies—and thus their capacity to breathe through their skin.

One species in the family Caliphyllidae, *Bosellia mimetica,* shows a further improvement in the breathing process. It has a surface network of blood vessels that is visible through the transparent outer layer of its body. The mollusk feeds exclusively on one species of green seaweed. When it is not moving, it assumes the flattened shape of its seaweed food and blends in with the environment. Its camouflage is all the more convincing because the configuration of blood vessels

ABOVE The shell-less mollusk, *Stiliger bifida*, has no gills, but breathes through its skin. The surface area of its body is increased by the presence of several large transparent lobes that jut out from the animal's back and function as gills.

near the surface of its body imitates the pattern of veins on the seaweed. When the animal moves, the shape of its body changes and becomes long and narrow.

Members of the family Stiligerae are largely Mediterranean species. Like the caliphyllids, they lack shells and true gills. Internally, their nervous systems are more advanced than those of other families in the order Sacoglossa. Some of their nerve centers are fused together and are concentrated in their heads.

In and out of water

Mollusks in the genus *Alderia* do not have hearts. *Alderia modesta* is a widespread species that exists in places as far apart as the Pacific coast of North America and the Atlantic coasts of Europe. It is less than 0.4 in. in length, and its back is covered with about 20 clubbed cerata or projections dotted with black and white markings. The rest of its body is light brown. The cerata pulsate, causing blood to circulate within them.

LEFT Sea hares of the genus *Aplysia* secrete a purple fluid, either as a screen against enemies or as a deterrent. The fluid is not a permanent dye, and although it will dye a handkerchief purple, it washes out easily.

BELOW LEFT In order to escape predators, *Tylodina perversa* hides inside the sponges on which it feeds. When sitting on the surface of the sponge, its brownish yellow coloring provides effective camouflage.

A different method of self-defense has evolved in the Pleurobranchidae family, whose members frequently lack shells or have internal ones. When attacked, they emit a strong sulfuric acid secretion.

The European species *Pleurobranchus membranaceus* has an internal shell of a membranous consistency. It has a broad, flat, light-brown foot that measures up to 5 in. long. The fold of skin, or mantle, that secretes the shell rests on its foot. It has a covering of tiny, retractable projections with dark markings. Underneath its mantle, on the right-hand side, it has a long gill.

Pleurobranchus membranaceus has a swimming technique that is strange but effective. It turns upside-down and beats first one side of the foot and then the other. Like all other members of its family, it feeds on sea squirts and sponges, which it attacks by boring a deep hole in their bodies and inserting its piercing mouthpart into their internal organs.

Berthella plumula, another European species in the family Pleurobranchidae, has projections that are fused together to form a flat structure known as a velum. Both its velum and its foot are able to take in large quantities of water. If the animal is attacked, it expels the water suddenly and its body shrinks dramatically in size. The species *B. aurantiaca* has another technique for protecting itself from attack: it rolls up into a ball.

Shelled sea butterflies

The order Thecosomata consists of 53 species in two suborders. Also known as shelled sea butterflies, they are tiny mollusks that range in length to little more than an inch. They are all free-swimming, marine creatures, and most live near the surface of the sea. Their feet are greatly modified for swimming by the presence of fins and swimming lobes.

Shelled sea butterflies do not actively move, and form part of the plankton on which they feed. They

Alderia are covered with algae and encrusting animals such as hydrozoa. At the rear of the mollusk, the top of a small tube—the end of its anal duct—is visible. Its fringed gill appears at the right of the anal duct opening. Its mouth consists of an incision at the front of its foot. Its eyes are contained in the two coiled, modified tentacles that jut out from its shell. It uses its tentacles to "taste" the water.

Clever forms of defense

The species *Tylodina perversa* belongs to the family Tylodinidae. To protect itself from attackers, it hides inside the sponge on which it feeds and disguises itself by imitating the brownish yellow color of the sponge.

have adapted to their exclusively planktonic life-style in numerous ways. Their shells and gills have undergone a progressive reduction in size. Their feet have expanded outward into wing-like structures that beat in time with each other, enabling the mollusks to hover at a certain depth below the surface of the water.

Shelled sea butterflies feed on planktonic mollusks and crustaceans. They capture them in feeding currents that they create by beating hundreds of microscopic hairs, or cilia, on the fronts of their bodies. Their stomachs have four strong, horny plates with which to crush the food. The tide often carries shelled sea butterflies toward the shore in huge numbers, where they form a staple diet for many fishes. Even whales draw much of the food they need from these tiny mollusks.

Sealed-in protection

There are two families of shelled sea butterflies in the suborder Euthecosomata. The family Limacinidae

ABOVE **The slug-like opisthobranch,** *Pleurobranchus mamillatus,* **has a thin, fragile shell. It is entirely enveloped by the mantle (seen here) and is never seen while the creature is alive.**
BELOW **The swimming motion of** *Pleurobranchus*

membranaceus **(A) is unusual in that the swimming lobe on one side of its body moves downward, while the one on the other side moves upward, causing the animal to roll. Its shell (B) is secreted from the small embyronic coil, visible at the top.**

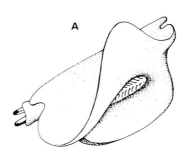

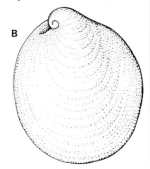

ABOVE The highly decorative *Pleurobranchus forskali* is a slow, slug-like opisthobranch that lacks a shell. It creeps slowly along the seabed feeding on sea squirts and sponges. It attacks its prey and bores a deep hole in its victim's body.

consists of eight species that inhabit all seas. They have retained well-developed, coiled shells that completely cover their bodies. As added protection, they can seal the openings with the horny pads (operculums) on their feet. On the top of their heads, they have a pair of tentacles, the right one much larger than the left. The sides of a limacinid's foot extend outward to form swimming lobes, and a fin-like lobe extends below the rear part of the foot. Limacinids lay their eggs in long, transparent, floating, jelly-like ribbons.

The family Cavoliniidae, also in the suborder Euthecosomata, consists of 23 species in seven genera. They have a planktonic life-style and inhabit temperate and warm seas all over the world. Members of the genus *Cavolinia* have flat shells that each divide into a top and bottom half and enclose the rear end of the sea butterfly's body. The front part of its body extends into two large lobes that serve a double function. They beat like the wings of a butterfly to help the mollusk swim, and they are equipped with microscopic hairs, or cilia, for gathering food. Although members of the genus *Cavolinia* are capable of remaining near the surface of the water, they often occur at depths ranging from a few hundred to 6500 ft.

Varied shell forms

The suborder Pseudothecosomata consists of 22 species in three families—the Peraclidae, the Cymbuliidae and the Desmopteridae. The shells of each family have developed in a different way. Members of the family Peraclidae, for example, have shells that are coiled in a spiral with a flattened spire. The central column of the shell extends into a curved beak, and its surface is covered with a meshlike texture. The opening can be sealed with a circular operculum. Two lateral swimming lobes at the front of the mollusk's body join together to form a continuous disk below its mouth. Because of the weight of its shell, the animal has to beat its lobes continuously in order to stay afloat.

Among species in the genus *Cymbulia*, the shells, mantles and gills have all disappeared. A cymbulian breathes through its skin, and instead of a shell it has a transparent, internal support called a pseudoconch.

Shaped like a boat and made of soft cartilage, it houses the animal's major body organs.

Members of the family Desmopteridae have dispensed with any kind of supporting structure. They are tiny creatures measuring no more than 0.08 in. in length, with two broad swimming appendages that extend into two ribbon-like tails at the back.

Naked sea butterflies

The order Gymnosomata—also known as naked sea butterflies—consists of about 50 species of mollusk in seven families. They are fast-swimming, predatory carnivores that live in the plankton. They have no shells or gills chamber but they sometimes have external gills. They capture their food in a highly specialized manner, frequently using tentacles equipped with suckers.

Naked sea butterflies are not easy to describe since they differ from all other Opisthobranchia and vary greatly from one genus to another. However, among their common characteristics, they are all active by day and collect in huge swarms, particularly in cold seas, where they feed on shelled sea butterflies. They, in turn, are preyed upon by fishes and whales.

ABOVE The bright red opisthobranch of the genus *Pleurobranchus* from the Red Sea reaches 6 in. long. A carnivore, it will usually feed rather than mate or sleep, but it will not feed while laying eggs because a hormone from its central nervous system suppresses its feeding instinct.

Specialized prey capture

The heads of naked sea butterflies are equipped with simple eyes and two swimming lobes that function like small wings. A whole range of organs have developed at the front of their bodies, serving as instruments for capturing prey. Their throats turn inside out to form long tubular mouthparts, with jaws and hooks to prevent the prey from escaping. The mollusks keep the hooks in special sacs and use their muscles to release the hooks into action when needed. At the base of their throats, they each have two or more feeding tentacles equipped with suckers on stalks. The mollusks use them to hold their prey while they eat it.

The species *Hydromyles globulosa* is the sole member of the family Hydromylidae. It can be found throughout the Indo-Pacific and has no tubular mouthpart or hooks. Instead, it captures its prey directly with its

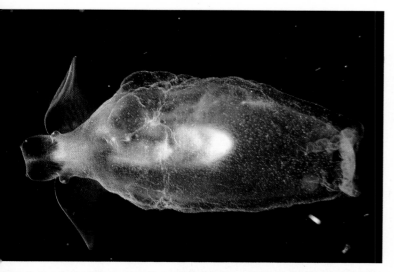

toothed tongue. Unique among the opisthobranchs, it has a special pocket near its anus that serves as an incubator. The larvae develop inside the pocket and emerge as fully developed individuals.

Tentacles and suckers

The family Pneumodermatidae consists of 17 species that live in warm, temperate seas. They have developed the most advanced method in their order of capturing prey. The Atlantic species *Pneumoderma atlanticum* catches its prey with two appendages that are each equipped with about 30 suckers. Having trapped its prey, it then shoots out its long, tubular mouthpart. *Pneumodermopsis ciliata,* which is common all over the world, has five tentacles, each equipped with a sucker at the end. *Cliopsis kroni,* a species belonging to the family Cliopsidae, has no suckers, but its tubular mouthpart can extend to three times the length of its body.

The best-known species of the family Clionidae is *Clione limacina,* which lives in the cold waters of the Arctic and sometimes appears in vast numbers along the coasts of northern Europe. Its tubular mouthpart is tiny, and it has no tentacles with suckers to help it capture prey. Instead, on each side of its mouth it has a sac containing about 15 hooks and three adhesive appendages. The animal swims quickly by beating its two swimming lobes in synchrony, and despite its poor sight, it preys upon mollusks of the order Thecosomata (particularly of the genus *Limacina*).

True sea slugs

True sea slugs belong to the four suborders and 66 families of the opisthobranch order Nudibranchia (the

TOP The naked sea butterfly of the genus *Cliopsis* belongs to the order Gymnosomata. It lacks a shell and has no mantle cavity. It is a free-swimming, planktonic creature, bearing various kinds of armament, such as pouches lined with hooks that it can push out to grasp its prey.
CENTER The delicate sea butterfly, *Cymbulia peroni,* belongs to the order Thecosomata. Unlike other thecosomes, it does not have a calcareous shell. Instead it has an internal, boat-like structure made of a soft gristle.
BOTTOM The naked sea butterfly, *Laginiopsis triloba,* has three fleshy lobes at the tip of its tubular mouthpart (A). Its head bears a pair of large cone-shaped tentacles (B). A pair of triangular fins spread out sideways from the front part of its rounded foot.

name means "exposed gills" from the Latin *nudus* meaning "naked," and *branchia* meaning "gill"). The 2500 or so species have a wide variety of body shapes and colors and include slugs with gaudy coloration and unusual appendages. Nudibranchs may be carnivorous or herbivorous: some species eat sponges, jellyfishes and sea anemones, while others eat seaweed. Except for the species *Ancylodoris baicalensis,* all sea slugs are marine creatures with short life spans—no more than a few months in some cases.

Nudibranchs are the most beautiful members of the class Mollusca and the most highly evolved of the opisthobranchs. The nervous systems of many species are concentrated into single brain-like masses above their throats; only a few nerve centers remain close to the major body organs, in the fashion of primitive mollusks. In adults, the gill chambers and shells have completely disappeared: breathing occurs either in secondary gills or through various flaps, plates or other fleshy extensions on the slugs' backs. As well as tongues, true sea slugs have unusual jaws consisting of two plates, each with two rows of teeth on one side. When a slug feeds, the plates rub together, crushing the prey between them. True sea slugs have developed highly specialized methods of camouflage and self-defense to compensate for their lack of shells.

ABOVE The transparent, naked sea butterfly, *Clione limacina,* has an elongate foot with two swimming lobes on its lower surface at the front end of its body. These beat simultaneously from side to side to propel the animal through the water.

The suborder Doridacea

The suborder Doridacea—the largest within the order Nudibranchia—contains 27 sea slug families within four superfamilies. Doridaceans inhabit most regions of the world's oceans, with species varying in size from less than 0.2 in. to more than 12 in. in length; some have protective, chalk-colored needles scattered over their skins. Although most members of the suborder feed on sponges, many species eat protozoans, marine worms, crustaceans and even other mollusks. All doridaceans are flat-bodied creatures. Their anuses—which open onto the centers of the rears of their backs—are surrounded by groups of gills arranged in the shape of flower petals. Many species can withdraw their "petals" when threatened.

Primitive doridaceans

The doridacean superfamily Gnathodoridacea contains two families of primitive nudibranch sea slugs. The first family—the Doridoxidae—is

2785

ABOVE The sea slug, *Hexabranchus sanguineus*, commonly known as the Spanish dancer, has a bright orange body with flecks of pink, white and yellow. The main part of its body is masked by the mantle which is folded up. Its head bears a pair of modified tentacles (rhinophores) on top.

Opisthobranchs (2)

The last three orders in the gastropod subclass Opisthobranchia are Thecosomata, Gymnosomata and Nudibranchia. The order Thecosomata (shelled sea butterflies) are small, free-swimming animals with reduced shells. Most live near the sea surface and feed on plankton. There are 53 species in two suborders. The suborder Euthecosomata consists of the families Limacinidae (with the single genus *Limicina*), and Cavoliniidae (including the genera *Cavolinia* and *Peraclis*).

The order Gymnosomata (naked sea butterflies) contains about 50 species of shell-less, fast-swimming, predatory mollusks. They are grouped into seven families, including the Hydromylidae of the Indo-Pacific region; the Pneumodermatidae (with the Atlantic species *Pneumoderma atlanticum*); and the Clionidae, which occurs in Arctic waters.

The final opisthobranchian order, Nudibranchia, consists of the true sea slugs. There are approximately 2500 species, divided into 66 families and four suborders: Doridacea, Dendronotacea, Arminacea and Aeolidacea.

monotypic, since it only contains the species *Doridoxa ingolfiana* of the deep Arctic waters on the east and west coasts of Greenland. The second Gnathodoridacea family is the Bathydorididae: there are six species and, since they all belong to the same genus, *Bathydoris,* the family is termed monogeneric. Members of the genus are usually small, rarely exceeding 1.2 in. in length. They thrive in very cold waters and live only in the Arctic, Antarctic or at depths beyond 13,000 ft.

The Anadoroidea

The doridacean superfamily Anadoroidea contains eight families of small to medium-sized nudibranchs. The 12 species of the obscure anadoroid family Corambidae live on the western coasts of Europe and on the Atlantic and Pacific coasts of North and South America.

The better-known family Goniodorididae contains 10 genera of nudibranchs that feed on sea squirts. Their natural coloration matches that of their prey and thus provides the sea slugs with near-perfect camouflage as they move within sea squirt colonies. Goniodoridids' eggs hatch in early spring, summer and early autumn. Members of the largest species may reach 1.5 in. in length.

Goniodoridid sea slugs have a wide distribution, and there are several European species. Two species of the

genus *Goniodoris,* for example, inhabit the seas of Britain: *G. castanea,* a distinctive reddish brown, white-flecked sea slug, lives off all British coasts except those of western Ireland. Like other true sea slugs, it has a cluster of secondary gills on its back: as many as nine plumed gills surround the anus; all match the coloration of the rest of the body. *G. castanea* has two rhinophores on either side of its head, each of which consists of up to 17 sections called lamellae (rhinophores are tentacle-like structures that sense the presence of chemicals in the seawater). Although *G. castanea* is not abundant, its distribution spreads from Europe to places as far away as Japan and New Zealand. Zoologists believe that members of the species traveled from Europe to new habitats by attaching themselves to the sides of ships.

Although the second British goniodoridid sea slug, *G. nodosa,* is fragile in appearance, it is a robust

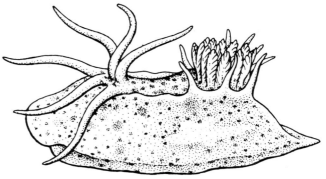

ABOVE In doridacean sea slugs, such as *Doris verrucosa* shown here, the anal openings at the animals' rears are surrounded by prominent clusters of feathery, secondary gills.
RIGHT The opisthobranch sea slug, *Okenia aspersa*, reveals its sensory tentacles, known as rhinophores, that pick up chemical signals emitted by nearby prey.
PAGES 2788–2789 Sea slugs of the order Nudibranchia (seen here in the Arabian Gulf) lay their eggs in long spiral ribbons.

creature. It grows up to 1.5 in. in length and has a translucent white body with faint yellow and pink coloration. Thirteen yellowish, feather-like gills surround its anus.

The young *G. nodosa* feeds mainly on bryozoans, while the adult feeds on sea squirts like other anadoroids. In the spring, sea slugs of the species mate in schools and lay curling masses of white eggs on colonies of bryozoa. Each egg mass contains as many as 32,500 eggs; each egg measures only 0.003 in. in diameter. Zoologists believe *G. nodosa* sea slugs to be annual organisms since they produce a new generation at the same time each year.

Immobility as defense

Most sea slugs of the genus *Goniodoris* ward off predators by secreting chemical repellents. However, the violet sea slug, *G. violacea*, is an exception since—like many other invertebrate animals—it remains completely immobile when threatened. In the face of attack, it shrinks back and keeps completely still in an attempt to discourage its predator. Since many predators are attracted to prey by their movements only, they often lose interest if their potential meals "play dead."

The great pretender

Ancula gibbosa—a species found on all North Atlantic coasts—has one of the largest geographical distributions of all nudibranch species. *A. gibbosa* protects itself from predators by mimicking a species of stinging mollusk: its body is translucent white, while

ABOVE The common British sea slug, *Polycera quadrilineata*, a member of the order Nudibranchia, has evolved a special trick for evading capture by a predator: if an enemy grabs it by one of its tentacles, the slug sheds it, leaving the attacker momentarily distracted.

FAR RIGHT While some sea slugs rely on camouflage to avoid detection, species such as *Chromodoris valencies* (above) and *Glossodoris luteorosea* (below) display vivid colors that warn predators of their foul taste or poisonous nature.

and, like many other nudibranchs, it shows a great variation in coloration, ranging from white or gray to reddish brown. *A. pilosa* lays huge numbers of eggs—approximately 170,000—none of which exceed 0.003 in. in length. The species occurs over a wide area, from the Bay of Biscay to northern Europe as far as the Arctic Circle. It inhabits the coasts of Greenland, Canada and the eastern seaboard of America, but seldom ventures into Mediterranean waters. A similar species lives in the Pacific near the Aleutian Islands.

British rarities

The family Trophidae contains what was, until 1972, one of Britain's rarest species of sea slug. *Crimora papillata* is white in color with bright orange tubercles all over its body; it feeds on bryozoans. In the 1980s marine biologists discovered large populations off the coasts of Devon, Cornwall and South Wales. *C. papillata's* eggs require a near constant temperature of 60.8°F, and, like the eggs of other British mollusk species, they take approximately 11 days to hatch.

Many-colored markings

Sea slugs of the genus *Polycera* (family Polyceratidae) inhabit many regions of the world, including the Pacific coast of America, the Mediterranean and the shallow coastal waters of western Europe. They are characterized by long, projecting nodules on the fronts of their bodies. The European species *P. quadrilineata* lives in shallow water where it feeds on the fronds of thin seaweed; it has two long orange tubercles on its back, next to its gills, and four long, orange, horn-like papillae at the front of its body. Most *P. quadrilineata* slugs have white bodies with rows of reddish orange markings on their sides and backs; their rhinophores and gills have a similar coloration. Some individuals, however, bear black, yellow and red speckled body markings in addition to their normal reddish orange pigmentation. The species' unusual coloration helps to break up its outline when it lies at rest in its natural surroundings, thereby making it less recognizable to predators.

Under threat of attack, *P. quadrilineata* employs two techniques of self-defense. When disturbed, its first reaction is to shrink and remain perfectly still and rigid. If, however, the predator continues undeterred, the sea slug flees, shedding its long tubercles as it moves; zoologists believe that internal muscular

the mouth tentacles, rhinophores and the row of long tubercles on its back are bright orange. The coloration closely resembles that of the aeolidacean species *Calmella cavolinii,* an animal avoided by predators because it can fire stinging cells removed from sea anemones during digestion.

Retractable rhinophores

Sea slugs of the doridacean family Lamellidorididae are similar in body structure to many other doridaceans. However, their rhinophores show an unusual development, since they can be drawn into special sheaths in the body. One such species, *Acanthodoris pilosa,* has a thick covering of white, elongated and conical tubercles (small rounded projections) on its back. It is about 1.5 in. in length

SEA SLUGS
— DEFENSE WITHOUT A SHELL —

During their evolution, many opisthobranchs (sea slugs) have progressively lost their shells. Although shells can provide valuable protection, they are also heavy and inflexible. The opisthobranchs that lack shells have become more mobile, they have adopted new life-styles and have conquered new habitats. Unlike shelled mollusks, or snails, sea slugs can swim and crawl into small cracks and crevices in rocks and corals in search of food and shelter. Opisthobranchs that have retained their shells use them as their first line of defense—by withdrawing their bodies into them when they are attacked. But opisthobranchs that lack shells are unable to do so, and being vulnerable, they have had to make many anatomical, functional and behavioral changes.

Camouflage and mimicry

A common form of defense among opisthobranchs is mimicry. Many species spend much of their lives living and feeding on medusae (jellyfishes), polyps and sponges and, by absorbing the pigments present in the bodies of their prey, they take on the same coloration. Some opisthobranchs mimic the shape of the substrate upon which they live, developing complicated outgrowths or cerata along their backs—opisthobranchs that employ this form of camouflage are known as homomorphic.

Some species of sea slugs have adopted a camouflage system known as "disruptive coloring." The upper surfaces of sea slugs from the suborder Doridacea (order Nudibranchia), for example, have several irregular markings on a background that blends in with the substrate. The markings have the effect of breaking up the sea slugs' shapes.

Floating upside-down

The suborder Aeolidacea contains two genera of pelagic sea slugs (Glaucus and Glaucilla) that float upside-down on the surface of the water, feeding on floating coelenterates such as those of the genera Physalia and Velella. The sea slugs have to hide from the marine predators that swim below them, as well as from birds that gather their

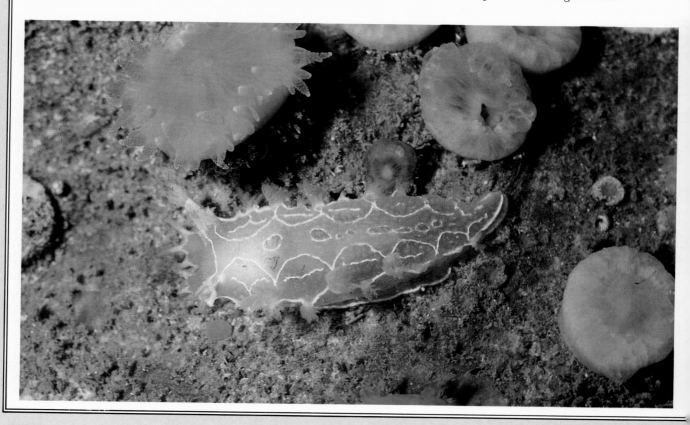

food from the surface of the sea. The undersides of the sea slugs' bodies are dark blue and blend in with the surface color of the water. Their backs, which are usually positioned downward in the water, are pale so they do not appear as a dark outline when observed from below.

Opisthobranchs that have developed poisonous or unappetizing chemicals in their bodies have adopted a different color scheme. Instead of hiding from predators, these sea slugs actively draw attention to themselves by displaying bright and vivid colors. Like bees and wasps, the sea slugs warn their attackers that they are dangerous or unpleasant to eat—a warning method known as aposematic coloring.

Chemical and biological warfare

Probably the most effective defense strategy developed by the opisthobranchs involves chemical and biological warfare. Many species of opisthobranch store concentrated sulfuric acid in special cells in their skin. If a predator applies pressure to such a sea slug by gripping it in its mouth, the poison cells in the sea slug rupture, pouring acid into the predator's mouth.

Many sea slugs feed on jellyfishes (medusae) that have stinging cells, called nematocysts. These sea slugs have developed a surprising line of defense. While feeding on a jellyfish, the sea slug stores the stinging cells in special sacs at the tips of its cerata, and can then use them for its own defense.

LEFT A sea slug, *Tritonia festiva*, moves among cup corals of the species *Balanophyllia elegans* off the Californian coast.
ABOVE RIGHT The sea slug, *Peltodoris atromaculata*, secretes acid substances to repel potential aggressors.
RIGHT The sea hare, *Aplysia punctata*, here crawling over the seabed off Ireland, exudes a purple fluid that may serve to screen it from enemies.

ABOVE **Although the sea slug, *Rostanga rubra*, stands out when placed on pale colored coral, it becomes almost invisible to humans and enemies alike when it feeds on the red coral that** forms its natural food. Because of this intimate link between food and body coloration, many sea slugs feed on only one type of food in order to blend with it, and so avoid predators.

contractions cause the detachment of parts of the body. The detached tubercles continue to move around for a while, often distracting the predator long enough for the sea slug to find a hiding place.

The swimming doridacean

The superfamily Eudoridacea contains 15 families of nudibranch sea slugs that vary in length from only 0.1 in. to as much as 12 in.

The genus *Hexabranchus*—the only genus in the family Hexabranchidae—has a distribution that extends throughout the Indo-Pacific from Africa to Hawaii, with smaller populations in the Caribbean. Although taxonomists have divided the family into 20 species, some specialists consider all hexabranchs to belong to only one species that embraces 20 varieties. The genus *Hexabranchus* contains some of the largest sea slugs—some weigh over 12 oz. and measure over 12 in. in length.

The hexabranchid sea slug *H. sanguineus*—an inhabitant of coral reefs—is the only doridacean species that has the ability to swim. Its wide, flat and beautifully patterned body spreads out into a thin, veil-like membrane at its edge. When the slug occupies the seabed, it rolls the membrane up onto its dorsal (top) surface and crawls along in the manner of all other doridaceans. However, for faster movement, it unrolls its veil-like sides and flaps them backward and forward. The flapping, coupled with rapid contractions of the back part of the body, provides enough force to propel the sea slug off the seabed and through the water.

The "sudden growth" scare

Although some opisthobranchs deter predators by reducing the size of their bodies, hexabranchids appear to expand their bulks when attacked. During the course of normal activities, such as feeding and traveling, the hexabranchid rolls up the flaps of flesh on its back. If attacked, it quickly unfolds them to reveal a white-banded, bright red inner surface. Predators often take fright when they see their victim is larger and more brightly colored than the one they initially attacked.

Changing colors

Many doridaceans undergo color changes as they grow older or change their diets. The genus *Chromodoris* (family Chromodorididae), for example, contains hundreds of species that change color at specific times in their lives; their distribution extends across all the world's seas and oceans. Many species share the same coloration during immaturity, but take on different colors as they approach adulthood. Consequently, a few species were not classified separately until studies had been made of specimens at different stages of development. A further unusual characteristic of some *Chromodoris* species is that they possess vivid blue coloration—a rare occurrence in the animal kingdom.

Seaweed imitators

Members of the genus *Rostanga* practice various forms of mimicry. The species *Rostanga rubra*, for example, mimics *Microciona atrasanguinea*, the red seaweed on which it feeds. Its red back is marked with a few black blotches and covered in short, hair-like

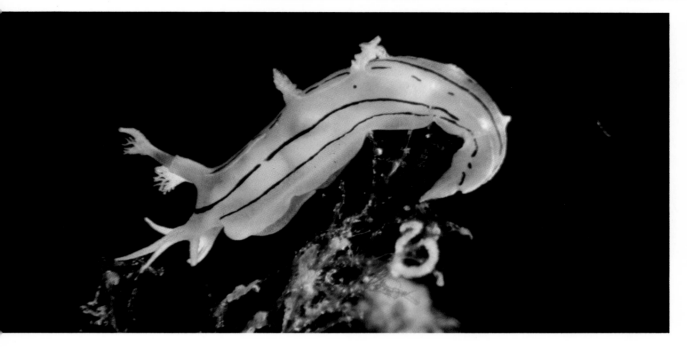

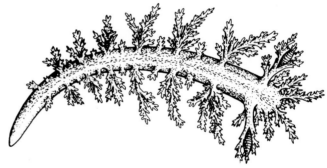

ABOVE Sea slugs lay large numbers of eggs at one time—sometimes more than 52,000—and each egg measures only 0.004 in. wide. The egg mass of every species has its own shape; that of *Tritonia plebeia,* seen here laying its eggs on a moss animal (bryozoan), resembles a white worm twisted into a spiral.

RIGHT The sea slug, *Dendronotus frondosus,* measures just over 2 in. long and has branched outgrowths—or cerata—that give it a resemblance to the coelenterate (sea anemone or coral) on which it lives.

papillae, while its plate-like rhinophores are yellow in color. To avoid the attention of predators, *R. rubra* usually lies hidden under stones or between the valves of empty oyster or clam shells, only emerging to search for food. The species inhabits the intertidal zones of coastlines from Norway to Portugal.

Rostanga pulchra, a species living along the Pacific coast of America and around Japan, eats red seaweed of the species *Ophlitaspongia pennata.* It imitates both the color and outward appearance of the seaweed—so its mimicry is both homochromous (color mimicry) and homomorphous (shape mimicry).

The family Archidorididae contains mainly western European doridaceans of the genus *Archidoris.* One species, *Archidoris tuberculata,* mimics the sponge *Halichondria panicea* on which it feeds. *A. tuberculata flammea*—another variety of the same species—feeds almost exclusively on the red sponge *Hymeniacidon sanguinea,* and is likewise red in color.

The small sea slug, *Rostanga coccinea,* of the family Rostangidae, has several sensory appendages—known as karyophilids—on its back. They take the form of tubercles shaped like upside-down cones, reinforced by chalky mineral secretions (spicules); each karyophilid contains a few sensory cells in its center.

Disruptive coloring

Doridaceans of the family Discordorididae employ a type of camouflage called disruptive coloring; as the family name implies, the species' color patterns are discordant with their surroundings. The species *Peltodoris atromaculatus,* for example, has a bright white body with large brown blotches covering its back. When it rests before a pale background, its dark pattern helps to break up its shape. Consequently, *P. atromaculatus* spends long periods without moving, in order to utilize its camouflage to the full. Its sole source of food seems to be the pale-colored sponge,

2795

Petrosia dura, on which it may remain immobile for several weeks.

The largest doridacean

Doridaceans of the family Halgerdidae inhabit the Caribbean and the tropical areas of the Indo-Pacific. Although most species are small in size, *Asteronotus cespitosus* grows up to 8 in. in length and weighs over 28 oz.—making it the largest doridacean.

The superfamily Porodoridacea

The doridacean superfamily Porodoridacea consists of only two families: the Phyllidiidae, which contains 20 species distributed throughout the Red Sea, parts of the Indian Ocean and along the coast of New Caledonia; and the Dendrodorididae, which inhabit the Atlantic Ocean, the Mediterranean and the Indo-Pacific.

LEFT While most nudibranchs creep over the seabed in a slug-like way, those of the genus *Dendronotus*, such as *Dendronotus frondosus* seen here, swim through the water by flexing their bodies from side to side.

BELOW LEFT Many sea slugs, such as this rare southwest European species *Antiopella praeclara*, have projections along their backs. These are called cerata (from the Greek *keras*, meaning "horn"), and often contain defensive stinging cells.

Dendronotaceans

The suborder Dendronotacea contains 10 families of nudibranch sea slugs. Unlike the doridaceans, all dendronotacean species have dispensed with the circular tufts of gills around their anuses. Some species breathe through gills at the sides of their bodies, while others exchange gases through their skins, having no gills whatsoever. Many dendronotaceans have rows of appendages and growths on both sides of their bodies; the structures probably assist the exchange of respiratory gases (there is little scientific evidence to support the theory). Members of all species can retract their chemical receptors and rhinophores into their bodies.

Coral eaters

Dendronotaceans of the family Tritoniidae live in temperate waters where they feed on the soft corals of the genus *Alcyonaria*, seizing the tiny polyps with their radulas and chitinous jaws. One of the largest European species—*Tritonia hombergi*—lives in close association with the coral *Alcyonium digitatum*, on soft areas of the seabed in tidal zones at depths down to 250 ft.; *T. hombergi* sometimes grows as long as 8 in. Its body is an elongated oval with an "oral veil" at its front—a fringed appendage that functions as an organ of touch and a chemoreceptor (an organ that senses the presence of certain chemicals in the water). The sea slug's back bears a covering of tubercles, while small clusters of gills open onto either side of its body. Coloration varies greatly among different *T. hombergi* individuals, ranging from shades of white to purplish browns—the colors tend to grow darker with age. Research shows that the species is one of the few members of the order Nudibranchia that secrete (when disturbed) irritant substances harmful to the skin of humans.

The other species in the genus *Tritonia* are smaller in size than *T. hombergi*. For example, *T. festiva* grows no

longer than 0.4 in.; it inhabits the coasts of America and Japan. *T. plebea*—an inhabitant of the French and Portuguese coasts—seldom measures more than 0.8 in. across.

Seaweed or sea slug?

Scyllea pelagica—a dendronotacean sea slug of the family Scyllaeidae—lives on floating brown seaweeds, particularly in gulfs. It mimics its host plants perfectly, being either green or brown in color with blue and gray markings and white or off-white stripes. *S. pelagica's* anatomy is unique among nudibranchs since its body has a vertically flattened appearance and a narrow foot that enables it to swim by striking the rear part of its body from side to side. The back bears numerous flat, leaf-like rhinophores and tubercles. Although *S. pelagica* lives among seaweeds, it is a carnivorous creature, feeding on small coelenterates and seaweed-collecting hydroids.

Changing color

Young specimens of *Dendronotus frondosus* feed exclusively upon the tiny polyps of a species of naked hydroid. Once they reach a certain length, they change their diet and begin to feed on more heavily protected hydroids. Their new diet affects their body coloration, and the sea slugs change from a dull yellow color to a vivid red. *D. frondosus* occurs along the Pacific and Atlantic coasts of North America, in Arctic waters and around the Atlantic coasts of Europe.

The family Tethyidae of the suborder Dendronotacea includes the genus *Tethys*. Members of the genus measure up to 1.2 in. long and have large veils that can be as wide as their bodies and half as long. They are basically white in color, and have two rows of papillae or small protuberances with dark red markings running along their backs.

They swim by rotating their entire bodies rhythmically, and flapping the broad sheaths that cover their rhinophores or sensory tentacles. The latter movement also enables them to move about on the seabed. They move in a curious manner, by leaning first on the front part of their veil and then on their feet. *Tethys* species are active predators, feeding on small fishes and crustaceans, such as the mantis shrimp, *Squilla*, which they cover with their veils. Since they have neither jaws nor toothed tongues (radulas), they swallow their prey whole.

ABOVE Arminid sea slugs, such as this *Armina tigrina*, are slow-moving hunters that feed voraciously on sea pansies—flat, invertebrate, marine animals living amid the silt and mud of the seabed. Since sea pansies glow (or become luminescent) when disturbed, the sea slugs that eat them absorb their ability to glow as well.

Variations on a theme

The family Dotoidae contains 12 species of sea slug that occur in British waters. The largest British species, *Doto fragilis,* measures up to 1.4 in. long. As with other species of sea slug, it changes color according to its diet. One variety feeds on the hydroid *Nemertesia antennina,* and is brown in color, while the other variety of *Doto* sea slug is white in color and feeds on the hydroid *Halecium muricatum.* Like other species of sea slug, *D. fragilis* lays large numbers of minute eggs. It may lay over 74,000 eggs in one batch, all of which measure less than 0.04 in. in diameter.

Planktonic parasites

The family Phylliroidae contains about 10 species of sea slug that measure less than 1.5 in. in length. They are all deep-sea dwellers, being planktonic. *Phylliroe bucephala* differs from other dendronotaceans both in shape and habits. Entirely

ABOVE The vivid colors of the Mediterranean sea slug, *Flabellina affinis*, warn predators of its bitter taste. The two serrated rhinophores (tentacles) that serve as chemical tasters can be seen extended at the front of the animal.

planktonic, it stays afloat by undulating its vertically flattened, fish-like body, which has no dorsal appendages. Its rudimentary eyes are sunk into its delicate, semitransparent and luminescent skin.

P. bucephala is probably the only external parasite in the subclass Opisthobranchia. While still immature, it lives on *Zanclea costata,* a small jellyfish only one-fifth its size. The sea slug clings onto its host with its foot and sucks out its organs.

Arminacea

Most members of the suborder Arminacea (order Nudibranchia) have smooth bodies, though a few have appendages. Their rhinophores or sensory tentacles are usually flat, or rolled in on themselves, and are not retractable.

The most primitive arminaceans belong to the superfamily Euarminiacea and are divided into three families, of which the family Arminidae is the most important. It contains approximately 30 species that are divided into five genera. One of the most widely distributed is the genus *Armina,* which contains oval-bodied sea slugs that lack dorsal appendages.

An arminid's back is covered in lengthwise furrows and it has two sets of gill plates between its foot and its dorsal mantle, or notum. It has two rows of plates on either side of its body, just behind its head, and another row of plates at the back of its body that contains extensions of its digestive glands.

A stinging response

Arminids have sting cells, or cnidosacs, that are situated at the edges of their notums. The sting cells are an effective method of defense and produce irritant sting threads, which the arminids fire if they are threatened. The species *Armina loveni* occurs on the northeast Atlantic coasts. It has a terra-cotta red back, decorated with about 50 white ridges that run along its length. It has two small rhinophores in front of its dorsal mantle.

A. tigrina is a more widely distributed species occurring around the coasts of Europe and America. It has a dark brown back with 25-45 lengthwise yellow stripes. It feeds on coelenterates and generally inhabits muddy or sandy areas of the seabed, where it buries itself. Some of the tropical species of arminid become luminescent as a result of feeding on the sea pansy.

Aeolidacea

The last suborder of the nudibranchs is the Aeolidacea. It is also one of the best known, since the aeolidacean sea slugs are a favorite subject for underwater photographers, partly because they are colorful and partly because they are easy to find. The suborder comprises three superfamilies: Pleuroprocta, Acleioprocta and Cleioprocta.

Aeolidaceans are all alike in body shape and feeding habits. Their elongated bodies, which are normally about 0.4-0.8 in. long, are equipped with numerous thread-like or clubbed projections (cerata) on the dorsal part of their bodies. They are usually arranged in rows or clusters. Aeolidaceans have two oral tentacles and two rhinophores that project from their heads, at the base of which are their eyes. Their radulas take the form of a single large tooth with numerous smaller teeth along each side.

Most aeolidaceans feed on coelenterates that possess sting glands. Instead of being digested, the sea slugs store the sting glands in a special part of their digestive glands. Situated inside their cerata, their digestive glands are connected to the outside by a small canal. If the sea slugs are disturbed, they expel the sting cells from their cerata, firing them at the intruder so that they cause a painful irritation. It is not yet understood how these sting cells enter the aeolidaceans' intestines, but it is thought that glands near to the entrance of their intestines secrete a mucus capable of rendering the sting cells temporarily harmless.

Pleuroprocta

The superfamily Pleuroprocta contains many primitive aeolidaceans. The family Coryphellidae contains small to medium-sized sea slugs—usually less than 0.3 in. in length. One of the best-known species of the genus *Coryphella* is *C. verrucosa*. It is less than an inch long and has a whitish, semitransparent body with seven or eight clusters of light red cerata with white tips arranged along either side.

Sea slugs of the genus *Coryphella* gather in large groups on the tiny polyps of hydroids on which they feed. Although the groups of coryphellans consist of many different species, all of them possess cnidosacs, or stinging cells, enabling them to sting predators. Aeolidaceans are always brightly colored, serving as a warning system; predators can easily distinguish them from other species and soon learn to avoid them. Known as aposematic coloring, it can also be seen in certain poisonous insects, such as the yellow and black bands on bees and wasps.

When a number of species with aposematic coloring come together, the warning signal becomes even stronger. Such behavior is defined as "group display." The Portuguese species *Flabellina affinis,* which belongs to the family Flabellinidae, has delicate mauve coloring and lives in close association with coryphellans.

Acleioprocta

The superfamily Acleioprocta contains the family Pseudovermidae—a group of sea slugs that have some unusual characteristics. They look more like worms than mollusks. However, their anatomical structures and their possession of radulas confirm that they are mollusks. They are classified in the suborder Aeolidacea because they have rows of cerata along their sides, although in many species these cerata are only vestigial. Pseudovermidans are just about 0.1 in. long and live among the grains of sand in tidal zones, where they feed on tiny coelenterates.

The family Fionidae contains only one species, *Fiona pinnata.* It occurs throughout the subtropics and has some strange habits. It spends its entire life on the surface of the high seas, where it feeds on a type of floating hydroid of the genus *Velella* or on small crustaceans, such as barnacles of the genus *Lepas,* that attach themselves to floating or barely submerged objects. *F. pinnata* lives on drifting matter, always in close proximity to its prey.

Although each of its cerata has an undulating membrane, it is unable to swim and never inhabits the seabed. It is thought that *F. pinnata* stopped swimming when it first began to lay its eggs on floating *Velella.* Like many other sea slugs, its body color changes according to its diet. After a meal of *Velella,* its cerata turn purple, and after a meal of *Lepas,* they turn dark brown.

Cleioprocta

Some of the most well-known opisthobranchs belong to the superfamily Cleioprocta, which includes

the family Glaucidae. Members of the two genera within this family, *Glaucus* and *Glaucilla,* have similar habits to the sea slugs of the genus *Fiona.*

Confined to the warmer seas of the world, glaucidans feed on floating coelenterates such as *Velella* and *Physalia.* They also collect their sting cells, which are powerful enough to pose a threat to humans. Aeolidacean sea slugs of the genus *Glaucus* have camouflaged body coloration that disguises them from both marine predators and sea birds. They have large cerata and gas-filled bodies, enabling them to float on the surface of the water. Their backs are usually positioned downward in the water, and are light colored, while the undersides, which lie upward, are purplish blue, so that seen from above, they blend in with the blue of the water.

Unlike other aeolidaceans, *Calma glaucoides* feeds on the eggs of small fishes that live close to the shore. It cuts through the outer covering of the eggs with its saw-like radula and extracts the contents with its jaws. *C. glaucoides* appears not to produce any waste matter from eating fish eggs, since it has no anus and its intestine has no outlet. Since it does not feed on coelenterates, it has no cnidosacs or sting cells.

Voracious carnivores

Favorinus branchialis of the family Favoriniae is a particularly voracious species of sea slug that feeds on eggs that have been deposited on vegetation by other gastropods. In some cases, it even eats its own eggs. *Aeolidia papillosa,* which belongs to the family Aeolidiidae, commonly occurs on the Atlantic coasts of Europe and America. It feeds on sea anemones, particularly *Metridium senile,* and the sea tomato, which it attacks by making broad wounds in its stalk. The sea slug *Spurilla neapolitana,* which inhabits the Mediterranean and the Sargasso Sea, also feeds on sea anemones.

Snails and slugs

Air-breathing snails and slugs belong to the gastropod subclass Pulmonata. They broke away from the marine prosobranchs (marine snails) and underwent changes that enabled them to conquer dry land and freshwater. However, they have not adapted to life on land easily, and many still require damp conditions in which to live. Other invertebrates that evolved from sea dwellers, such as arachnids (spiders), have been more successful and inhabit a wider range of habitats.

TOP The sea slug, *Coryphella iodenia,* also known as the Spanish dancer, has yellow-tipped cerata (finger-like projections) that contain stinging cells. The cells have been taken into the sea slug's body from its coelenterate prey, such as sea anemones. They continue to serve as a form of defense for their new owner.

ABOVE A tiny nudibranch, *Favorinus japonicus,* from the Marshall Islands in the South Pacific, is dwarfed by the vast folds of the prey on which it is feeding— the ribbons of eggs laid by a far larger nudibranch (*Coryphella* sp.). Nudibranchs usually feed on only one type of prey.

In moving away from the sea, the pulmonates have continued a trend set by the early mesogastropods. The oldest types of mesogastropod, such as the periwinkle of the genus *Littorina,* moved away from the sea and colonized intertidal zones and areas above the shoreline. Other mesogastropods, such as the land winkles of the genus *Pomatia,* established themselves on dry land. Pulmonates and opisthobranchs (of the phylum Mollusca) are thought to have branched off from these early mesogastropods. The pulmonates managed to conquer dry land by undergoing certain changes such as the transformation of their mantle cavities into lungs.

The family Ellobiidae of the order Archaeopulmonata is thought to contain the earliest pulmonates, from which all the others developed. A few of the later pulmonates then ventured into freshwater by adapting their mantle cavities.

Obtaining and conserving water

The first problem land-dwelling pulmonates had to overcome was how to maintain the balance of fluids within their bodies. In their new environment, water

ABOVE Several species of sea slug, such as *Spurilla neapolitana* shown here, supplement their diet by taking up the algae that live in their prey. The algae continue to function in the sea slug's digestive gland, producing food by photosynthesis. The sea slug then feeds on the nutritious by-products of the algae's food-building activity.

became a precious commodity, and it had to be used carefully. Many physiological and behaviorial changes took place, enabling the pulmonates to control their fluid levels.

Pulmonates obtain most of the water they need from their food. Their diet normally consists of succulent vegetation that contains a high percentage of water. Their bodies are covered by a coating of mucus that serves to lessen water loss through evaporation. A covering of this sort acts as a type of waterproofing, sealing the fluids underneath its thick layers. However, this is less effective than a waterproof cuticle, and pulmonates are, on the whole, unable to survive in places that have long, hot, dry periods. Land-dwelling pulmonates also conserve water by excreting solid, undiluted uric acid.

TOP The bright orange, yellow-tipped cerata of the sea slug, *Aeolidiella sanguinea,* warn predators such as fishes of its ability to protect itself with stinging cells and sulfuric acid — either secreted through the skin or vomited through its mouth.
ABOVE In sea slugs of the genus *Facelina,* the cerata occur in clusters along their bodies.

Despite their physiological changes, pulmonates cannot survive in all types of environment or climate. They have learned to carry out their daily activities during the coolest, wettest periods, such as at night or after heavy rainfall. During the warmest part of the day they hide in damp places, such as under stones, among vegetation or in the ground.

Long periods of inactivity

Pulmonates remain inactive throughout the hottest and driest as well as the coldest seasons. In temperate latitudes they hibernate for three or four months of the winter, and they undergo a similar period of inactivity, known as estivation, during the driest months of the summer. When entering these dormant phases, they usually dig themselves a hole in the earth. The common garden snail digs a hole 8-12 in. deep,

but some species of slugs that live in exceptionally dry areas go down as deep as 3 ft. or more. While they are hibernating, their metabolism slows down and some species almost stop breathing. A mucus secretion from their mouths solidifies into a layer known as the epiphragm, which seals the apertures of their shells, leaving a tiny hole for the air to pass through. Some species of slugs cement their shells to the substrate using mucus.

In many cases, not even these adaptations are sufficient to prevent water loss. Like all gastropods, pulmonates move around on a layer of mucus that they renew all the time, with consequent loss of fluid. So, in order to survive in a dry atmosphere, these creatures remain immobile for most of the time. Experiments show that in dry air, the great gray slug loses 2.4 percent of its initial body weight per hour, or 58 percent per day, but if forced to move, it loses up to 16 percent per hour.

If the temperature is very high, continuous evaporation of the body fluids takes place in order to keep the body temperature down. In this way, the garden slug *Arion ater* can maintain a body temperature of 69.8°F when the temperature of the air is about 91.4°F. The adaptation of body fluid evaporation has enabled *Sphincterochila* species to survive in the Negev desert at temperatures of 149°F. In some dry areas, where the highest temperatures occur on the ground, many pulmonates climb the highest stalks they can find and withdraw into their shells. The species that do this usually have pale shells that reflect sunlight.

Respiration

The breathing methods of snails and slugs have undergone profound changes in the course of evolution. Most species have lost their gills, and their mantle cavities have transformed into lungs that are connected to the outside by a small aperture called a pneumostome. Their mantles have become thickly veined, and the exchange of gases occurs through the covering film of water.

The bottom of the mantle cavity is muscular and acts as a diaphragm. With each contraction, the bottom of the cavity flattens, increasing the amount of space inside and drawing in air through the open pneumostome. The pneumostome then closes and the muscles relax, so that the cavity grows smaller. In this way, the pressure of the gases increases inside the

cavity, enabling oxygen to enter the blood vessels inside it. Many species of pulmonate that have returned to living in the water have developed secondary gills in place of their lungs.

Reproduction

Reproductive methods have adapted to meet the requirements of the pulmonates' land-dwelling life-style. The early stages of molluscan larval life, the trochophore and veliger stages, take place inside the egg. The young pulmonates hatch into tiny replicas of the adults. Only a few families do not develop in this way. The primitive freshwater and marine snails of the families Ellobiidae and Onchidiids, for example, have a larval stage, or veliger, that they spend in the open sea. All pulmonates are hermaphrodites, and some species undertake self-fertilization. Mating can last for several hours, and land slugs and snails of the order Stylommatophora perform long courtship rituals before mating.

All pulmonates store sperm inside their bodies until the moment of use, which can occur up to a year later. Most pulmonates reach sexual maturity after a year, but the largest species may take up to four years. Only about 5 percent of all slugs and snails reach maturity. Of the largest species, only about half survive every year. They can reach a maximum age of 8 to 10 years.

With or without a shell

The shell structures of pulmonates vary according to the species, but they are generally rounded spires or helixes (as in the common edible snail). Pulmonate shells lack the striking ornamentation typical of marine mollusks. Because they need to be well camouflaged, pulmonate shells are usually drab in color. However, not all pulmonates have shells. Slugs of the family Limacidae have internalized their shells, and those in the family Arionidae have lost their shells completely. Coloring and behavior may vary considerably among members of the same species. Although most pulmonates live on land or in freshwater, a few species live on the coast.

The subclass Pulmonata is divided into four orders: the first is Archaeopulmonata (primitive snails), the second is Basommatophora (pond and marsh snails), the third is Systellommatophora (tropical slugs) and the fourth is Stylommatophora (land snails and slugs). The first order contains mainly freshwater species, although

TOP Land-dwelling snails are vulnerable to drying out in the heat. They have, therefore, kept their shells and retract into them when it gets too hot. Once inside, they seal the opening with quick-drying mucus. **ABOVE** Slugs have lost their protective shells, and most species occur either in cool temperate countries (where they live under rocks or fallen trees) or in humid, tropical jungles. They usually avoid the sun by leading nocturnal lives, and keep their eggs moist by burying them in soil.

Snail sp. (*Delima itala*)

Giant African land snail (*Achatina fulica*)

Variable grove snail
(*Cepaea hortensis*)

Amber snail
(*Succinea putris*)

Great slug (*Limax maximus*)

Common red slug
(*Arion rufus*)

Cuban snail (*Polymita pict*

Great ramshorn snail (*Planorbis corneus*)

Great pond snail
(*Lymnaea stagnalis*)

2804

Tree snail (*Liguus dryas*)

Edible snail (*Helix pomatia*)

a few genera live by the sea and in estuaries. Pond and marsh snails of the order Basommatophora have eyes that are situated at the base of their retractable tentacles, whereas the eyes of the land snails and slugs of the order Stylommatophora are always positioned on the end of stalks. The orders Systellommatophora and Stylommatophora contain mainly land-dwelling pulmonates, although some species live in freshwater.

Primitive snails

The order Archaeopulmonata contains one superfamily, the Ellobiacea. Divided into two families, it contains primitive snails that occur along the coastline. The family Ellobiidae contains about 21 genera of terrestrial, intertidal and estuarine snails.

Snails of the genus *Carychium* have tall shells and occur along the banks of rivers and in other moist places throughout the world. They can be found at altitudes of over 6000 ft. The family Otinidae contains only one species of snail, *Otina otis*. A minute species with a shell no longer than 0.1 in., it only inhabits the rocky coasts of Britain and France. Unlike members of the family Ellobiidae, *O. otis* is unable to retract its body completely into its shell.

Pond and marine snails

The order Basommatophora contains seven superfamilies and 15 families, with fewer than 1000 species of aquatic snail. They vary widely in size, but rarely measure more than 4 in. They usually live in freshwater, though some occur along the coastline.

The superfamily Siphonariacea contains limpet-like snails that occur throughout the tropical and equatorial zones of the Southern Hemisphere. The superfamily contains about 80 species that are divided into two families.

The snail *Siphonaria ferruginosa,* which belongs to the family Siphonariidae, has a shell resembling that of a limpet. It takes the form of a flattened cone and has ribs of varying thickness running down from the apex. The ribs protrude outward, giving the rim of the shell a wavy outline. A slanting crest runs from the dorsal part of its shell toward the outer edge. *S. ferruginosa* breathes through gills, and has a tentacle-like structure called an osphradium, which functions as a chemoreceptor. The osphradium is situated inside the snail's reduced lung cavity, suggesting that the snail evolved from land-dwelling pulmonates.

MOLLUSKS CLASSIFICATION: 12

Pulmonates (snails and slugs) (1)

The third and final subclass within the order Gastropoda is the Pulmonata, a large group of air-breathing mollusks that live on land, in freshwater or in the sea. There are four pulmonate orders—the Archaeopulmonata, Basommatophora, Systellommatophora and Stylommatophora. The Archaeopulmonata contains two families of primitive freshwater and marine snails—the Ellobiidae and the Otinidae (which has just one species, *Otina otis*, of Britain and France).

The second pulmonate order, Basommatophora, consists mainly of aquatic snails grouped into seven superfamilies and 15 families. They include the Siphonariidae (limpet-like pulmonates); the Amphibolidae (operculate pulmonates) of eastern Asia and Australia; the Lymnaeidae (pond snails, such as the great pond snail, *Lymnaea stagnalis*, of Eurasia, North Africa and North America, and the mud snail *Lymnaea truncatula*); and the Physidae (bladder snails). The family Planorbidae (ramshorn snails) are freshwater animals and include the great ramshorn, *Planorbis corneus*, from Europe and western Asia; while the Ancylidae (freshwater limpets) occur worldwide. (See mollusks classification box 13 for the remaining two pulmonate orders.)

The snails *S. normalis* and *S. alternata* inhabit the rocky coasts of islands in the Indian and Pacific oceans. Like limpets, they feed on the microscopic algae that cover the surface of cliffs. The tides regulate the snails' activity. When inactive, the snails withdraw into shallow depressions that they dig in the rock, ensuring that the edges of their shells fit perfectly against the rock surface.

Varied behavior

The behavioral habits of these snails vary from species to species and among individuals of the same species. Some move from their hiding places as soon as the tide leaves them uncovered, while others only move once the tide has covered them. Their

behavior is also determined by weather conditions and conditions at sea. High temperatures, a dry atmosphere and rough seas all discourage activity in siphonarian snails.

Snails of the family Amphibolidae occur all over eastern Asia, as far as Australia. They live partly buried in the sand near river mouths. Snails of the genus *Amphibola* are the only pulmonates to have retained operculums, although the shells have the helical shape like those of the land-dwelling pulmonates.

Freshwater snails

The superfamily Chilinoidea contains only a few species of freshwater snails. *Chilina fluctuosa* of South America has certain primitive characteristics. For example, its pneumostomes are sometimes missing. Many zoologists consider *Chilina* species to be the most primitive of the basommatophores, from which many species, such as the pond snails of the family Lymnaeidae, descended.

The family Acroloxidae contains only a few species of snails. The apexes of their plate-like shells bend over at the back and on the left-hand side. On the right-hand side, toward the back of their shells, they have pseudobranchiae, but they breathe through their skins. Snails of the genus *Acroloxus* occur over a vast

ABOVE The limpet-shaped *Siphonaria grisea* is a primitive pulmonate that lives in tropical areas on rocks at the sea edge or in estuaries.
BELOW The map shows the distribution of a few basommatophoran species in the family Lymnaeidae (pond snails).
BELOW RIGHT The map shows the distribution of various species of freshwater snails of the family Planorbidae.

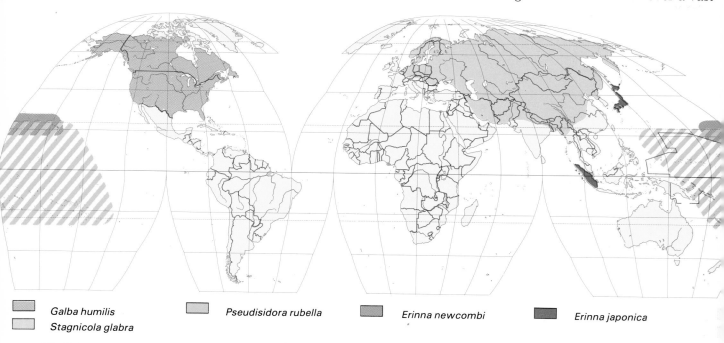

Galba humilis
Stagnicola glabra
Pseudisidora rubella
Erinna newcombi
Erinna japonica

area covering Europe, Central Asia and North America. Like many other species of basommatophore, *A. lacustris* inhabits stagnant water. Aquatic snails belonging to the order Basommatophora usually surface at regular intervals to take in air from the atmosphere, enabling them to survive in water containing a high level of organic waste (and as a consequence a low level of oxygen).

Pulmonate snails of the genus *Acroloxus* breathe only oxygen contained in water; they require clean ponds with high oxygen content for their survival. The snail usually lives near a pond's bottom; if, however, the water's oxygen content drops—due to a rise in temperature or an accumulation of dead matter—the snail moves nearer to the oxygenated surface vegetation of the pond. It returns to deeper water only after conditions improve.

Lymnaean pond snails

Pond snails of the family Lymnaea are some of the most common freshwater mollusks in the world. The great pond snail, *Lymnaea stagnalis,* for example, lives in still or slow-running water in many parts of Europe, Asia, North Africa and North America. Large groups of great pond snails usually live and feed on shallow water vegetation.

The shells of great pond snails form tapering, bluntly pointed spirals, the last whorls of which broaden into single, wide openings (peristomes). Minor details of shell structure, however, vary according to the environment in which individual snails develop. For example, snails that live on hard-stemmed aquatic plants develop two notches on the edges of their peristomes, which rest on the plant stalks.

Since the pond snail lacks gills, it has to rise to the water's surface at regular intervals to fill its pulmonary cavity, or "lung," with air; the need for air restricts its habitat to within a few yards of the surface.

Zigzagging herbivores

Lymnaean pond snails are usually herbivorous animals that feed by browsing through algae and other plants with side-to-side movements of their heads. Browsing snails leave zigzag trails on rocks, or on the glass of fish tanks (humans use them to reduce algae growth in ornamental ponds and aquaria). Most pond snails live in waters rich in vegetation, feeding on filaments of algae, fibrous algae and water plants such as pondweeds (*Potamogeton*), water crowfoot (*Ranunculus*) and reed mace (*Typha*). Unlike many pulmonates, pond snails are not disadvantaged by the need to search their surroundings for particular

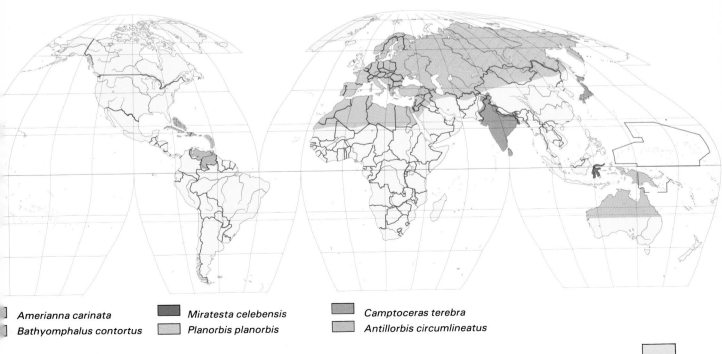

Amerianna carinata	Miratesta celebensis	Camptoceras terebra
Bathyomphalus contortus	Planorbis planorbis	Antillorbis circumlineatus

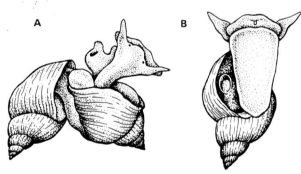

A   B

ABOVE The ear-shelled water snail lays its eggs in a jelly-like envelope on the stems of plants (seen to the right of the animal). The developing young are vulnerable to predation, but the jelly is distasteful and stops predators from eating the eggs.
LEFT The drawings show two pond snails (genus *Lymnaea*) in the process of mating (A); and a bird's-eye view of a pond snail as it crawls along the underside of the pond surface, feeding on floating detritus (B). The snail's oval breathing hole, known as a pneumatophore (seen to the left of the foot) pierces the water surface and allows the snail to breathe in air.

species of plants: they simply move about at random until they encounter vegetable matter.

Since lymnaean pond snails have light shells, they are able to hang upside-down from the surface film of a pond and feed on protein-rich surface scum, leaving clear trails in the water as they travel to and fro. They break down vegetable matter with their sharp tongues, or radulas, which consist of approximately 100 rows of minuscule teeth, with 130 teeth in each row. If food is abundant, pond snails move slowly, but if nourishment is scarce, they move more quickly, covering a wider area.

The lymnaean pond snail occasionally needs to supplement its vegetable diet with animal matter—although it eats most types of carrion, it prefers dead insects and crustaceans. The pond snail detects the odor of rotting organic matter with olfactory receptors (organs similar to taste buds) in its tentacles and in the front part of its foot. Since carrion is relatively scarce, the snail moves toward it as soon as its olfactory receptors detect the unmistakable scent.

Spirogyra eaters

Pond snails of the lymnaean genus *Stagnicola* are common throughout North America, Asia and Europe. Although they eat many types of algae, they prefer spirogyra; like other lymnaeans, they possess olfactory receptors with which they detect decaying flesh. The species *S. reflexa* and *S. palustris* inhabit North America, while *S. glabra* occurs throughout Europe and Asia.

Parasite carriers

Several species of pond snails act as hosts for the parasitic larvae of flukes—flatworms (platyhelminths) that invade the livers of large mammals, causing serious disease. The mud snail species *Lymnaea truncatula,* for example, acts as an intermediary host to the larvae of the liver fluke *Fasciola hepatica.* Liver fluke eggs carried in the excrement of the primary host—often a sheep—hatch into larvae that actively seek mud snail hosts. After burrowing into a snail, the larvae enter its organs, where they pass through several stages of growth. Upon completion of their growth, they leave the snail for the protection of vegetation, where they develop hardy, encysted body coverings. When eaten by primary hosts, such as sheep, horses, cattle and humans, the cysts hatch into mature larvae that enter the liver to complete their final development into adulthood. Adult liver flukes complete their life cycle in the liver, laying as many as 20,000 eggs a day.

Bladder snails

Bladder snails comprise the few genera of the lymnaean family Physidae. Although the different physidan species vary only slightly, large bladder snail populations inhabit most regions of the world. *Physa acuta* and *P. fontinalis,* for example, inhabit European ponds, streams and rivers, while *P. acuta* is widespread in Mediterranean countries and in western Europe.

Widespread in the north

Bladder snails of the species *P. fontinalis* inhabit northern Europe and northern Asia; they occur in great numbers in the streams, ponds and rivers of Siberia. *P. fontinalis* has a light, thin shell that spirals to the left (viewed from the foot); the oval-shaped shell may reach 0.5 in. in length, with its final whorl making up about four-fifths of the total bulk. The wide opening of the shell has a slightly dilated front with a fragile outer lip. While most of the shell surface is light yellow in color, the lip of the columella (the tube leading to the shell's center) and part of the last whorl are white. The snail explores its environment using two long tentacles on its head.

ABOVE The great pond snail is one of the largest members of the freshwater snail family Lymnaeidae, growing up to 2 in. in length. It feeds on algae, plants and other aquatic animals such as sticklebacks, newts and water beetle larvae. Since it breathes air, it has to come to the surface periodically to renew the oxygen in its lungs.

Auxiliary breathing system

Like other lymnaeans, the *P. fontinalis* bladder snail regularly rises to the water's surface to breathe. Although it has the lung-like mantle cavity typical of most pulmonates, it absorbs additional oxygen through two specialized mantle lobes that protrude over the shell. In well-oxygenated water, the lobes remain retracted and invisible; in water containing very little dissolved oxygen, however, they spread to their full extent, vastly increasing the surface area through which the snail absorbs oxygen.

The amount of dissolved oxygen in the water affects *P. fontinalis*'s behavior in several ways: in highly oxygenated water, it fills its mantle cavity with air about once an hour; in the absence of large amounts of oxygen, however, it rises to the surface once every few minutes. Sometimes, the snail stops immediately below the water's surface and extends the

ABOVE A pair of bladder snails, *Physa fontinalis*, rasp their way across the algae covering a dead leaf. As with the genus *Lymnaea,* the members of the genus *Physa* also have to crawl to the surface at intervals to take in fresh air in an exchange of gases. Both genera belong to the order Basommatophora, and can be identified by the eyes at the bases of their tentacles (unlike snails of the order Stylommatophora which carry their eyes on the tentacle tips).

edges of its shell opening into the air to form a short, makeshift siphon.

P. fontinalis sometimes moves to the surface quickly by releasing its grip on vegetation and floating upward. However, this is an inconvenient method of obtaining oxygen, since the snail has difficulty in returning to the pond floor if it surfaces in the middle of the pond.

Mucus trails

Bladder snails of the family Physidae commonly inhabit ponds and ditches and, to a lesser extent, the sides of fountains and cattle troughs where they feed on algae. The calm surfaces of many small bodies of water may conceal thousands of *Physa* bladder snails as they make routine journeys to and from the surface to replenish their oxygen supplies. Like their marine prosobranch cousins, they mark distinct paths along the rocks, stones and vegetation of their habitats. Each snail leaves a trail of mucus that it can follow on subsequent journeys.

Since the *Physa* water snail lives among thick vegetation, its journey to the surface is potentially difficult: it has to crawl through dense algae, often retracing its steps along plants that cease their growth before reaching the open air. However, once it finds a suitable route to the surface, the snail makes subsequent journeys by following the scent of its original trail of mucus. Mucus trails benefit the entire *Physa* population of a pond, since all snails, if lost, can reach the surface by following the routes of others.

Chemical signposting

Physa mucus marks not only a trail but the direction in which the trail-making snail traveled. Zoologists believe that the mucus contains an agent that pulls certain chemicals to one side of the trail, allowing snails to orient themselves correctly; however, there is no scientific evidence to substantiate the theory. The submerged freshwater vegetation contains a complicated labyrinth of *Physa* snail tracks; the more frequently snails pass along certain routes, the greater the mucus deposits. Thus, tracks become "lanes," and "lanes" merge into "main roads"—this cuts down on the number of major routes to the surface or to certain areas of pasture, thereby conserving energy and food supplies and increasing the snails' chances of meeting for the purposes of mating.

For a fast ascent to the surface, the *Physa* snail simply releases its grip on the pond floor and floats upward. However, since such an ascent makes for a difficult descent, the snail confines its use to emergency situations such as attacks from predators.

Leeches—the main enemies of water snails—often become frightened when a snail swings its shell violently from side to side.

Ramshorn snails

The family Planorbidae (of the order Basommatophora) contains the pond-dwelling pulmonates commonly known as ramshorn snails; planorbidans inhabit many regions of the world, including Africa, South America and Southeast Asia. Several species act as hosts to the parasitic larvae of the blood fluke *Schistosoma,* the cause of the dangerous disease schistosomiasis (known also as bilharzia). Schistosomiasis is a major disease that continues to spread through many areas of the Third World: the African *Bulinus* snail, for example, carries larvae of the blood fluke *S. haematobium.* The *Schistosoma* species *S. mansoni* inhabits Africa, South America and the Caribbean, and is spread by the pulmonates *Biomphalaria* in Africa and *Australorbis* and *Tropicorbis* in

America. *S. Japonicum* occurs in Japan and Southeast Asia where it parasitizes the pond snail *Oncomelania.*

Schistosomiasis infects humans, and, although it seldom kills, it absorbs much of the body's food intake, depriving its victims of energy. The disease causes the daily loss of millions of work hours in the areas that most need them—the developing countries of the Third World. Ironically, much of the technical aid donated by the First World—such as dams and irrigation systems—helps to spread schistosomiasis, since it provides ideal habitats for infected ramshorn snails.

Flattened and spiral shells

Most ramshorn snails of the genus *Planorbis* have flattened, spiral shells, although a few species have cone-shaped shells. In the species *P. contortus* and *P. carinatus,* the last whorl of the shell bears a thickened central ridge, while the shell of *P. crista* bears a patterning of diagonal ridges. *Planorbis* snails are small creatures, measuring 0.1-0.6 in. in length. They live in stagnant pools or slow-moving water rich in vegetation. The snails eat detritus and algae, which they find in the vegetation or on the muddy bottom.

Back-up gills

Like other lymnaeans, the ramshorn snail periodically rises to the surface to fill its mantle cavity with oxygen. However, it can supplement its air supply by using a gill on the left side of its foot. The gill is useful in stagnant water, where a generally low oxygen presence in the water may lead to an almost total lack of oxygen at night, due to the activity of plants and decaying bacteria. Ramshorns eat vegetable matter and—to a lesser extent—decaying animal flesh.

The great ramshorn

The great ramshorn snail, *Planorbis corneus,* occurs throughout Europe and western Asia. It has a flat, spiral shell that it holds vertically when moving across the pond floor or climbing up vegetation. The great ramshorn has a dark coloration—often tinted red due to the presence of the red, oxygen-carrying pigment hemoglobin in its blood. Although most mammals carry hemoglobin in their blood, the pigment occurs very rarely in lymnaeans. Most mollusks use hemocyanin—a pigment containing the chemical copperas—to transport oxygen from the gills and skin

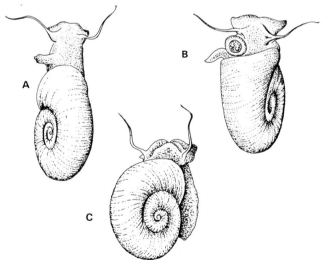

TOP A ramshorn snail, *Planorbis umbilicatus,* makes its way up an underwater plant stalk. Ramshorn snails are named for the distinctive whorl of their shells. They have lungs and belong to the order Pulmonata.

ABOVE The great ramshorn snail *Planorbis corneus* absorbs oxygen through a respiratory lobe between its tentacle and the shell on its left side (A), or through a breathing pore (pneumostone) (B). Both structures are hidden as the snail crawls along (C).

SNAILS AND SLUGS
— SLIMY COURTSHIP —

Snails and slugs have surprisingly elaborate reproductive procedures, involving complex courtship behavior. They usually mate in spring, although some species that live in dry environments take advantage of winter's moisture to preserve their eggs. Although most snails are active by night, they tend to mate by day. Since mating can take many hours, they seek safe, moist places—usually below layers of large, damp leaves.

Since much commercial activity centers around the edible snail, Helix pomatia, its courtship has been closely studied. Like most of its relatives, it is a hermaphrodite, so reproduction mainly involves the exchange of spermatophores. At the start of courtship, the two snails investigate one another with their tentacles and mouths. They edge gradually closer and rear up at right angles to the ground with the bases of their feet in full contact. Supported by the tip of their shells and the hind part of their feet, they sway back and forth, caressing each other with their tentacles. At the same time, the male and female both open their orifices.

A game of darts

After some time, each snail extends its tentacles forward, turns a light blue color in front, and stabs its partner with a chalky, sharp dart extruded from the front part of its foot. The dart does not always penetrate the target and often falls to the ground. If a partner is impaled, it withdraws briefly and then returns the favor. The exact function of the dart is uncertain, but it is clear that many aspects of a snail's behavior rely on specific acts or events to stimulate the next stage within a complicated sequence of actions.

Eventually, the snails turn their heads to the left to align their genitalia, and exchange spermatophores. Then they separate and withdraw slightly into their shells, a position that they may maintain for several hours. About four to six weeks after mating, each snail lays 40-50 eggs in a shallow excavation in moist soil. The eggs are about 0.2 in. in diameter. They are greenish white at first but become dull white with time. After 20-30 days, they hatch into miniature snails, with shells about 0.4 in. in diameter.

Hanging by slime

Slug courtship can be equally elaborate, and the behavior of the great gray slug, Limax maximus, is typical. Prospective mates circle one another, flapping their mantles in a courtship display on the underside of a large leaf or branch until they have generated a substantial base of slime. They suspend themselves from a rope of slime, writhing energetically and winding themselves around one another. Then they extrude their sexual organs and wrap them together until they have exchanged sperm. The pair then drop to the ground or eat their way back up the rope of slime. They lay soft, amber eggs, about 0.2 in. in diameter, in damp places such as holes under stones or among roots. The eggs hatch about a month later.

FAR LEFT The edible snail lays 40-50 eggs. After they have been laid, the snail buries them in the soft soil, and they hatch after 20-30 days.

TOP Although snails are hermaphrodites, having both male and female sex organs, they usually transfer sperm from one to the other in order to fertilize their eggs. During the first phase of courtship of *Eobania vermiculata,* seen here, the snails feel each other with their tentacles.

ABOVE RIGHT The drawings show the mating of two snails (*Helix* sp.) as they rear up with the soles of their feet pressed together (A, B and C).

RIGHT During the final stage of the great gray slug's mating ritual (D-G), the entwined animals hang from a branch by means of a mucus cord. As they hang there, they unfurl and entwine their penises (shaded areas) into a knot, allowing them to exchange sperm. After mating, they either fall to the ground or climb back to the branch, eating the cord as they go.

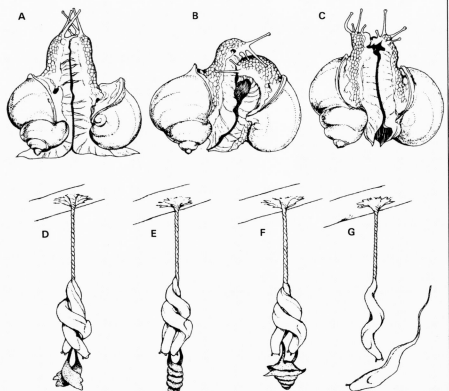

A   B   C

D   E   F   G

to the body tissues. If the great ramshorn lives in stagnant water, it stores oxygen in the iron contained in its hemoglobin.

Great ramshorn snails seldom make use of their hemoglobin since they usually inhabit water that is well oxygenated enough to allow normal respiration. Like the great pond snails, they often carry air bubbles, or "reservoirs of air," from the surface. The great ramshorns' skill in retaining air bubbles allows them to remain underwater for considerable periods of time.

Saltwater dwellers

The great ramshorn differs from many other aquatic pulmonate snails in that it tolerates slightly salty water, with a salinity of up to 3 parts per 1000 (salinity at sea averages 1.3 oz. per 220 gals.). A few species can even live in water with a salinity of 8 parts per 220. If ramshorn snails live in slightly saline environments—such as some areas of the Baltic Sea—they seldom achieve full growth.

Mud as food and refuge

The term "detritus" conveniently covers all the silt, mud and rubbish that gathers wherever vegetation dies, and is a useful description of the diet of many animals. Researchers have tried to establish exactly what part of the detritus animals feed on. An examination of the stomach contents of *P. contortus* shows that the snail probably uses its bacterial, rather than its structural, elements. When sediment has been treated with chemicals that kill bacteria, the mollusk will not feed on it.

Apart from its food value, mud also serves as a protection for the mollusk. Various species of *Planorbis* often have to face long periods when the pools or places where they live dry up. Most species react to these difficult times by gathering in the deeper parts of their homes and burying themselves in the mud. They then go into a state of lethargy that can last several months. Only when their habitat is flooded do they begin to move again. Defense behavior of this kind allows the snails to penetrate some very harsh environments; some non-European species of *Planorbis,* such as *P. montanus* and *P. andecolus,* live in high mountains, at altitudes of up to 13,000 ft., although the record is held by the pond snail *Lymnaea hookeri,* which has been found in the Himalayas more than 18,000 ft. above sea level.

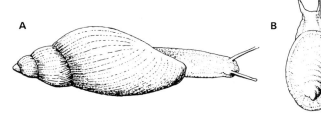

A   B

FAR LEFT **The great pond snail finds much of its food in the algae that grows on the pebbles covering the pond bottom.**
TOP **The shell of the great pond snail is quite unlike those of the ramshorn and bladder snails, and has the twisted spire pointing to the rear.**

ABOVE **The shapes of pulmonate shells vary according to where the animals live. The bulky shell of *Galba palustris* (A) identifies a snail that lives in still water; the streamlined shell (B) belongs to a river limpet from fast-flowing water.**

Mating at a snail's pace

Most water snails are hermaphrodites, and any individual snail can produce both eggs and sperm. They seldom fertilize themselves, although they occasionally do so in times of ecological hardship when the snails may be isolated from one another. In nearly all land-dwelling pulmonates, mating is preceded by a long and complicated courtship. With basommatophores (the pond and marsh snails), things are simpler. The animal that happens to be playing the role of the male at any given time climbs onto its partner's shell. After some time, it manages to insert its penis in the appropriate orifice and releases the sperm. The animal playing the role of the female takes no active part in the mating, but continues to move along or to eat. Multiple mating sometimes occurs; in this case, each snail acts as a male for the one in front of it, and as a female for the one following it.

Feeding by smell

Most aquatic pulmonates cannot identify plant food from any distance. The planorbid, *Biomphalaria glabrata*, of South America is an exception. It can detect algae or other vegetable substances by picking up the chemical stimuli that they emit. The ability to smell is not as developed in the pulmonates as it is in marine prosobranchs, and their source of food must be no more than an inch away. As soon as the snail perceives the chemical signal given off by the food, it starts to swing its head from side to side, sampling the water around it in order to identify the zone in which the stimulus is strongest.

The chemosensory cells that are receptive to the food stimulus lie just behind the base of the tentacles, on either side of the head. As with the positioning of human ears, these sites are ideal for establishing direction. In addition to the cells, cilia (hair-like organs) on its tentacles and head beat continually to propel a current of water toward these chemo-receptive areas. As well as picking up food smells, snails of the genus *Biomphalaria* can follow the traces of mucus left by other snails.

Freshwater limpets

The family Ancylidae, often known as the freshwater limpets, has members that are common all over the world. Nearly all of them live in fast-flowing, well-oxygenated water, attaching themselves to rocks and other firm objects on the streambed. The species *Ancylastrum sumingianum* is typical of Tasmania, the genus *Burnupia* occurs in Africa, and the genus *Ferrissia* in North and Central America. The river limpet *Ancylus fluviatilis* is Europe's representative.

The river limpet has a cap-shaped (patelliform) shell with an oval base and a backward-pointing apex. Like its marine namesake, it has limited movement, spending much of its time securely attached to the bottom, using its foot as a sucker. Here it feeds on the layers of algae that cover the rocks. Such a stationary life means that it does not rise to the surface for air. Instead, it relies on the rich amounts of oxygen dissolved in the water to breathe. Respiration takes

BELOW The map shows the geographical distribution of various species of the pulmonate family Zonitidae. The **pulmonates are the most advanced of the gastropods and are adapted for breathing air through their lungs.**

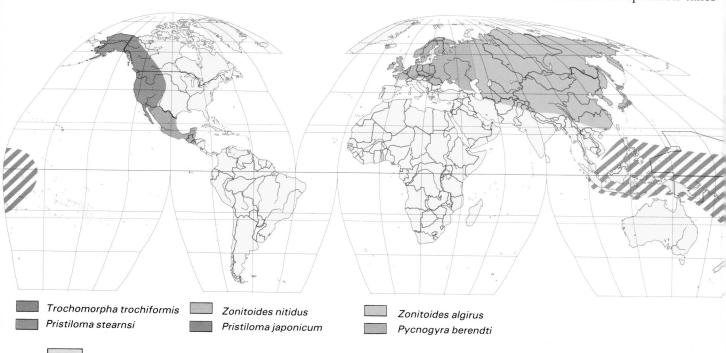

Trochomorpha trochiformis

Pristiloma stearnsi

Zonitoides nitidus

Pristiloma japonicum

Zonitoides algirus

Pycnogyra berendti

place through its skin, supplemented by the action of a pseudobranch. In fast-flowing water, *A. fluviatilis* usually positions itself facing the current, in order to offer the least possible resistance. The nature of the surrounding water has a distinct influence on the shape of freshwater limpets: those species that live in calm water have deeper, more pointed shells—those living in fast-flowing water have flatter shells.

Land snails and slugs

The snails and slugs that are encountered on land differ in shape from their aquatic relatives. Land mollusks have two pairs of tentacles on their heads, and their eyes are mounted on the tips of the hind pair. Such mollusks belong to the order Stylommatophora ("stalk eyes"), and they are therefore known as stylommatophores.

Although the advantages of eyes held as high as possible may seem obvious in a crawling animal—every 0.04 in. upward must expand horizons enormously in their miniature world—the snails do not always hold them vertically. For example, when the animal climbs up a plant in the search for food, it holds its eyed tentacles at 90 degrees to its body—that is, parallel to the ground rather than the plant stem. When the snail descends, it lowers the tentacles, extending them forward—toward the ground. No satisfactory explanation for this behavior has been offered, but it is possible that, while the mollusk is climbing upward, its priority is to identify a suitable grazing area. By pointing its tentacles sideways, it can enlarge its field of vision, enabling it to explore its surroundings more effectively. On the return journey down the plant, it is may be more important to follow the trail and to inspect the ground for possible predators. At the least sign of danger, the snail swiftly retracts its eyes.

Sticking to their zones

Stylommatophores live in nearly all habitats, from forests to rocky mountains, from the seashore to the meadows. Although certain species vary in color according to slight variations in habitat, the majority of species occupy a limited habitat. Thus, one that lives in rocky areas cannot live in a damp environment that is rich in vegetation, while species that inhabit coniferous woods cannot live in deciduous woods, and vice versa.

MOLLUSKS CLASSIFICATION: 13

Pulmonates (snails and slugs) (2)

The third order in the mollusk subclass Pulmonata is the Systellommatophora, a group of shell-less snails from mainly tropical regions. They belong to three families—the Veronicellidae, the Rathousiidae and the Onchidiidae—that are closely allied to the final order Stylommatophora.

The order Stylommatophora contains land-dwelling snails and slugs in a number of superfamilies. They include the Achatellinacea, which contains minute tree snails, such as those living on Hawaiian banana trees; the Vertiginacea (including snails of the genus *Vertigo*); the Succineacea (amber snails); the Achatinacea, which includes the African giant snail, *Achatina fulica*, originally from East Africa and the island of Mauritius; the Endontacea, which contains garden slugs of the genus *Arion*; the Helicacea, containing the edible snail, *Helix pomatia*, and the brown-lipped snail, *Cepaea nemoralis*; and the Zonitacea, which includes the great gray slug, *Limax maximus*, and the gray field slug, *Agriolimax reticulatus*.

Snails of the world

Most animals are classified according to ideas of evolutionary progress. Those closest to the ancestors are considered to be the most primitive; those furthest away are thought to be the most advanced. Snails, however, are divided according to the anatomical details of their genital and excretory systems. While this provides a convenient means of dividing them into groups, it does not always reflect their degree of evolutionary development.

The first three families in the subclass Pulmonata—the Veronicellidae, Rathousiidae and Onchidiidae—belong to a distinct order, the Systellommatophora. It consists of mollusks without shells that inhabit only the hot regions of the world. The genus *Onchidium* is unusual among pulmonates. Common on the coasts of the Indian and Pacific oceans, a typical member of the genus lives between the high- and low-water marks, and possesses small projections (papillae) on its back that serve as secondary gills.

2817

LEFT The tiny pupilloid snail *Abida* sp., typical of the drier zones of southern Europe, hangs from the shady side of a rock, sheltering from the heat. BELOW LEFT *Clausilia dubia* belongs to a group of snails that seldom exceed 0.6 in. in length.

BOTTOM LEFT A few snail shells and some of their lengths: *Vertigo alpestris*, 0.08 in. (A); *Pupilla muscorum*, 0.2 in. (B); *Zebrina detrita*, 0.8 in. (C); *Acanthinula aculeata*, 0.08 in. (D); *Vallonia costata*, a side view (E); *V. costata*, from below (F).

Stylommatophores

The order Stylommatophora is the fourth and final order of the pulmonate subclass, and contains a number of superfamilies, including the Achatellinacea, Vertiginacea, Succineacea, Achatinacea, Endontacea, Helicacea and Zonitacea. The superfamily Achatellinacea includes some of the most primitive stylommatophores. Small mollusks with microscopic shells, they live mainly in the eastern Pacific Ocean. Some species live on fruit trees; in Hawaii, for example, many congregate on banana trees.

Vertiginacean mollusks

The superfamily Vertiginacea includes a large number of species scattered around the world. They are usually tiny mollusks that only rarely reach a length of 0.4 in. Although most of them have a shell, it is sometimes only 0.08-0.1 in. long. The shell is usually oval or subcylindrical, and the shell's margin is often thickened and sunken toward the outside edge. The inner margin of the opening nearly always presents a series of folds and indentations that identify the different species. Some members of this group can be oviparous (laying eggs containing embryos at an advanced stage of development) or even viviparous (bearing their young alive)—a characteristic that is rare in terrestrial pulmonates.

Cool snails

Pupilla muscorum, a snail only 0.1-0.16 in. long, inhabits the cooler regions of the world, such as northern North America, Asia and Europe. It lives in exposed, arid environments that are rich in calcium, such as rock faces, areas of gravel and meadows. It even ventures onto coastal sand dunes, an extremely inhospitable environment due to the lack of water and succulent vegetation, the high salt content of the ground, and the drastic temperature difference between night and day. The snail species

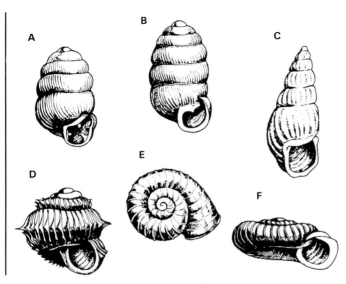

P. alpicola lives only in wet areas, usually at an altitude of more than 3500 ft. above sea level.

Abida polvodon is a Mediterranean species that inhabits dry fields and scrub on chalky soil. It has a large number of notches and folds in its shell. *Gyliotrachela hungerfordiana* is a small mollusk from the Moluccas and Java. Seen from the side, the opening of the shell points upward, so that when the snail is moving, its shell is probably held upside-down with its apex aimed toward the ground.

Mollusks of the genus *Vertigo* are widespread. Its species are tiny, measuring a maximum of 0.08 in. long. *Vertigo moulisiana* inhabits marshy areas beside lakes and rivers in central, southern and western Europe, where it often lives on marsh reeds of the genus *Phragmites*. Unlike most mollusks, *V. moulisiana* does not readily hibernate, and it is rare to find specimens whose shells are sealed by the epiphragm (a solidifed mucus secretion). When the weather becomes cold, *Vertigo* mollusks prefer to shelter under large leaves. *Vallonia costata,* a common species in North America and Eurasia, has an exceptionally elegant shell. It is tiny and flat, with a large number of ribs forming an attractive pattern.

A fluke carrier

One species of the superfamily Vertiginacea causes a degree of economic damage. *Zebrina detrita,* in the family Enidae, lives in the Mediterranean region on chalky ground and is a prime intermediate host of the parasitic fluke *Dicrocoelium denditicum,* which attacks sheep. The parasite's larvae assemble in balls of slime in the snail's breathing chamber; when they fall out of the pneumostome (the respiratory pore), ants gather them up and take them to their nests for food. The next larval stage infects the ants, which are then eaten accidentally when sheep crop the grass.

The families Cionellidae, Amastridae and Partulidae are also included in the superfamily Vertiginacea. The cionellids live almost exclusively in temperate zones in Europe, northern and central Asia and North Africa; the amastrids are confined to the Hawaiian Islands; and the partulids inhabit the Indian and Pacific Ocean region.

Snails of the family Clausiliidae occur throughout Asia, North Africa, South America and Europe, where they are most common in the Balkans and the Caucasus. Their numbers diminish toward western

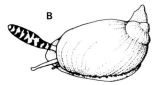

TOP The amber snail *Succinea putris* lives close to water in Europe and Siberia and preys on other pulmonate snails.
ABOVE One tentacle of the amber snail may be infected with the larva of a parasitic trematode fluke. The larva, which is colored with black and white rings, alters the snail's appearance; these drawings show the mollusk viewed from the side (A) and from above (B). The wriggling, worm-like tentacle is designed to attract a bird, which will then eat the snail and, in turn, become the final host of the parasite.

Europe; six species occur in the French Pyrenees and only three species inhabit Britain.

The European members of the family Clausiliidae rarely measure more than 0.6 in. in length. They have tapering shells made up of numerous whorls that increase regularly in size. The insides of their peristomes have a complex system of indentations, folds or notches. All snails of this family have a flexible spoon-shaped, calcareous plate, the upper part of

ABOVE Among the largest snails in the world, Achatina achatina may grow to more than 8 in. in length. It leads a nocturnal life in the tropical forests of New Guinea.

which is attached to the columella (the central axis of the shell spiral) by an elastic ligament. Although the plate, known as the clausilium, is not attached to the foot, it serves the same purpose as an operculum. When the snail withdraws into its shell, it closes the opening to prevent predators and other animals from entering.

Amber snails

The superfamily Succineacea comprises a group of snails that occur in wet areas throughout the world. Snails of the family Succineidae are unable to withdraw completely into their shells; although the last whorls of their shells are greatly expanded, their peristomes are large and take up a lot of space. Their shells tend to be fragile and are usually a translucent, light brown color. Their front tentacles are reduced.

Amber snails inhabit damp places, such as dark woods or among the vegetation on the banks of lakes or rivers. Some species even venture underwater and are amphibious. Although they usually eat algae and organic waste, some species of amber snail are predatory, attacking and eating other pulmonates and their eggs. Amber snails are prey to other gastropods, frogs and small ants.

Succinea putris, an amber snail common throughout Europe and Siberia, feeds on aquatic plants at the edge of the water or on vegetation on the banks. It lays clusters of 20-40 eggs among leaves or on damp ground. *S. putris* is the intermediate host of the trematode fluke *Distomum macrostomum,* which in its adult state lives as a parasite in the digestive tract of birds. Using the amber snail as a stepping-stone to its final host, the fluke alters both the appearance and the behavior of the snail. One of the fluke's larval stages, known as a sporocyst, enters one of the snail's tentacles. The sporocyst enlarges the tentacle and causes it to pulsate, so that it resembles a wriggling worm. After it has been infected by the fluke, *S. putris* leaves its damp environment and enters a sunny field, making itself conspicuous to birds. The false worm or the whole snail is then eaten by birds, ensuring the continued development of the parasite.

The European amber snail *S. elegans,* distinguishable by its black body, lives on aquatic plants. The hardy snail *S. oblonga,* which occurs in Asia and in Europe, inhabits rocky environments.

SHAPELY SHELLS

Atoracophoridae

Snails of the family Atoracophoridae in the superfamily Succineacea occur in well-defined areas throughout the world. *Triboniophorus graeffi*, for example, inhabits Australia and New Guinea, while *Anietella virgata* lives in the archipelago of the Bismarck Islands in the Pacific. They live in vegetation, often in trees. Their shells are reduced to small, calcareous pieces dotted on the epidermis or outer layer of the skin, and they have a single pair of tentacles. Their pneumostomes (the aperture to the mantle cavity), their anal openings and their renal pores open separately on their backs. Their lungs resemble the respiratory systems of arthropods and consist of a system of tubes known as trachea. All snails that possess this characteristic lung structure belong to a group known as Tracheapulmonata. A short duct leading from the pneumostome divides into narrower respiratory tubes that extend into the different organs.

Achatinacea

The superfamily Achatinacea, belonging to the order Stylommatophora, includes many different species of snails. When alive, the European snail *Caecilioides acicula* has a smooth, shiny, transparent shell, but when it dies, its shell becomes white and opaque. Although rarely seen alive because of its subterranean habits and its size (it rarely measures more than 0.1 in. long), *C. acicula* lives under the roots of plants, sometimes several inches deep, or in deep cracks in rocks, where it hunts small invertebrates. Empty shells are found in large numbers in the detritus that accumulates when rivers flood, and in ants' nests that are built mainly of pine needles.

Shedding its shell

The snail *Rumina decollata*, which is common in the Mediterranean, measures up to 1.4 in. in length. Each year in early summer, the snail cuts away the most recent whorls of its shell. As the weather warms up, it builds an internal calcareous partition or septum and its shell develops a narrow flaw. When the snail knocks against an obstacle, the shell breaks off at the point of weakness. The discarded shell is subcylindrical in shape and lacks an apex, and the shell opening is closed by a septum.

ABOVE The body of the giant African snail, *Achinata fulica*, grows to a length of almost 12 in., while the shell may reach 8 in. in length. Giant African snails are indigenous to East Africa, where they feed mostly on decaying vegetation. However, the activities of humans have spread the species to south Asia, Indonesia and many Pacific islands, where it causes widespread destruction of agricultural crops.

A giant pest

The superfamily Achatinacea contains the giant African snail. Native to Mauritius and parts of East Africa, it has spread to many of the warmer areas of the world, where its voracious appetite has caused a great deal of damage to the green vegetation on which it feeds. Its large, strong, brown shell may measure up to 8 in. in length and is marked with lengthwise patterns of purple, green, pink or white. The snail may weigh up to 18 lbs.

In its native habitat, the giant African snail caused little damage. It was well controlled by predators and by the local people who valued it as food and used its shell to make spoons. However, in the mid-19th century, some specimens were taken to India. By the turn of the century, the giant African snail had spread to Ceylon (Sri Lanka), where it became a major pest in tea

ABOVE **The familiar land slug, *Arion ater*, can grow up to 8 in. in length and inhabits gardens throughout Britain and Ireland.**

Since coloration varies greatly between individuals, some taxonomists classify red and black *Arion ater* slugs as separate species.

gardens. It was introduced to the Indonesian islands where it began eating rubber trees in Java and Sumatra. Valued as a food source and for medicinal purposes, it became established in Japan. By the end of World War II it had reached nearly all the Pacific islands. The giant African snail has also been transported to the USA and has a foothold in Europe.

Giant African snails have become major agricultural pests because they spread quickly; a snail in its female phase (like all pulmonates, it is hermaphroditic) lays about 300 pea-sized eggs a month, and may produce up to half a million tons of snails in five years. Many attempts have been made to eradicate the giant snail, but it has proved to be highly resistant. The introduction into infested territory of predatory snails that hunt the giant African snails' young has had a limited degree of success. However, the hasty introduction of these pulmonates to many islands, such as Moen island (part of the Truk islands, a group within the Caroline islands in the Pacific Ocean), has endangered the native snail species.

Predatory snails

The family Streptaxidae belonging to the superfamily Streptaxea contains snails that occur in South America, Africa and the Indo-Pacific area. *Discartemon sangkarensis*, a species that lives in Indochina and in the Celebes, has a pyramid-shaped shell that measures about 0.4 inch long. It has a wide shell opening, the upper edge of which is curved inward, rendering the shell opening almost triangular. *Edentulina affinis* and *Gonaxis kiweziensis* are large, carnivorous snails that hunt the young of the giant African snail.

Land-dwelling snails

Within the order Stylommatophora, the superfamily Buliulacea includes land-dwelling snails that are common in Central and South America, Africa and the southwestern Pacific Ocean. Many species hibernate in winter, using their sticky secretions to attach their shells to the bark of trees. However, some species retain an opening in their shells and continue to feed on a reduced scale throughout the winter. *Placostylus fibratus*, Dryptus moritzianus and *Ligmes vettatus* are some fairly common species of snails in the superfamily Buliulacea.

Endodontacea—snails and slugs

The stylommatophoran superfamily Endodontacea contains both snails and slugs. A slug is basically a snail with a reduced shell and no operculum—the flap that closes the entrance to the snail's shell when the animal is retracted—or no shell at all. Without these moisture-conserving devices, slugs tend to inhabit damp environments, and are usually seen after rain or when dew lies on the ground at dawn or dusk.

The superfamily Endodontacea includes three families: the Endodontidae, Arionidae and Philomycidae. The family Endodontidae contains snails whose normally developed shells rarely exceed 0.4 in. in length. These pulmonates are found worldwide, generally in shady, damp environments. Slugs in the family Philomycidae have no shells at all.

The family Arionidae mostly contains slugs whose shells are partially or completely covered by the mantle. Slugs in the genus *Binneya* are an exception, however. These slugs from Central and North America have external spiral shells that are usually reduced to an oval plate on the skin on their backs.

Only two genera of slugs in the family Arionidae live in Europe. One of them, *Geomalacus*, is represented by the single species *Geomalacus maculosus*, which occurs in Mediterranean countries and in Ireland, where it feeds on rock lichen and tree bark.

The other genus of European slugs in the family Arionidae is *Arion*. The typical slug in this genus has a shell that is reduced to small, chalky granules on its

ABOVE A garden slug of the species *Arion ater* in its red phase. The white, circular organ is the creature's pneumostome, or breathing pore. The granular area beneath the pneumostome is the remnant of the shell—now buried within the mantle.

skin. It has a mucus gland under its tail, a slightly raised mantle on its back, and a pneumostome that opens on its right side about halfway along its mantle. Two species in the genus *Arion* have been introduced to countries outside Europe—*Arion ater* to New Zealand and *A. subfuscus* to the United States.

A. ater is one of the most conspicuous slugs of northern Europe, commonly seen in woods, meadows or gardens in the early morning or after summer rain. It is large—up to 8 in. long—and seems to appear from nowhere and disappear as soon as the ground dries out. Because *A. ater* varies greatly in color—from black through gray to red—some naturalists have divided the genus into two species, *A. ater* (black) and *A. rufus* (red).

Eating one's own family

The Arionidae are usually herbivorous. They feed on vegetables, fruit or fungi, and sometimes climb the trunks of trees to forage for lichen and algae. However, they also eat organic waste, such as the excrement of herbivorous vertebrates or the dead bodies of insects and other animals. *A. subfuscus* is smaller than *A. ater*, reaching only 2.8 in. in length. It is distinctively marked, with a dark streak running down both sides of its brown body. Some American researchers have recently discovered that it becomes predatory in its adult life, attacking, killing and devouring members of its own family. Other European species may also behave in the same way.

Slug reproduction

Reproduction in the species *A. ater* has been closely studied. Like most pulmonates, it is a hermaphrodite, but it passes through distinct sex phases. In the first month of its life, it behaves like a male; from the second to the fifth months, it is a hermaphrodite; thereafter, it behaves exclusively as a female. During mating, animals exchange fleshy, crystalline "darts" that probably help to stimulate the later stages of copulation. As the darts differ from species to species, it is likely that they also prohibit mating between different species.

A. ater lays its eggs in early autumn, placing them under dead leaves or stones or in some other damp and sheltered place in the ground. The eggs, which are about 0.2 in. in diameter, usually hatch after 30 days. However, if they are laid late in the year, they do not hatch until the following spring. The slugs rarely live longer than two years since they do not usually survive the winter following their birth.

Colored to suit the climate

The superfamily Zonitacea contains a great variety of snails and slugs. Many of them belong to the families Helicarionidae and Limacidae. The family Helicarionidae contains the species *Euconolus fulvus*, which lives in temperate climates. It occurs in a wide range of habitats—from fields and marshes to deciduous and coniferous woods—and varies somewhat in shape according to its location. All individuals in the species reach a maximum length of 0.2 in. and have slightly conical shells with a waxy sheen and five and a half whorls. However, those that develop in damper places usually have dark brown shells that are larger and taller than those of specimens from drier environments.

Species of pulmonate shell that are distributed over a wide area tend to be larger in the hotter zones. High humidity also encourages bulk, although shells become thinner and more fragile in such areas. In regions that are hot and sunny, the shells tend to develop bright pigmentation. In colder regions, they are usually a dark color or black.

Glass snails and shelled slugs

The superfamily Zonitacea also includes the delicate glass snails of the genera *Zonites* and *Vitrina*, as well as a vast array of slugs. *Vitrina pellucida* is found all over Europe—living in damp environments, woods, fields or among rocks. It feeds mainly on organic waste and does not look like a typical pulmonate. Its extremely thin, translucent shell consists of only three whorls and is a light green color. Like all species that do not retract completely into their shells, it has a large peristome. Its mantle protrudes from the front of its shell, extending forward to cover part of its back and backward onto the shell as far up as the apex.

Species in the genus *Oxychilus* are also characteristic of the superfamily Zonitacea. They have shiny, transparent shells that turn a whitish, opaque color when the animal dies. They inhabit extremely damp places, with some even living in caves or spending their entire lives underground. The blue-colored snail *Oxychilus allarius* is one of the few pulmonates that can tolerate slightly acidic soils, and can therefore live in coniferous woods. It is notable for its curious habit of emitting a pungent odor that resembles garlic when it is alarmed.

Species of the genus *Daudebardia* occur in the Mediterranean area, in central Europe and in the Caucasus. They are small mollusks, only about 0.1 in. long, but exclusively carnivorous nonetheless. *Daudebardia rufa* and *D. brevipes* are the two most common species in the genus, and both live under leaves or stones, in soft earth or in woods.

Summer confrontations

Members of the slug family Limacidae resemble the Arionidae, apart from the fact that they have retained a

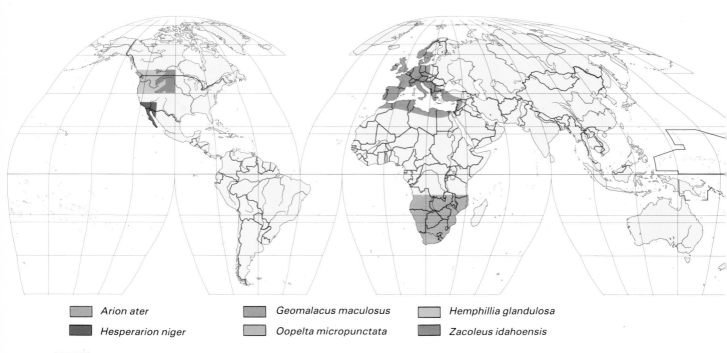

Arion ater	Geomalacus maculosus	Hemphillia glandulosa
Hesperarion niger	Oopelta micropunctata	Zacoleus idahoensis

residual shell that is a fragile and completely internal calcareous plate. The opening of their peristome is further forward than it is in snails. Most slugs in the family Limacidae live in Europe and western Asia. Only a few genera such as *Deroceras* and *Agriolimax* inhabit the New World and North Africa as well. The great gray slug, *Limax maximus*, although only recently introduced to the United States, is now common there. It feeds mainly on vegetables, especially ripe fruit and fungi, which it can identify from some distance using its senses of sight and smell.

Gray slugs, like some related arionid slugs, do not hesitate to attack other species that they encounter during their nighttime foraging. One American species, *Deroceras caruanae*, although only an inch long, attacks pulmonates twice or three times its size, often with fatal consequences.

Without a doubt, the most aggressive species of gray slug is *Limax maximus*, which kills and eats a wide range of other slugs. Its aggressiveness is closely linked to the animal's stage of development and to the season: it is only aggressive as an adult, and then only during the hottest and driest period of the year. Great gray slugs usually congregate in winter, starting to hunt for food during the night at the onset of spring when the environment becomes warmer and damper.

In summer, each slug has to find a suitably deep and damp refuge in which to rest during the day. The shelters must also be reasonably close to a source of food, since summer nights—when the slugs forage—are relatively short and the animals must return to the safety of their shelters at daybreak. The number of suitable shelters diminishes in the summer, and competition to possess a home triggers the slugs' aggression.

A typical fight

In a typical fight between great gray slugs, the aggressor approaches a smaller relative, lifts the front part of its body and extends it tentacles to identify its opponent accurately. Then it strikes its victim repeatedly with its jaws and radula, causing deep wounds on the posterior part of the opponent's body. The attacked slug reacts by shaking its tail vigorously to the left and right, striking its tormentor and trying to escape. However, the attacker does not give up. It pursues its victim by following the trail of mucus that it leaves behind. Then it attacks from the front. The opponent

ABOVE The great gray field slug, *Agriolimax reticulatus*, has the ability to withstand severe cold: it can move and feed at temperatures slightly **above freezing point. FAR LEFT The geographical distribution of several species of the slug family Arionidae.**

curls up and emits great quantities of mucus, fixing itself to the ground to dissuade its enemy from further attack. However, the great gray slug keeps biting until its quarry is dead and then eats it.

Slugs are preyed upon by hedgehogs, badgers, other mammals and some birds. Many insect larvae are particularly fond of slugs, and larvae of the glowworm *Lampyris noctiluca* are among their fiercest predators. However, slugs are far from prime prey for most predators, since their slime seems to render them unpalatable. Birds, especially, often leave them only partially eaten.

Slugs with shells

The superfamily Oeleacinacea contains one family, the Testacellidae. Slugs of this family occur in Western Europe and along the Mediterranean coast of North Africa. However, some species of slugs belonging to the genus *Testacella* have been introduced into America. The shell of a testacellid slug is reduced to a plate that is situated at the back of its body, above its mantle. Three species belonging to this genus live in Europe. The largest of them, *T. mangei*, measures up to 4 in. in length. A nocturnal slug, it remains inactive for much of the year. As the weather gets cooler, or a period of dry weather begins, *Testacella* slugs bury themselves deep in the ground, where both the temperature and the humidity are more constant. *T. scutulum* digs to a depth of 9 ft. below the surface.

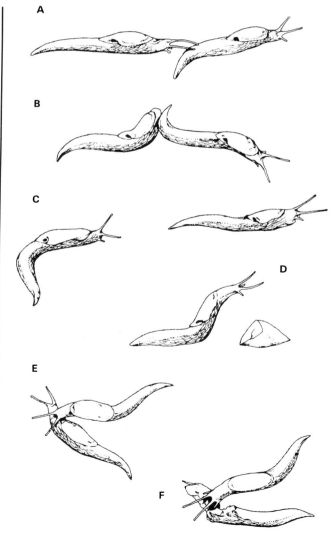

A

B

C

D

E

F

ABOVE LEFT The common limaciud slug, *Deroceras laeve*, lives among rotting vegetation on damp ground.
ABOVE The great gray slug, *Limax maximus*, preys on other slugs, including those of its own species.
LEFT A great gray slug pursues its prey: the predator approaches from behind (A) and, undeterred by tail lashing (B), sets off in pursuit of its intended victim (C). The predatory slug raises its body (D), strikes a deadly blow with its sharp radula (E) and enjoys its well-earned meal (F).

Testacellid slugs are strictly carnivorous and feed on earthworms. They commonly occur in cultivated gardens, where the continually disturbed and organically enriched soil encourages the presence of worms. A slug attacks its prey at night when the earthworms emerge from the ground. The slug has sharp teeth on its radula, which curve backward, enabling it to maintain a strong grip on its prey. The earthworm wriggles violently in an attempt to escape, but usually fails. The slug eats its prey slowly, sometimes taking all night.

Helicacea

The superfamily Helicacea is the largest of all pulmonate superfamilies. It contains 180 genera of snails, a vast number of which have reached the evolutionary peak of all the stylommatophores (including the familiar garden snail and the edible snail).

Snails that belong to the superfamily Helicacea—with the exception of snails in the family Caeminidae—possess dart sacs as part of their sexual anatomy. Used during mating, a dart sac serves as the delivery apparatus for a small, calcareous, arrow-shaped

needle. The snail performs a complex mating ritual whereby it fires a dart into its partner's body before inserting its penis.

The families Helicellidae and Helicidae contain snails that account for nearly half of Europe's pulmonates. Their numbers increase from northern Europe to the Mediterranean area.

Avoiding the hot sun

Snails of the family Helicellidae are common throughout the western temperate regions including America, where they were probably introduced in agricultural imports. The genus *Helicella* of the family Helicellidae contains snails that are particularly well adapted to life in a dry or arid environment. Many species, such as *Helicella ericetorum*, *H. intersecta* and *H. virgata*, even live in the sparse, tough bushes that grow on sand dunes by the sea. These species, as well as *Euparypha pisana*, also a member of the family Helicellidae, have adapted in a way that enables them to resist the strong summer sun.

Since the ground-level temperature may be high, these snails climb up the tallest stalks or bushes in the early hours of the day. When they reach a height where the temperature is lower, they secrete mucus that hardens on contact with the air, and secure

ABOVE During daylight hours, snails of the genus *Helicella* avoid the high temperatures at ground level by resting on the stems of tall plants, sealing their feet to the stem with sticky mucus secretions. After sunset, the snails descend to the ground to feed during the cool night hours.

themselves to the stalks. They often attach themselves to each other, sometimes in large groups containing up to 100 individuals. The snails return to the ground in search of food when nightfall brings cooler, damper conditions. However, such behavior can prove dangerous. When the snails remain immobile on vegetation, they become easy prey for birds and the rat *Rattus norvegicus*. These rats have become especially common in coastal marine environments during the last few decades and have quickly learned that they need only bend the stalks to reach the snails.

The edible snail

The family Helicidae contains the familiar garden snail and the edible snail that inhabit temperate regions. The edible snail, *Helix pomatia*, is familiar to many people throughout the world who eat it and consider it to be a delicacy. It occurs throughout Europe, and in Britain it is especially common in southeast England. The edible snail lives in open

LEFT The eyes of the edible snail, *Helix pomatia*, are in the tips of its tentacles. They—like the eyes of most other gastropods—detect changes in general light intensity, but cannot perceive movement or color. Each eye consists of a lens that covers a tiny chamber of light-sensitive cells.

RIGHT When introduced to new habitats, giant African land snails of the species *Achatina maculata* undergo huge population explosions. Shortly afterward, however, their growth rate declines dramatically and levels off. Zoologists are unable to explain the phenomenon.

sometimes even for longer than a day. When a pair of edible snails meet to mate, they rear up, pressing the soles of their feet together. Then, supported by the rear end of their feet and the tips of their shells, they rock from side to side, caressing each other with their tentacles. Eventually each snail plunges a calcareous dart into the sole of its partner's foot. Zoologists believe that the dart stimulates the snails to exchange sperm.

Once the snails have exchanged sperm, they separate. Each snail stores the sperm until its own eggs are ready to fertilize. Edible snails lay between 60 and 80 greenish white eggs, which they bury in a small hole. The eggs hatch in 25-37 days, depending on the weather. The newly hatched edible snails eat the remains of their eggshells before progressing to their adult diet. They become fully grown in one to three years.

The edible snail has a rounded, thick-walled shell, approximately 2 in. in height and breadth with five whorls. Its shell may be cream, gray or pale yellow in color, with up to five indistinct, brownish, spiral bands.

The garden snail

The family Helicidae also contains the garden snail, *Helix aspersa*. Common in Britain, its shell has five whorls and measures up to 1.5 in. across. It has five dark brown spiral bands on a fawn, yellow or buff background. Made of calcium carbonate (chalk), the shell is covered by a glaze of protein material that wears off with age.

Because they need calcium for their shells, garden snails flourish where soils and rocks are rich in calcium. The garden snail occurs in most of Europe, and it has been introduced into North and South America, Australia and southern Africa. It is

woodland, scrub, hedgerows, old quarries and grassy downland, but is more dependent than most snails on an abundance of calcium in the soil and is particularly associated with chalky soils. In France, it often occurs in fields or vineyards.

Though becoming scarcer because it is a food delicacy and is used in laboratory research, the edible snail flourishes better on the continent than in Britain, where it spends half the year hibernating. In captivity the edible snail will eat fresh lettuce, oats and many other kinds of vegetation, but in the wild it feeds on decaying vegetation, fungi and various herbs.

Courtship rituals

Although edible snails are hermaphroditic, self-fertilization is rare. These snails perform elaborate courtship rituals that can last for several hours,

widespread in Britain, except in the north of Scotland, and is most abundant in southern England, especially near the sea. It lives in gardens, hedges, quarries, areas under cliffs and banks and in old walls.

Garden snails feed on the leaves of many plants, including lettuce, hops, primrose, nasturtium, alder, holly and nettle. They also eat fruit, and sometimes dead slugs and earthworms. Garden snails have a well-developed homing instinct and regularly return from their foraging expeditions to the same roosting place, which is often communal. Like most snails, they spend a greater part of the year in hibernation, especially during dry periods and in winter. They mate throughout the spring and summer and lay up to 100 oval-shaped eggs that hatch within four weeks.

Adapting to the environment

The brown-lipped snail of the family Helicidae has interested naturalists since the 19th century. The interest was aroused by the variations in the snail's coloring in certain environments—known as chromatic polymorphism. Its shell may be plain yellow or light brown, or may be decorated with between one and five dark spiral stripes. It was clear from the beginning that color and decoration are genetically determined, but it was not easy to relate color or pattern to particular climatic or geographic circumstances.

Today, it is thought that the climate, or the microclimate, of a given area influences the coloring of the mollusk through a process known as natural selection. For example, a large proportion of snails with pale yellow shells occur in valleys between dunes—the light color reflects the sun's rays better than darker colors. Snails that live in wooded hills have shells that are darker or striped. In an environment that maintains the same climatic conditions (such as the dunes), the snails adopt only one genetic trait, and therefore only one color. But in a varied and complex environment, such as a damp wood with sunny glades and rocky outcrops, the snails exploit the numerous genetic possibilities and colors in order to adapt themselves to their surroundings.

Although many snails are distributed over wide areas, some snail species belonging to the genus *Helicigona* have evolved to live in cold climates and only occur on certain mountain ranges. When the glaciers receded at the end of the last Ice Age, helicigonan snails remained isolated on the highest peaks.

TOP The brown-lipped snail's muscular foot lends it extraordinary agility of movement. A mucus covering on the foot prevents dehydration and enables the snail to glide across most surfaces.
ABOVE The shell markings of brown-lipped snails, *Cepaea nemoralis*, vary greatly among species. Like most other stylommatophoran snails, the brown-lipped snail is a herbivore that feeds on live or decaying plants. During mating, it uses a flexible calcified dart to stimulate its partner. The brown-lipped snail lays its eggs on moist ground, often in soil under decaying leaf material.

HINGED FILTER FEEDERS

Mussels, oysters, scallops and clams—mollusks recognizable by shells that are divided into two shallow, hinged valves—lead largely immobile lives on the sea floor or on coastal rocks, filter feeding on tiny organisms in the water

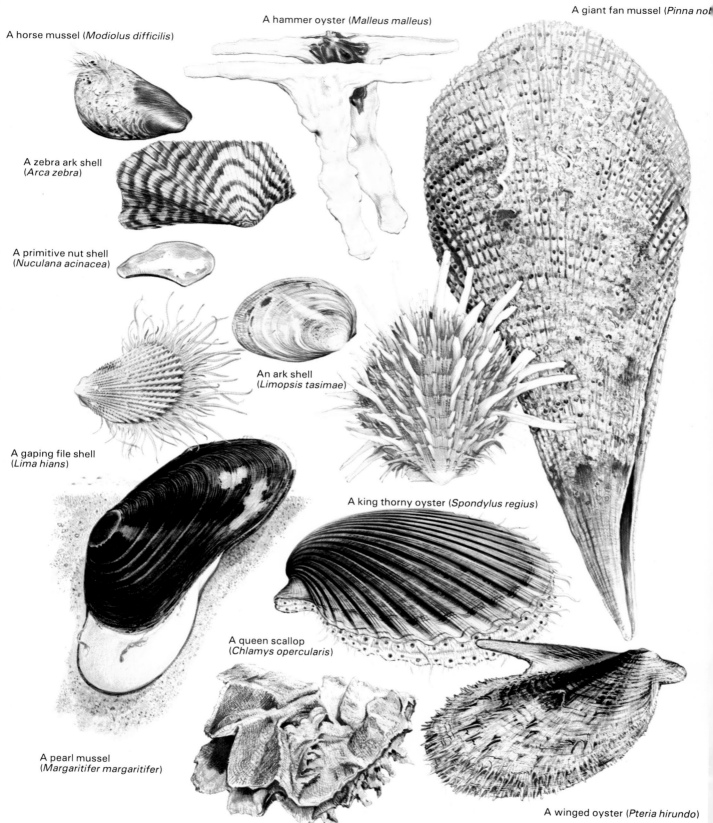

A giant fan mussel (*Pinna nobi*

A hammer oyster (*Malleus malleus*)

A horse mussel (*Modiolus difficilis*)

A zebra ark shell
(*Arca zebra*)

A primitive nut shell
(*Nuculana acinacea*)

An ark shell
(*Limopsis tasimae*)

A gaping file shell
(*Lima hians*)

A king thorny oyster (*Spondylus regius*)

A queen scallop
(*Chlamys opercularis*)

A pearl mussel
(*Margaritifer margaritifer*)

A winged oyster (*Pteria hirundo*)

A roofed oyster (*Ostrea crystagalli*)

Millions of years ago, some mollusks left the rocky seabeds around the coasts to inhabit more varied and softer floors of sand, mud or detritus. Burying themselves in the sediment was a convenient way to avoid predators, but it was impossible to search for food while buried. So, at the same time that the mollusks began to bury themselves, they also began to feed exclusively on microscopic particles.

The evolution of bivalves

The changing habits and behavior of mollusks clearly reflect the structure of bivalves or lamellibranchs. It is easier for an animal to burrow into the sediment if its body is laterally compressed, so mollusks with compressed bodies and shells that extended downward to enclose their entire bodies survived in greater numbers. Their shells began to split lengthwise, assuming the shape of a clasp. The two halves were held together by the periostracum, the horny covering of the shell that thickens into an elastic ligament on the back of the clasp. The elastic ligament holds the shell open when the adductor muscles are not in action.

The class Bivalvia

The class Bivalvia contains 15,000-20,000 species of mollusk, including clams, mussels and oysters. They are classified according to physical characteristics that are common to the entire class—their gills, clasps and muscle structure. The six major subclasses into which they are divided are the Paleotaxodonta, Cryptodonta, Pteriomorpha, Paleoheterodonta, Heterodonta and Anomalodesmata.

The subclasses Paleotaxodonta and Cryptodonta are sometimes classed together as the Protobranchia. They include some of the most ancient species of bivalve, with gills that closely resemble those of the gastropods. The gills of bivalves in some of the other subclasses consist of a series of filaments joined by cilia or connective tissue. Bivalves in the small subclass Anomalodesmata include deepwater species that have no gill filaments; they exchange respiratory gases through the surface of their mantles.

Among protobranchs, the two lobes of the mantle are always separate; in the other subclasses, they are fused, enabling the animal to pump water more effectively. The lobes remain separate, however, where the foot and the byssus threads emerge and where water enters and leaves the shell. Moreover, in this part of the animal's body, the mantle is often elongated to form two siphons.

Functional muscle fibers

Bivalves have two muscles holding their shells together. The anterior (front) muscle is often tiny—or missing, as is the case with scallops of the genus *Pecten*. Both muscles are unusual in that they consist of two types of fiber—striated and smooth—with two separate functions.

Bivalves use their striated muscles to close their shells as quickly as possible when threatened by an attacker. However, these muscles require a lot of energy to function, and many species need to keep their shells closed for long periods of time. Certain mussels that are exposed to air at low tide, for example, may need to keep their shells closed for several months. If they used their striated muscles the entire time, they would soon be depleted of energy. Instead, they rely on their smooth muscle fibers, known as catch fibers, to hold the shells shut for long periods since they require very little energy to function.

Carefully selected nourishment

Nearly all bivalves feed on microscopic particles such as plankton, obtaining them from both vegetable and animal sources. Many species choose their nourishment carefully, selecting specific types of particles to suck in through their inhalant siphon. Others restrict themselves to particles of a certain size. They all avoid vegetable cells that contain substances toxic to bivalves.

By far the majority of adult bivalves live in the sea, attached to rocks or buried in sediment. Only a few species have invaded freshwater environments, where conditions are far more unstable. Some species of bivalve have managed to survive long periods of drought in dried-up tropical pools by burying themselves in the mud, closing their shells so as not to let in air and slowing down their metabolism. In northern climates, by contrast, some lamellibranchs can live imprisoned in ice, at a temperature of 23°F in the case of the genus *Anodonta* or at 14°F in such species as the common orb-shell cockle, *Sphaerium corneum*.

The growth of mollusks is conditioned by extremes in the environment. In the less salty waters of the Baltic Sea, where salinity decreases from west to east, the size of bivalve shells diminishes correspondingly. The common mussel *Mytilus edulis*, for example, grows up to 4.4 in. long at the western end of its range but reaches only 0.8 in. in length at its eastern end.

Paleotaxodonta and Cryptodonta

The two subclasses Paleotaxodonta and Cryptodonta have various characteristics indicating that they are the two most primitive groups in the class. Species in the subclass Paleotaxodonta possess a clasp with long rows of interlocking teeth on both halves of the shell, rather like a cog, whereas the Cryptodonta have more advanced clasp mechanisms.

Within the subclass Paleotaxodonta, the order Nuculoida is one of the most ancient bivalve groups. It contains a huge number of species, with representatives in nearly every sea. However, they are difficult to identify. Species in the shallow-water nutshell genus

Nucula have a single pair of feathery gills. They use their gills solely to breathe, while members of the more advanced Cryptodonta and most of the rest of the class Bivalvia use their gills for feeding as well.

Efficient water circulation

The circulation of water inside the mantles of bivalves in the subclass Paleotaxodonta has changed considerably during the course of evolution. Initially nutshells, which usually live buried just below the surface, would create a current of water that used to enter the front of their bodies, pass over their gills, and leave at the rear. However, such a type of circulation prevented the bivalves from burying themselves deeper in the seabed and they soon abandoned it. Now, in nutshell species such as *Nuculana fragilis* and *Yoldia limatula*, which live along the European coastline, and *Y. arctica*, which inhabits the Arctic seas, water both enters and leaves at the rear of the animals' shells, allowing them to bury themselves deeper.

Nutshells have two labial palps that are similar to tentacles and long enough to protrude from their shells. They use them to gather their food, which consists of algae, protozoa and detritus. Each palp contains a cilia-lined groove that acts like a conveyor belt, transporting the food to the nutshell's mouth.

BELOW **The map shows the world distribution of ark shells.** PAGE 2831 **The queen scallop,** *Chlamys opercularis*, **escapes from an attacker by closing** its shell and forcing a jet of water through the opening in its mantle cavity. By doing so, it can push itself through the water in fast, jerky movements.

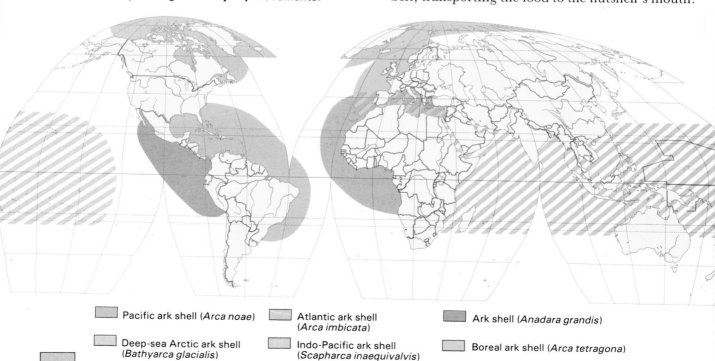

| Pacific ark shell (*Arca noae*) | Atlantic ark shell (*Arca imbicata*) | Ark shell (*Anadara grandis*) |

| Deep-sea Arctic ark shell (*Bathyarca glacialis*) | Indo-Pacific ark shell (*Scapharca inaequivalvis*) (also found in the Adriatic) | Boreal ark shell (*Arca tetragona*) |

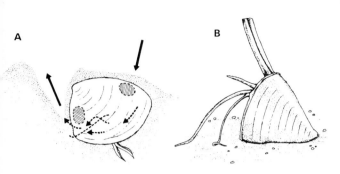

Cryptodonta

The family Solemyidae belongs to the more advanced subclass Cryptodonta. However, members of the family retain some primitive characteristics, such as having feet that are shaped like those of the prosobranchs. A solemyid does not use its foot to move along, but it can join the two sides of the sole together to form a slender organ that is ideal for burrowing.

A member of the genus *Solemya* can disappear into the mud with just two brisk movements of its foot. The outer layers, or periostracum, of *Solemya togata*, a species found around the coast of Portugal, extend outside the shell and form a thin veil, while those of *S. borealis*, present along the Atlantic coast of the United States, are elongated like fingers. These bivalves probably feed by absorbing dissolved organic substances directly from the water.

Pteriomorpha — mussels and oysters etc.

The subclass Pteriomorpha is a large group of mostly marine bivalves that display both highly advanced and surprisingly primitive characteristics. The subclass contains the most well-known bivalves in two major orders — the Arcoida and the Mytiloida — and includes ark shells, mussels, oysters and scallops. They live attached to solid surfaces, securing themselves in position either with secretions from their feet that harden into strong threads called byssus threads, or by fusing one-half of their shells to the surface.

The common mussels of the genus *Mytiloida* and the ark shell *Arca noae* are among the bivalves that secrete byssus threads to fix themselves to stones and shells on the seabed. However, ark shells do not necessarily remain fixed to the same place for their entire lives. Like mussels, an ark shell can move by extending its foot out of its shell, breaking the threads one by one and simultaneously secreting new ones. In this way, it

TOP The primitive nutshell, *Nucula nucleus*, secures itself to the seabed using its specially adapted foot. By pressing the two sides of the sole of its foot together, the nutshell forms a shovel-like wedge. It then pushes the wedge into the substrate, unfolds it and uses it as an anchor.

ABOVE Ark shells of the species *Arca senilis* have strong, thick, heavy shells with prominent radial and concentric decoration. They often bury themselves in the mud or sand of seabeds, or attach themselves to rocks.

ABOVE LEFT The primitive nutshell (A) has small gills that it uses only for respiration. It sucks in water in the opposite direction to most other bivalves. The nutshell feeds by shoveling detritus into its mouth using its labial palps. The primitive bivalve, *Yoldia limatula*, (B) feeds by wedging half its shell into the soft seabed. With its posterior pointing up, it holds its siphons out, stirs up the mud with its ciliated "palp appendages" and takes small particles of food in through its siphons.

can move not only on a horizontal plane but also up and down slopes and vertical walls.

Within the order Arcoida, the family Glycimeridae consists of two unusual species. The dog cockle, *Glycimeris glycimeris*, is almost completely circular, and *G. pilosa* has scales on its periostracum that give it an almost hairy appearance.

The famous mussel

The order Mytiloida consists of five superfamilies and includes mussels, pen shells, scallops and oysters. The best-known species in the family Mytilidae, or mussels, is the edible common mussel, *Mytilus edulis*. Since ancient times, it has been famous for its use in cooking throughout the world. It can be found along the coasts of Europe and the western United States, in the Arctic seas and in Alaska. The similar southwest Mediterranean mussel, *M. galloprovincialis*—as its name suggests—inhabits the Mediterranean Sea.

Members of the genus *Mytilus* live on solid surfaces, including man-made ones such as ship hulls, between the high- and low-water marks. They are extremely resistant to conditions at low tide that would harm other mollusks, such as when the sun is hot. Like more primitive types of bivalve, they minimize the likelihood

ABOVE Mussels often congregate in large numbers on rocks. Once secured by byssus threads, they rarely move and are difficult to dislodge. When the tide retreats they close their shells tightly until it returns and covers them again.

of overheating because the water inside their shells partially evaporates.

Clogging up the canals

The bivalve *Limnoperna fortunei* has recently become famous—not for its taste but because of the damage it is causing to the water supply system of Hong Kong, a city that takes the water for its millions of inhabitants from several rivers in Chinese territory. *L. fortunei* lives in the Chinese waterways and has recently entered the canals of Hong Kong, completely covering their walls and thus slowing down the flow of water.

The common, cigar-shaped species in the genus *Lithophaga* are perhaps the bivalves best suited to living in rock. A lithophagan creates cylindrical, polished holes in the rock not by mechanical erosion but by means of an acidic mucous solution that it secretes. *L. mytiloides* is common in the Mediterranean Sea.

Species in the family Pinnidae, known as pen shells, are particularly notable for their large size. *Pinna nobilis*, which is 31.5 in. long, is the largest bivalve in Europe. It

lives with the rear of its wedge-shaped shell buried in the sediment, anchored by its byssus threads. The rest of the shell, two-thirds of its entire length, remains above the surface in a vertical position.

The pearl makers

The family Pteriidae includes one species of mollusk that is economically important—the pearl oyster, *Pinctada margaritifera*. It produces natural pearls of such beauty that in Japan it is raised for the production of cultivated pearls. A pearl is made when the mollusk reacts to the introduction of a foreign body into its shell. The oyster first secretes a periostracum around the object, then a calcareous layer, and finally a layer of mother-of-pearl.

Another member of the family Pteriidae is the hammer shell, *Malleus malleus*, from the Indo-Pacific. Its shell is one of the strangest of all the bivalves—an upside-down T-shape. *M. vulgaris*, also from the Indo-Pacific, and *M. albus* both possess similar, oddly shaped shells. Some species that live as parasites inside other animals—for example *Vulsella rugosa*, which lives inside the cavities of sponges—belong to the same family.

ABOVE The bivalves of the species *Lithophaga aristata* have long, cylindrical shells that resemble cigars. The mollusks bore their way into rocks by producing acidic secretions. The bivalves are protected from the acid by the protective outer covering on their shells.

PAGES 2838-2839 The shell of the calico scallop, *Argopecten gibbus*, is fringed with tentacles, among which it has about 50 bright blue eyes. The tentacles are sensitive organs of touch, while its eyes sense changes in light intensity. Together they serve to warn the scallop of predators.

MOLLUSKS CLASSIFICATION: 14

Bivalves (1)

The class Bivalvia consists of many familiar mollusks such as clams, mussels and oysters. There are approximately 15,000-20,000 species, and they are divided into six major subclasses: Paleotaxodonta, Cryptodonta, Pteriomorpha, Paleoheterodonta, Heterodonta and Anomalodesmata. This classification box deals with the first two subclasses and part of the third.

The bivalve subclass Paleotaxodonta contains some of the most ancient bivalves in the order Nuculoida, such as the nutshells (genera *Nucula* and *Yoldia*). The subclass Cryptodonta contains slightly more advanced bivalves in the family Solemyidae (genus *Solemya*—for example, *Solemya togata*).

The subclass Pteriomorpha contains the most important of the bivalves in two major orders: the Arcoida and the Mytiloida. The Arcoida contains the superfamily Arcacea, within which are the families Arcidae (ark shells, such as *Arca noae*), and Glycimeridae (dog cockles).

The order Mytiloida includes five superfamilies: the Mytilacea, Pinnacea, Pectinacea, Anomiacea and Ostreacea. The Mytilacea contains the family Mytilidae (mussels—for example, the common mussel, *Mytilus edulis*, of Atlantic, Pacific and Arctic waters, the Mediterranean mussel, *M. galloprovincialis*, the horse mussel, *Modiolus modiolus*, and the bearded horse mussel, *M. barbatus*). The superfamily Pinnacea contains the families Pinnidae (pen shells) and Pteriidae (which includes the pearl oyster, *Pinctada margaritifera*, and the hammer shell, *Malleus malleus*). The superfamily Pectinacea includes the families Pectinidae (scallops, such as the great scallop, *Pecten maximus*; tiger scallop, *Chlamys tigerina*; and queen scallop, *C. opercularis*), and Spondylidae (the thorny oyster, *Spondylus gaederopus*, of the Indo-Pacific region). (See mollusks classification box 15 for the remaining mytiloidan families.)

Scallops

The superfamily Pectinacea contains many species of bivalves known as scallops. Except for file shells of the family Limidae (superfamily Anomiacea), scallops are the only bivalves that swim. They normally lie free on the seabed and will swim away when a predator approaches. They seem to swim at other times for no special reason. Some scallop species fasten themselves to solid supports by a byssus or mass of fine threads, while others can walk by expanding and contracting their feet.

Unlike other bivalves, a scallop has only one adductor muscle positioned in the center of the shell, to hold the two valves or shell halves together. The principal ligament consists of tough cartilage that is fixed to two depressions in the shell at the center of the clasp. When the shell is closed, the ligament remains compressed, but as soon as the adductor muscle relaxes, the ligament stretches, pulling the two halves of the shell apart.

Good swimmers

Scallops of the genus *Pecten* are especially good swimmers. They are able to move backward and forward by closing their valves to different degrees. When a scallop has opened its shell and taken in

ABOVE The great scallop or edible scallop, *Pecten maximus*, with its shell half-open, reveals its foot and the tentacles that extend from its mantle. It has a thick, solid, almost circular shell and up to 15 widely spaced, broad, round-topped, ridged ribs. The large, convex, lower (right) valve slightly overlaps the flat, upper (left) valve.
BELOW The map shows the world distribution of mussels of the family Mytilidae.

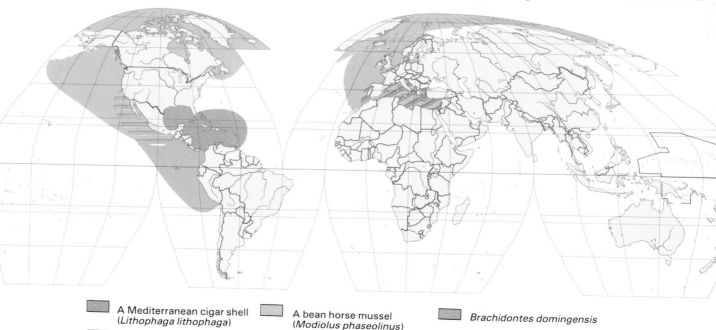

A Mediterranean cigar shell (*Lithophaga lithophaga*)

Crenella faba

A bean horse mussel (*Modiolus phaseolinus*)

Rhomboidella columbiana

Brachidontes domingensis

A large horse mussel (*Modiolus capax*)

water, its mantle edges come together leaving an opening at the front. If the valves come together quickly, water is forced out through the opening left at the front, driving the scallop backward. Alternatively, the mantle edges may close leaving two openings at the rear, one on either side of the hinge. When water passes through these, the scallop is driven forward.

A pecten scallop has 30 to 40 blue eyes arranged around the rim of its mantle, each of which is made up of a cornea, a crystalline lens and a retina. New eyes may develop at any time, and any lost through injury are replaced by new ones. Although the eyes cannot form a full image, they are able to detect changes in light intensity, which may indicate the presence of an obstacle or predator. The tentacles around the edges of the mantle are touch-sensitive organs, and a scallop has a well-developed chemical sense that enables it to taste and smell.

ABOVE The gaping file shell, *Lima hians*, occurs in northern Britain, Anglesey and the Isle of Man. It is unable to withdraw its long, orange-red sensory tentacles into its shell, **which even when closed has a wide gape. The file shell derives its bright red color from the hemoglobin (the red, oxygen-carrying pigment) in its blood.**

Spiny shells

Like the scallops of the genus *Pecten*, the thorny oyster of the family Spondylidae has well-developed eyes. However, it is not free-swimming and cements itself to corals by producing a byssus or beard (a bunch of horny threads) from a gland in its foot. The top surface of its shell is covered with spines that act as camouflage and as a defense against predators.

The superfamily Anomiacea contains the families Limidae, Anomiidae and Placunidae and includes some of the most remarkable byssus-producing bivalves.

ABOVE The duck mussel, *Anodonta anatina*, one of the largest bivalves in Europe, reaches a length of about 6 in. It is a freshwater mussel with a strange growth cycle. Young duck mussels, called "glochidia," attach themselves to fishes using either spines on their shells or byssal threads. They feed on the tissues of the fishes until they undergo metamorphosis. Then they break free from the fish and begin their independent existence.

File shells

The file shells of the family Limidae occur in tropical seas. Some species are able to swim like scallops, by rapidly closing their shells. A mass of long, sensory tentacles adorn the edges of their mantles and hang from the shells resembling a bunch of colorful streamers. Some species, such as the gaping file shell, build themselves a "nest" on the floor of tropical seas. They collect pieces of shells, pebbles and detritus, arrange them around their shells and join them together with byssal threads. It is not unknown for some species to hide inside cavities that are ready-made, such as the cavities of sponges.

File shells build their nests to protect themselves from predators. Some species can also cast off their limbs or their tentacles (a process known as autotomy) as a means of defense. If a file shell is attacked, it immediately shuts its shell, often cutting off parts of its tentacles, which will continue to wriggle, distracting the predator. While the attacker is busy eating the tentacles, the file shell escapes by means of sudden jumps.

The windowpane oyster, *Placuna placenta*, of the family Placunidae inhabits the Indo-Pacific regions. It has a large, flat, translucent shell that was once used by people of the Philippines to make small windows. The common saddle oyster of the family Anomiidae is one of only a few species of anomiids to occur in European waters. The common saddle oyster sits, raised above the sea floor, on a column of byssal threads that grow so hard that they resemble stone.

Oysters

The order Mytiloida contains the superfamily Ostreacea, with just one family of oysters, the Ostreidae. Oysters are generally untidy and irregular in outline (often made more so by a variety of encrusting animals and plants growing on them). Their two valves differ, the left-hand valve being more concave than the right one. It is generally anchored to the seabed or some other solid object. Oysters of the genus *Crassostrea* have elongated shells distinguishing them from the round-shelled oysters of the genus *Ostrea*.

The European flat oyster of the genus *Ostrea* occurs along the Atlantic coast of Europe from Norway to Morocco and also in the Mediterranean and the Black Sea. An adult oyster remains in one place, feeding by filtering bacteria, protozoa, algae, eggs, larvae and vegetable fibers from the water. It also absorbs salts through the walls of its body. The beating cilia on its complex, lattice-like gills draw a current of water over its body. However, it does not pump water continuously, but adopts a pulsating rhythm that is dictated by the salinity of the water, its temperature and the density of organisms in the water.

Fussy about food

Oysters do not feed on all organisms that float suspended in the water; many species have a specific diet and will only eat organisms of a certain size. A bivalve that has siphons selects its food using its palps, which are situated at the entrance to its inhalant siphon. If the bivalve rejects the food particles, they are pushed away by a jet of water.

The cilia present on the gills of oysters only send the most suitable particles of the material they ingest to the mouth. The rest is expelled, undigested, as pseudofeces. The labial palps (on the lip or thickened margin of the aperture of a gastropod shell) carry out a second selection. They "taste" the material before it reaches the mouth. Once in the stomach, or style sac, enzymes break down the food.

The enzymes are released by the protostyle (an organ present in all bivalves that consists of a translucent stick composed of protein and carbohydrates, held

MOLLUSKS CLASSIFICATION: 15

Bivalves (2)

The order Mytiloida in the subclass Pteriomorpha—the third major grouping in the class Bivalvia—contains two other important superfamilies, apart from those containing the mussels and scallops (covered in mollusks classification box 14). They are the superfamily Anomiacea, which contains the families Limidae (file shells, such as the gaping file shell, *Lima hians*), Anomiidae (saddle oysters, such as the common saddle oyster, *Anomia ephippium*), and Placunidae, which includes the windowpane oyster, *Placuna placenta*. The superfamily Ostreacea contains the family Ostreidae (oysters) whose members include the European flat oyster, *Ostrea edulis*, and the giant oyster, *Crassostrea gigas*.

The fourth bivalve subclass, Paleoheterodonta, contains two orders—the Unionoida and Trigonoida. The Unionoida are all freshwater bivalves, and they include the painter's mussel, *Unio pictorum*; the swan mussel, *Anodonta cygnaea*; and the pearl mussel, *Margaritifer margaritifer*. The order Trigonoida contains the single family Trigoniidae with the genus *Neotrigonia*. (The first part of the next bivalve subclass Heterodonta occurs in mollusks classification box 16.)

ABOVE The European flat oyster, *Ostrea edulis*, is a sedentary animal. Soon after it has completed its larval stage, it cements itself to the seabed by the convex, lower (right) valve of its shell. It remains attached to its base, slowly becoming encrusted by acorn barnacles and other marine creatures.

BELOW File shells of the species *Lima* collect detritus with their tentacles and build protective nests (A). Small pieces of wood or stone are bound together with byssal threads (B) forming a shelter in which the file shells can hide from predators (C).

together by mucous protein). The protostyle, which wears down quickly but regrows at the same rate, is spun around once every five seconds by the cilia in the style sac, dragging the ingested material into the stomach and releasing the enzymes.

Freshwater and marine bivalves

The subclass Paleoheterodonta comprises two orders of bivalves including mussels and pearl oysters: the Unionoida, which contains freshwater bivalves; and the Trigonioida, which contains both marine and freshwater species.

The order Trigonioida contains bivalves that belong to the family Trigoniidae. Some species, such as the primitive *Neotrigonia margaitacea*, occur in the seas around Australia. All the other species live in freshwater. The large order Unionoida contains a group of freshwater bivalves that are familiar to many people as they occur in all waterways, even the smallest ditches.

Freshwater bivalves reproduce using a method resembling that of the prosobranchs that have invaded freshwater. Certain gill filaments that temporarily cease functioning as gills form pouches in which the bivalves store their eggs. In the summer, the males release spermatozoa into the water to fertilize the eggs. The egg pouches have special channels ensuring that they have a permanent flow of freshwater over them. In the spring, the larvae leave via the exhalant siphons. They attach themselves to the flesh under the scales of fishes using hooks and adhesive thread, and here they complete their larval stage.

2843

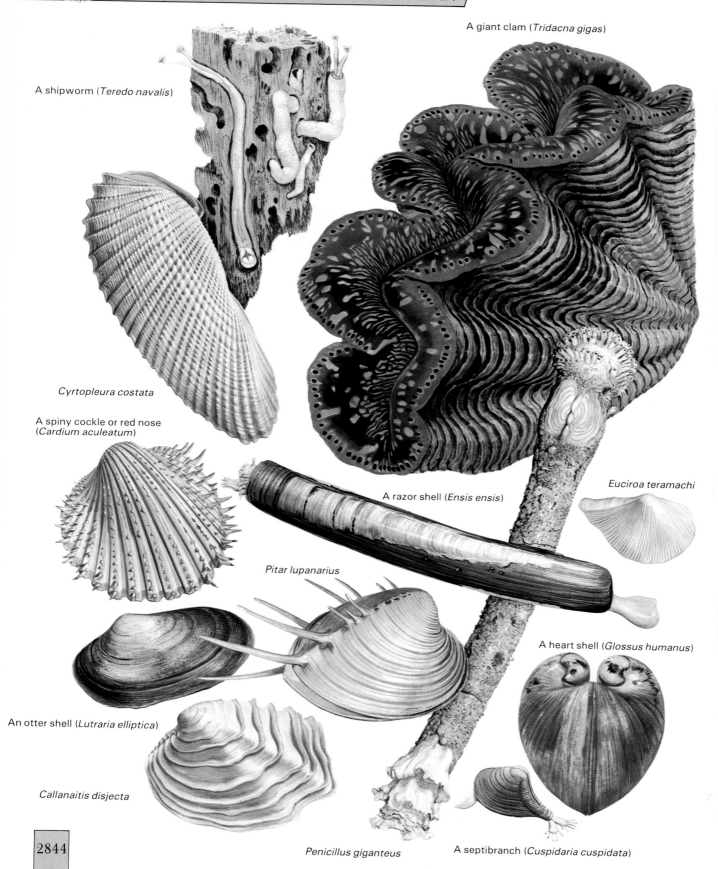

A shipworm (*Teredo navalis*)

A giant clam (*Tridacna gigas*)

Cyrtopleura costata

A spiny cockle or red nose
(*Cardium aculeatum*)

Euciroa teramachi

A razor shell (*Ensis ensis*)

Pitar lupanarius

A heart shell (*Glossus humanus*)

An otter shell (*Lutraria elliptica*)

Callanaitis disjecta

Penicillus giganteus

A septibranch (*Cuspidaria cuspidata*)

2844

Cockles, clams and shipworms

Most of the shells found on sandy beaches belong to members of the subclass Heterodonta, which contains more than 10,000 species. It is split into two orders of living species: Veneroida and Myoida. A third order contains only fossils. The cockles, clams and shipworms within the subclass have clasps that consist of one to three teeth on each side of their shells and some lateral, blade-shaped teeth.

Veneroida

The superfamily Astartacea contains the family Astartidae, which includes some species of bivalve that live in deep, cold waters. *Astarte borealis*, for example, occurs in the Pacific and Atlantic areas of the Arctic. Most bivalves within the family keep their mantles wide open, and some possess short siphons.

The superfamily Carditacea contains bivalves that incubate their eggs in a special pouch. The egg pouches of the Australian species *Thecalia concamerata* and the American species *Milneria minima*, for example, are formed from the inner edges of their shells, which bend inward forming a small chamber. The superfamily contains several freshwater genera such as *Adacna*, the Caspian Sea cockles.

The superfamily Sphaeriacea includes bivalves that live in fresh and brackish water. The population of *Corbicula manilensis*, a tropical species belonging to the family Corbiculidae (which was accidentally introduced into the North American continent during the 19th century), has increased enormously. It is now the most common species in this part of the world and has invaded most of the waterways. As bivalves of the genus *Corbicula* are commonly eaten in the Far East, it is thought that some specimens of this species were originally imported by immigrants.

Internal development

The larvae of many cockles of the family Sphaeriidae live inside their mothers until they are completely developed. It has proved difficult to classify the bivalves that make up this group as they are extremely small, measuring no more than about 0.1 in. long. The common orb-shell cockle inhabits flowing water, while *Sphaerium lacustre* lives in ponds. However, both move in a way that resembles the movement of caterpillars or leeches. The common orb-shell cockle first uses the front part of its long foot

ABOVE European flat oysters occur on the southwest and southeast coasts of England and on the west coast of France. They congregate in large numbers in the shallow water of estuaries and bays. Although a fairly common species, the European flat oyster has become extinct in some areas due to pollution, severe winters, over-fishing or destruction by predators.

as a sucker, and then the rear part. It extends the front part of its foot, attaches it to the substrate and then contracts it, dragging its shell along with it.

The superfamily Cyprinacea includes the bivalve species *Cyprina islandica*. It now only occurs in the North Sea and in the Baltic, but fossil evidence has shown that during the Ice Age of the Quaternary period, *C. islandica* was common in the Mediterranean.

The superfamily Dreissensiacea contains only one family, Dreissensiidae. These bivalves have unusual characteristics for freshwater mollusks: they have planktonic larvae, and they produce byssal threads.

Commensalism in bivalves

Although parasitism and commensalism (living in a mutually beneficial partnership) are rare in the bivalves, they do occur among members belonging to the superfamily Erycinacea. Many species of the family Lasaeidae live on other organisms, although it has not been proven whether they are true parasites. Species that belong to this family are divided into several genera. The genera *Kellia* and *Lasaea* both contain commensal species. These small bivalves live inside the bodies of certain echinoderms, such as urchins and sea cucumbers, but do not appear to harm their hosts. Bivalves belonging to the genus *Entovalva* are

2845

ABOVE **The prickly cockle, *Cardium echinatum*, occurs off the coast of Britain where it lives in muddy sand. It has a thick shell with numerous curved, backward-pointing, short, triangular spines, connected at their base by a ridge. The exhalant** channel on the right is clearly visible. A small sea anemone that was unable to anchor itself directly to the sand has adhered itself to the cockle's shell.
BELOW **The map shows the world distribution of the cockle family, Cardiidae.**

possibly the only parasitic bivalves alive today. They are small mollusks that live in the digestive tracts of sea cucumbers. It is not certain whether they harm their hosts, but it is thought that they steal food particles from inside the sea cucumbers' stomachs.

The edible common cockle

The superfamily Vardiacea is divided into two greatly differing families of bivalve—the Cardiidae, containing the cockles, and the giant clams of the family Tridacnidae.

The common cockle is the most widespread species of cockle in Europe, living on muddy or sandy seabeds. It is especially prevalent near estuaries and brackish lagoons, where many other mollusks cannot live owing to the low salinity of the water. It inhabits waters from Iceland to the Mediterranean and West Africa, and also occurs in the Caspian and Azov seas.

All species in the family Cardiidae have two well-developed but short siphons and a type of eye. They use their two siphons to explore the world above the surface of the mud or sand, retracting them beneath the sediment at the slightest disturbance. All cockles can use their long, robust feet to jump, and the jumping cockle, *Laevicardium crassum*, is the most expert jumper.

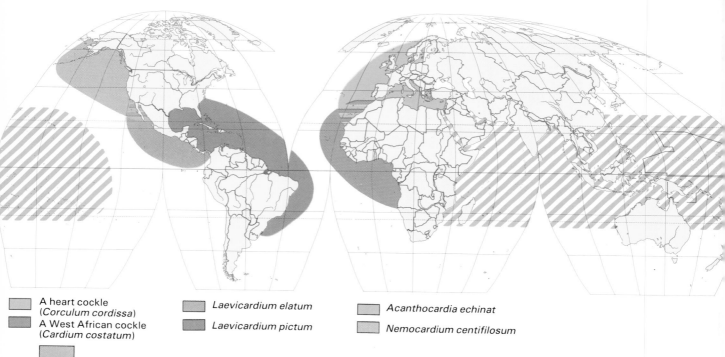

A heart cockle
(*Corculum cordissa*)
A West African cockle
(*Cardium costatum*)

Laevicardium elatum

Laevicardium pictum

Acanthocardia echinat

Nemocardium centifilosum

MOLLUSKS CLASSIFICATION: 16

Bivalves (3)

Subclass Heterodonta—the fifth subclass in the class Bivalvia—contains over 10,000 species, among which are the cockles and giant clams. Heterodonta is divided into two living orders: Veneroida and Myoida. A third order contains only fossils.

The order Veneroida includes the following superfamilies: the Astartacea, with the family Astartidae and genus *Astarte*; the Carditacea, containing Caspian Sea cockles of the genera *Adacna* and *Diadacna*; the Sphaeriacea, containing the families Corbiculidae (genus *Corbicula*), and Sphaeriidae (with the common orb-shell cockle, *Sphaerium corneum*, and pea-shell cockles of the genus *Pisidium*); the Cyprinacea, which has the species *Cyprina islandica*; the Dreissensiacea, containing the family Dreissensidae and genus *Dreissensia*; the Erycinacea, including the family Lasaeidae (genera *Kellia*, *Lasaea*, *Entovalva* and *Montacuta*); the Cardiacea, which is divided into two families—the family Cardiidae (cockles, such as the common cockle, *Cardium edule*, and its Mediterranean variant, *C. edule lamarcki*, and the jumping cockle, *Laevicardium crassum*), and the family Tridacnidae (containing the giant clam, *Tridacna gigas*); the Veneracea, which includes the family Veneridae (members include the pullet carpet shell, *Venerupis pullastra*, and Venus clam, *Venus gallina*), the genus *Petricola* (such as the American piddock, *Petricola pholadiformis*) and the common piddock, *Pholas dactylus*; and the Tellinacea, containing the families Tellinidae (including the Baltic tellin, *Macoma baltica*, and zebra tellin, *T. fabuloides*) and Donacidae (the coquina shell, *Donax truculus*).

Clams famous for their size

Clams of the family Tridacnidae have been famous for hundreds of years due to their size. The giant clam, *Tridacna gigas*, for example, can reach a length of 51 in. and a weight of 2425 lbs. Not all members of the family reach such a size, however. *T. crocea*, a species capable of tunneling into rock, grows to a maximum length of 4 in., and *Hippopus hippopus*, which lives in sand, is no more than 10 in. long.

ABOVE The giant clam, *Tridacna gigas*, lives in the shallow water of Indo-Pacific coral reefs. It is the largest bivalve in the world, growing to a length of 5 ft. and weighing up to 500 lbs. The shell of a giant clam is thick and heavy and the animal is often unable to move. Wedging itself firmly into coral, with its hinges facing downward and the margins of its valves facing upward, it displays the brilliant colors of its mantle.

Perforating rock and shell

The superfamily Veneracea contains a large number of species, about 3000 of which belong to a single family, the Veneridae. They include the pullet carpet shell, *Venerupis pullastra*, and the venus clam, *Venus gallina*. The genus *Petricola* contains bivalves that perforate rock with the front of their shells. The American piddock, *P. pholadiformis*, a species that is common in the River Thames in Britain, prefers calcareous rocks, but also burrows into the thick shells of other animals.

Fragile, egg-shaped shells

The superfamily Tellinacea consists of bivalves that have long, well-developed siphons. One of the most numerous families in the group is the family Tellinidae, which includes 350 species, all difficult to identify. They have attractive shells, with two halves that usually differ in size and are sometimes extremely fragile. The shells are mostly egg-shaped, sometimes nearly triangular, with a wedge-shaped rear edge.

A tellinid bivalve has an extremely well-developed inhalant siphon as an adaptation to the way in which it feeds. It protrudes out of the sediment and explores the seabed, sucking in any tiny organisms that it can

MOLLUSKS CLASSIFICATION: 17

Bivalves (4)

The second order in the bivalve subclass Heterodonta is the Myoida (the first, Veneroida, is covered in mollusks classification box 16). Myoida is divided into four superfamilies. They include the Myacea, which contains the sand gaper, *Mya arenaria*, of the family Myidae, and the family Corbulidae (with the species *Lentidium mediterraneum*); and the superfamily Asdemacea, which contains the families Pholadidae (including the common piddock, *Pholas dactylus*), the Xylophaginidae (with the wood piddock, *Xylophaga dorsalis*), and the Teredinidae (with the shipworm, *Teredo navalis*). Other species in the order include the Atlantic razor shell, *Ensis directus*, the common razor shell, *E. ensis*, the pod razor shell, *E. siliqua*, and the razor shell, *Solen arcuata*.

The sixth and final bivalve subclass is Anomalodesmata. Its single order, Pholadomyoida, contains the superfamilies Poromyacea and Clavagellacea. The Poromyacea includes the family Pandoridae (with the pandora shell, *Pandora albida*), and the family Cuspidariidae (with *Cuspidaria rostrata*). The superfamily Clavagellacea contains the watering-pot shell, *Clavagella aperta*.

find. Representatives of the family are numerous in sand and mud, with some species demonstrating unique adaptations to their environment.

The coquina shell, *Donax truculus*, a species in the family Donacidae, lives exclusively on sandy seabeds between Scandinavia and Senegal. It is particularly well adapted to its environment. Unlike most bivalves, it does not always remain buried in the sand, but emerges at high tide and allows the waves to roll it up the beach. When the tide goes out again, the bivalve goes with it and buries itself once more.

Myoida

The second order in the bivalve subclass Heterodonta is the order Myoida. It contains widely differing species, including some that burrow into rock and

TOP The warty venus shell, *Venus verrucosa*, of the superfamily Veneracea occurs below the lower shore, where it burrows in shell debris, gravel and sand. The warty venus clam has a heavy, rounded shell with thick, close-set concentric ridges that form warts or tubercles.

ABOVE The coquina shell, *Donax rugosus*, is ideally adapted to life in a sandy environment. Its elongated, glossy valves and pointed foot enable it to burrow in the wet sand.
FAR RIGHT The map shows the world distribution of various species of the family Veneridae.

others that bury themselves in the seabed. The order Myoida is divided into four superfamilies, the first of which contains only the one family, the Solenidae.

The razor shells of the genus *Ensis* are the most common members of the family Solenidae in Europe. They have elongated shells that are slightly open at both ends and can be perfectly straight or curved, depending on the species. Their siphons, which are fused together near the shell, are often extremely long. Some members of the family Solenidae, such as the Atlantic razor shell, *Ensis directus*, have narrow shells that enable them to live at depths of 3 ft. below the seabed. Other species include the common razor shell, *E. ensis*, and the pod razor shell, *E. siliqua*, which is the largest British species at almost 8 in. long.

A strange bivalve that belongs to the family Hiatellidae is the geoduck, *Panopea generosa*. It lives along the Pacific coasts of the United States and Alaska, buried up to 3 ft. deep in the mud. While its shell is only about 4 in. in length, its sturdy siphons can be extremely long, making up half of the weight of the mollusk. The siphons are so long, in fact, that the bivalve cannot completely retract them into its shell, which has an opening at either end.

The family Corbulidae includes both marine and freshwater species. They are usually small, with the right-hand shell larger than the left-hand one. On beaches around the Mediterranean, it is not uncommon to walk on a thick layer of empty shells, each no more than about 0.1 in. long, that have been thrown up by rough seas. They belong to *Lentidium mediterraneum*, a species endemic to the Mediterranean and the Black Sea. It lives just below the low-water mark, either half buried or, more commonly, with the larger, right-hand side of its shell resting on the seabed.

Rock-boring bivalves

Among the mollusks that erode rock, bivalves in the families Pholadidae and Teredinidae, and the superfamily Asdemacea, are typical borers. They have no ligaments or teeth on their shells, so they use muscles alone to hold the sides of the shells together. The common piddock, *Pholas dactylus*, belongs to the family Pholadidae. It holds its shell open through an action of the anterior adductor muscle on an extension of the shell. It keeps the shell closed using the posterior adductor.

The common piddock manages to burrow into hard clay and soft rock by alternately opening and closing its shell. Like other members of its family, the piddock possesses calcareous platelets to protect its anterior adductor muscle, which is on the outside of its shell. It normally feeds on plankton.

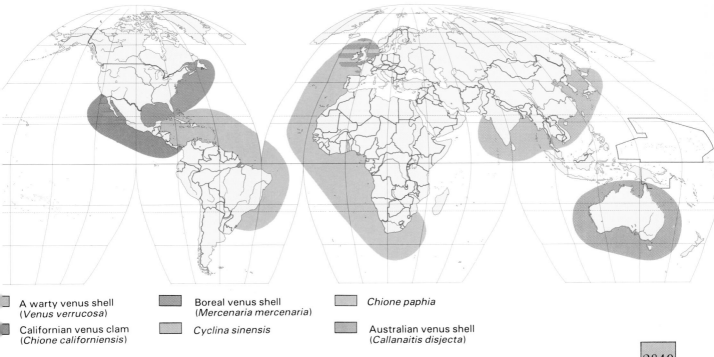

☐ A warty venus shell (*Venus verrucosa*)

■ Californian venus clam (*Chione californiensis*)

▨ Boreal venus shell (*Mercenaria mercenaria*)

▨ Cyclina sinensis

▨ Chione paphia

▨ Australian venus shell (*Callanaitis disjecta*)

Wood-eating bivalves

Bivalves in the family Teredinidae have modified their anatomy even more than the true piddocks to suit their life-style. Their soft, unprotected bodies, which in some species can be up to a yard long, are covered by a calcareous layer. They have shells solely on the fronts of their bodies, and they use them exclusively for boring. Whereas mollusks in the family Pholadidae filter water, all species in the family Teredinidae eat wood. They digest part of the cellulose, and do enormous damage to wooden underwater structures such as the wooden hulls of boats.

Within the family Teredinidae the shipworm, *Teredo navalis*, is the dominant species in the Black Sea, while *T. utriculus* is the most common in the Mediterranean, and *Bankia bipalmulata* can be found in the Indo-Pacific area.

Flat and curved shells

Anomalodesmata is the final subclass of bivalves, consisting of a single order, Pholadomyoida. It contains the two superfamilies Poromyacea and Clavagellacea, and just a few species. The Pholadomyoida generally have dissimilar valves. The pandora shell, *Pandora albida*, which inhabits sheltered bays on the south coast of England, is a good example. The right-hand side of its shell is flat, while the left-hand side is curved.

The superfamily Poromyacea, until recently called the order Septibranchia, is the last in the class Bivalvia. Once again, its classification is based on gill structure, although this group has no gills as such. They have been replaced on either side by a perforated septum that acts as a diaphragm. When it contracts, it pumps in water, thereby capturing small organisms.

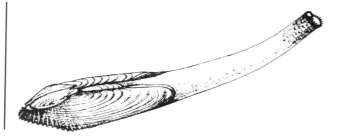

TOP **The pod razor shell, *Ensis siliqua*, measures up to 8 in. in length. It lives in soft mud and sand, in which it digs downward rapidly with its powerful foot. When the tide returns to cover the sand, the pod razor shell rises to the surface to feed and breathe, projecting its siphon through the sand.** CENTER **The bivalve *Tapes decussatus* occurs in many coastal lagoons around the Mediterranean. Unlike many other species of bivalve, it is able to endure great variations in the salinity of the water and so can obtain food with little competition.** BOTTOM **The common piddock, *Pholas dactylus*, has an elongated shell with up to 50 rows of spines. Its siphons are fused together along their length, providing the piddock with enough support to burrow deeply into the seabed.**

TENTACLES IN THE DEEP

The most highly evolved of all the mollusks are the nautiluses, cuttlefishes, squids and octopuses. Equipped with sharp eyesight, muscular tentacles, jet propulsion for swimming, and intelligence, they are effective oceanic predators

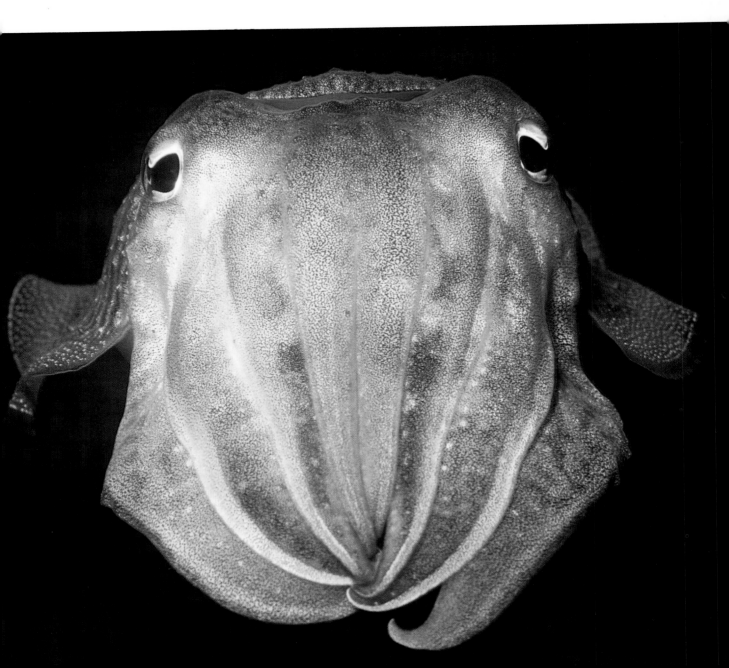

The mollusk class Cephalopoda contains about 700 species of nautiluses, squids, and octopuses. Cephalopods—the most highly evolved of all mollusks—differ from other members of their phylum in anatomy, physiology, life-style and feeding habits (they are carnivores). All cephalopod species are marine animals: some inhabit shallow waters, some are deep-sea swimmers and many—such as octopuses and cuttlefishes—dwell on the seabed. They cannot tolerate low salinity and consequently do not live in seas with a low salt content, such as the Black Sea and the Baltic.

The different species resemble each other in appearance, since most show similar evolutionary adaptations to a pelagic, predatory life (pelagic refers to the environment between the seabed and the surface). Humans have shown an interest in cephalopods for thousands of years: the earliest known drawings of the creatures are paintings of octopuses that decorate Cretan vases dating from about 1500 BC.

Superior predators

The most noticeable difference between cephalopods and the other mollusk classes is the superior development of the former's nervous system and sensory organs. They eyes of an octopus, for example, are complex

PAGE 2851 The common cuttlefish, *Sepia officiallis*, — an inhabitant of the Atlantic and the Mediterranean—is the world's most commonly occurring cuttlefish species. Like the chameleon, it has the ability to change color in response to color changes in its environment. Tiny structures called chromatophores contain multicolored pigments that transmit various colors through the cuttlefish's skin.
ABOVE A common cuttlefish takes on a coloration of brown and white stripes. The pattern provides effective camouflage when the cuttlefish swims near the seabed.
BELOW The distribution of six common octopus species.

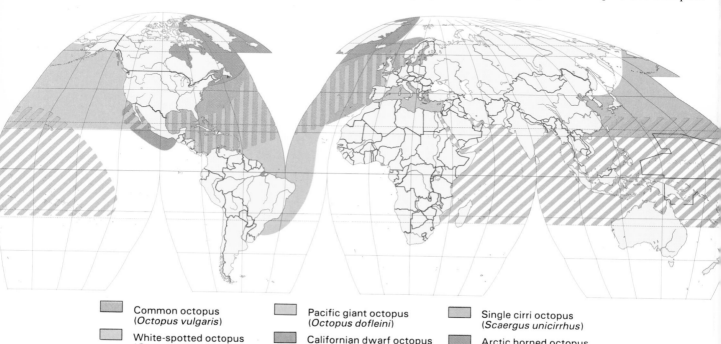

| Common octopus (*Octopus vulgaris*) | Pacific giant octopus (*Octopus dofleini*) | Single cirri octopus (*Scaergus unicirrhus*) |
| White-spotted octopus (*Octopus macropus*) | Californian dwarf octopus (*Octopus hubbsorum*) | Arctic horned octopus (*Bathypolypus arcticus*) |

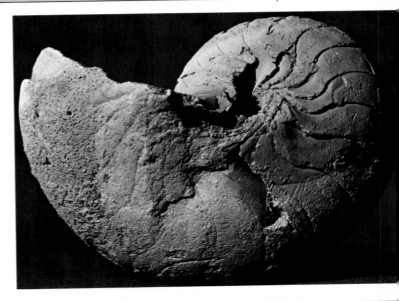

structures that resemble those of humans in both appearance and internal structure. In keeping with the requirements of a predatory existence, cephalopods developed highly effective muscles, limbs and sensory capabilities. Their hunting abilities rival those of many vertebrate animals, and, in many cases, cephalopods are stronger, faster and more intelligent than their vertebrate counterparts. Although cephalopods constitute only a small percentage of the world's mollusk population, they play an important ecological role as predators on one of the highest rungs of the marine food chain.

Early cephalopods

The earliest ancestors of cephalopods are thought to be members of the class Ellesmeroceratidae, which appeared in the Upper Cambrian period, some 550 million years ago. About 450 million years ago, during the Ordovician period, the Ellesmeroceratidae evolved into three different subclasses: the Endoceratoidea, the Actinoceratoidea and the Nautiloidea. The subclass Nautiloidea is the only group that has survived to the present day.

The ammonites

During the Devonian period (405 million years ago) —and to a lesser extent in the rest of the Palaeozoic era—a group of Nautiloidea developed into the ammonites (Ammonoidea). Some ammonite fossil shells—such as that of the giant Cretaceous species *Pachydiscus septemarodensis*—are enormous, reaching diameters of over 6 ft. 6 in. The ammonites constitute some of the most common animal fossils, numbering over 163 families, each containing many species.

Ammonites had flat, conical shells consisting of several whorls, each one—except the final whorl—contained within the one after it. The general body and shell structures of ammonites resembled those of other nautiloids: their shells possessed several air chambers, each of which was sealed from the others by a septum. Siphuncles, or air tubes, passed through small holes in the septa and linked each chamber. Ammonites regulated the gas content of each of their chambers and thus controlled the depths at which they floated in the water.

The ammonite lived in its final shell chamber and could retract itself into its shell, closing the opening with a calcareous trap-door, or operculum. When

TOP One of the first cephalopods was the nautilus, *Nautilus disculus*, a mollusk that lived approximately 550 million years ago. The species' foot extended into two tentacles similar to those of modern cephalopods.

ABOVE The shell of the New Caledonian pearly nautilus, *Nautilus macromphalus*, bears a strong resemblance to that of *N. disculus*. However, zoologists are unable to ascertain whether its body resembles that of its ancient predecessor.

An odd-eyed squid (*Histioteuthis reversa*)

A whiplash squid (*Mastigoteuthis glaukopi*

A hook-tentacled squid
(*Abraliopsis chuni*)

A jeweled squid (*Lycoteuthis diadema*)

A deep-sea squid (*Bathyteuthis abyssic*

A pearly nautilus
(*Nautilus pompilius*)

Galiteuthis suhmi

A stalk-eyed squid
(*Bathothauma lyromma*)

A ramshorn cuttlefish
(*Spirula spirula*)

An arrow squid
(*Chiroteuthis pic*

A common cuttlefish (*Sepia officinalis*)

A common squid (*Loligo vulgaris*)

swimming, it held its shell with the opening pointing downward, and propelled itself by squirting water from its mantle cavity. As the ammonites evolved, their numbers expanded until they colonized every sea and ocean in the world. However, some 70 million years ago, at the end of the Cretaceous period, the ammonites became extinct; zoologists cannot explain their disappearance.

The Belemnoidea

About 260 million years ago, at the end of the Palaeozoic era, a cephalopod group called the Belemnoidea began to evolve separately from the Nautiloidea—its original subclass. While the early nautiloids had four gills, four auricles and four kidneys, the Belemnoidea differed in that they possessed only two gills and two auricles. Although the Belemnoidea became extinct, they gave rise to the present-day subclass Coleoidea (formerly known as Dibranchiata), which contains the cuttlefishes, squids and octopuses.

The earliest known coleoids were teuthoideans with reduced shells, such as the common squid, *Loligo vulgaris*. The order Sepioidea emerged after the teuthoideans and included, among other creatures, the common cuttlefish (genus *Sepia*) and the pelagic cuttlefish (genus *Spirula*), which has an internal spiraled shell. The last emerging orders were the Vampyromorpha (vampire squids) and Octopoda (the octopuses), which contained animals devoid of all traces of a shell. Unlike their belemnoidean ancestors—which were inhabitants of open water—the coleoids live in cracks on the seabed, between rocks or in very deep water.

The genus *Nautilus*

Modern cephalopods fall into two subclasses according to their gill characteristics: members of the subclass Nautiloidea (formerly Tetrabranchiata) possess four gills while those of the subclass Coleoidea (formerly Dibranchiatea) have two. The genus *Nautilus* belongs to the first group and is considered to contain "living fossils" that have survived to the present day in a form almost identical to that of their Paleozoic ancestor. However, it is possible that the genus *Nautilus* is becoming extinct, since only three of its former 3000 species remain in existence—all three inhabit the Indo-Pacific area.

MOLLUSKS
CLASSIFICATION: 18

Cephalopods (1)

Some 700 species of nautiluses, cuttlefishes, squids and octopuses belong to the class Cephalopoda. They are marine creatures that are found in all seas from the polar regions to the Equator. The class Cephalopoda is divided into two subclasses: the Nautiloidea (nautiluses) and the Coleoidea (cuttlefishes, squids and octopuses). (The nautiluses and cuttlefishes are dealt with here; squids are covered in the mollusks classification box 19, and octopuses are dealt with in mollusks classification box 20.)

Nautiluses

The subclass Nautiloidea contains only one genus, *Nautilus*, whose three known species occur in the Indian and Pacific oceans. They are the pearly nautilus, *Nautilus pompilius*; the wrinkled nautilus, *N. scrobiculatus*, of New Guinea; and *N. macrophalus* from the Solomon Islands.

Cuttlefishes, squids and octopuses

The subclass Coleoidea contains four orders: the Sepioidea, Teuthoidea, Vampyromorpha, and Octopoda. The Sepioidea (cuttlefishes) has five families, including the Spirulidae, which has just one species, the ramshorn cuttlefish, *Spirula spirula*; the Sepiidae, containing the common cuttlefish, *Sepia officinalis*, the elegant cuttlefish, *S. elegans*, the smallest cuttlefish, *S. typica*, and the lesser cuttlefish, *S. orbignyana*; and the Sepiolidae, which contains the genus *Sepiola* and such species as the Mediterranean deepwater sepiolid, *Heteroteuthis dispar,* and the African whip sepiolid, *Austrorossia mastigaphora.*

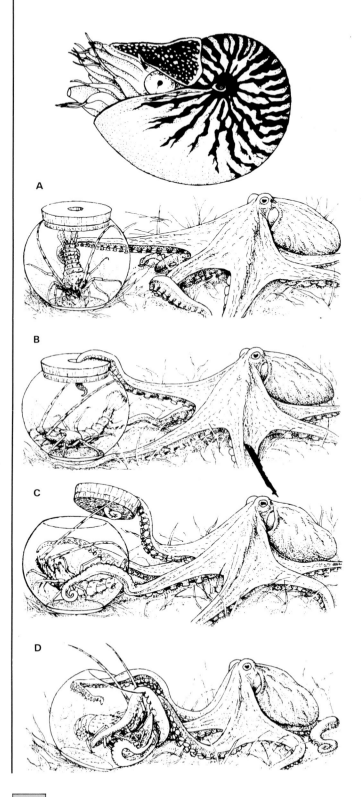

A
B
C
D

LEFT Unlike most other cephalopods, the pearly nautilus, *Nautilus pompilius*, hunts slowly, since its blunt, heavy shell prevents it from swimming swiftly through the water in pursuit of prey. Its preferred diet consists of slow-moving, bottom-dwelling crustaceans such as crabs and shrimps.
BELOW LEFT In a laboratory experiment, an octopus demonstrates its intelligence by taking only a few minutes to overcome a problem wholly new to it: after observing its prey (a lobster) within a sealed jar (A), the octopus discovers that it can pry the lid off by inserting a tentacle through a hole in the lid (B). It then removes the lid with its long tentacle (C) and grasps its prey (D).

The nautilus has a flat, spiral shell that consists of several whorls, each whorl containing the one before it. As in the shells of prehistoric nautiloids, several calcereous plates, or septa, divide the modern nautilus shell into various chambers, the last of which contains the animal's body. The siphon—a narrow tube (about 0.1 in. wide) made up of a thin layer of cells containing an artery and a vein—runs through every chamber, passing through small holes in the septa. The shell chambers contain small amounts of liquid and a mixture of gases—principally nitrogen, but also argon, oxygen and water vapor. The nautilus controls its depth by passing gases and liquids through its siphon, adjusting the content of each shell chamber until it achieves its desired position in the water. Like all cephalopods, the nautilus moves horizontally by squirting jets of water from the mantle cavity through a tube, or funnel, on the underside of its body.

Specialized tentacles

The original molluscan foot of the nautilus evolved into tentacles and a funnel-like structure for directing water jets. Dozens of tentacles surround the nautilus' mouth, forming groups that perform various functions. Those closest to the mouth are known as "labial" tentacles, while "branchial" tentacles form two groups of 17 on either side of the head. Two wide, arm-like tentacles act as stabilizing fins that bend over the nautilus' back forming a lid, or operculum, that closes the shell entrance when the occupant withdraws. Each tentacle consists of a basal part (without suckers) that can be elongated into a slender filament.

Male and female nautiluses differ in several respects: the female possesses 90 or more tentacles, while the male has only about 60; the opening on the male's shell

flares more widely than the female's; and four of the male's tentacles fuse into an appendage used in mating.

Unlike other cephalopods, the nautilus has inefficient eyes, each of which contains only a pupil and a retina. During normal activity, seawater enters the eyes and fills the eye cavities. When the nautilus moves along the seabed with a gentle, swaying movement, its eyes rotate in the opposite direction to its body's motion.

The nautilus feeds on crustaceans and dead or dying fishes, using chemical receptors to detect its prey. The tentacles have some chemical detection ability while four chemoreceptors are located near the creature's four gills.

Three species

The most common of the three known nautilus species is the pearly nautilus, *Nautilus pompilius*, an inhabitant of the area of the Pacific between America and the Fiji Islands. The wrinkled nautilus, *N. scrobiculatus*, is a rough-shelled cephalopod that lives in the waters around New Guinea. *N. macrophalus* inhabits the seas around the Solomon Islands.

Coleoids

Most cephalopods fall into one of the four orders of the subclass Coleoidea—the group that contains the octopuses, squids and cuttlefishes. Although the Mediterranean contains large coleoid populations, the 200 or so known coleoid species have a distribution that extends to many parts of the globe.

Members of many coleoid species lead solitary existences, and some, such as the octopuses, show strong territorial instincts. However, several species that inhabit the pelagic zone (the area between the seabed and the water's surface) form large shoals in order to follow the migrations of fishes. Some deep-water species periodically migrate upward in order to reproduce and to feed. Since coleoids have missing or reduced shells, they are vulnerable to attacks from creatures such as whales, dolphins, porpoises, seals, penguins and sea birds.

Superior intelligence

Coleoids are the most intelligent of all mollusks; their nervous systems show a high degree of centralization, forming brains within the backs of their heads. Zoological experiments have proved that octopuses possess memories that provide them with

ABOVE Ramshorn cuttle-fishes live in the tropical waters of the Atlantic and western Pacific, moving between depths of 30 and 1500 ft. They determine their depth by regulating the gas content of their shell chambers. Since the cuttlefishes' shells are lighter than water, they float after the cuttlefishes have died; thousands may wash up onto beaches.

the ability to learn new behavior. For example, under laboratory conditions, the creatures learned to respond to sight and touch and to distinguish between rough and smooth objects.

Triple-hearted mollusks

All coleoids have two gills, two kidneys, one heart and two branchial, or gill, hearts. The gills "suck" water in at high pressure and thus do not require cilia to aid water flow. When breathing, the coleoid first draws water in over its gills to extract oxygen. After passing through the gills, the water flows through the anus and the opening of the kidneys, before leaving the body as a jet of water ejected through the funnel.

Coleoid "ink"

The coleoid's intestine contains a diverticulum—a tubular outgrowth—known as the ink sac, since it is filled with an ink-like blue-black liquid. When under attack, the coleoid empties its "ink" first into the intestine and then into the mantle cavity. As soon as the liquid enters the mantle cavity, the coleoid violently squirts it into the water in a thick cloud that distorts the attacker's sense of smell.

All members of the orders Sepioidea (cuttlefishes) and Teuthoidea (squids) have eight arms of similar length and two tentacles that grow to much greater lengths than the arms. Both the arms and tentacles

possess between two and four rows of suckers running down their entire lengths—the suckers resemble shells with rigid outer rims. A flexible cushion at the base of each sucker allows the squid or cuttlefish to grip tightly to almost any surface.

Cuttlefishes

Cuttlefishes are flat-bodied coleoids with spongy, internal shells. They inhabit most regions of the world, often resting on the seabed and occasionally swimming in the pelagic zone.

The ramshorn cuttlefish, *Spirula spirula*,—a small, deepwater coleoid with a cylindrical body—is the only member of the sepioidean family Spirulidae. It has red or dark brown coloration patterned with light brown markings; the body seldom grows to more than 2.4 in. in length. Ramshorn cuttlefishes inhabit the tropical and subtropical seas and—to a lesser extent—the seas of the temperate zones.

The ramshorn cuttlefish has an internalized, flat, spiral shell similar in structure to that of a nautilus: the shell's interior consists of several chambers separated by septa and connected to the body by a siphon. Each chamber contains a small amount of liquid and a mixture of gases. By adjusting the gas content of its chambers, the cuttlefish varies the shell's weight, causing

ABOVE Cuttlefishes—cephalopods closely related to squids—rely on their internal shells to keep them buoyant. While squid shells consist only of thin shards of bony material, cuttlefishes have large, calcereous shield-shaped internal shells. When increasing depth, the cuttlefish forces liquid through its shell's small holes in order to displace gas. When rising to the surface, it performs the action in reverse.
RIGHT The coloration of the little cuttlefish (a member of the genus *Sepiola*) blends with colors on the seabed. When attacked, sepiolids often bury themselves by shifting sand with jets of water from their funnels.

its body and shell to float upward or downard at will. It usually travels along a vertical path, moving between depths of about 30 ft. to as much as 1500 ft. below the sea's surface.

The common cuttlefish

The coleoid family Sepiidae contains over 100 species of cuttlefishes, many of which inhabit the Atlantic coasts of Europe, while being unknown on the eastern seaboard of North America. The common cuttlefish, *Sepia officinalis*, lives in the Atlantic and the Mediterranean and is, as its name suggests, the world's most commonly occurring sepiidaen. It has the unusual ability to change color rapidly in order to

2859

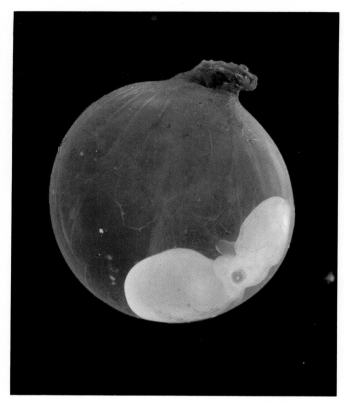

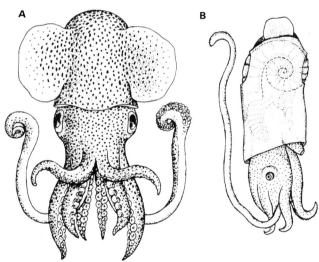

TOP The soft, transparent cuttlefish egg soon hardens and turns black with ink from the embryo's ink sac. The young feed on yolk and break free from the egg after they reach lengths of approximately 0.4 in.

ABOVE One arm of the squid species *Semirossia tenera* is coated with a sticky membrane to compensate for its lack of suckers (A). The internal shell of the ramshorn cuttlefish is visible through its outer skin (B).

blend in with the seabed. Tiny structures called chromatophores lie in the common cuttlefish's dermis—a deep-lying layer of skin—where they contract or dilate when stimulated.

Multicolored courtship rituals

Like all members of the class Cephalopoda, cuttlefishes perform courtship rituals before mating. The male cuttlefish attracts his intended mate by changing color several times and displaying his hectocotylus—an arm used for transferring sperm to the female's reproductive opening. During mating, the male uses his hectocotylus to insert spermatophores (capsules containing sperm) through the female's funnel, which contains the reproductive organs. After a few hours, the female cuttlefish leaves the male and lays her fertilized eggs on seaweed or coral. Cuttlefish eggs resemble bunches of black grapes.

The genus *Sepiola*

Cuttlefishes of the genus *Sepiola* have short bodies with two rounded, well-developed fins. All sepiolids use their fins as rudders for steering, and some use them for both steering and swimming—providing themselves with additional means of propulsion through the water. While most sepiolid cuttlefishes live in the pelagic zone, some, such as the Mediterranean species *Heteroteuthis dispar* and the African whip sepiolid, *Austrorossia mastigaphora*, live at great depths beneath the ocean's surface. Like other cuttlefish genera, the sepiolid ejects a cloud of ink when attacked. If, however, the attacker continues his offensive, the sepiolid attempts to bury itself in the seabed, shifting sand with blasts of water from its funnel.

Squids

Squids are coleoids with torpedo-shaped, streamlined bodies and well-developed posterior fins; their suckers differ from those of other coleoids in that they contain short, curved hooks. Unlike the often solitary cuttlefishes, squids frequently travel in shoals in pursuit of fishes such as sardines. Their internal shells are reduced to thin, membranous structures that resemble the gladius, or Roman short sword. Oceanic or "flying" squid species—which propel themselves through the water's surface—include some of the fastest of all marine invertebrates. Squids comprise 25 families within the two suborders of the order Teuthoidea.

The family Loliginidae

The family Loliginidae contains squids with slender, elongated bodies and two triangular fins at their tail ends. Loliginids include some of the most numerous squids, such as the common squid (*Loligo vulgaris*), the forbes squid (*L. forbesi*), the long-tailed squid (*Alloteuthis subulata*) and *A. media*; all four species inhabit the Mediterranean Sea. The Atlantic square-toothed squid (*Loligo pealei*) lives in the eastern coastal waters of North America, while the opalescent squid (*L. opalescens*) inhabits the west coast.

The reef squid (*Sepioteuthis sepioidea*)—an inhabitant of the Indian Ocean and the seas around Central America—differs from other loliginids in structure: it has a flattened body with lateral fins along the length of its mantle. The reef squid lives on or near the seabed, where its coloration—yellow or brown with red markings—provides camouflage against predators.

Massed mating shoals

For two or three days each year, tens of thousands of loliginid squids congregate in huge mating shoals near coastal areas. The different species use various methods of communication to indicate their intention to mate. For example, the male opalescent squid (*Loligo opalescence*)—a pale-colored coleoid of no more

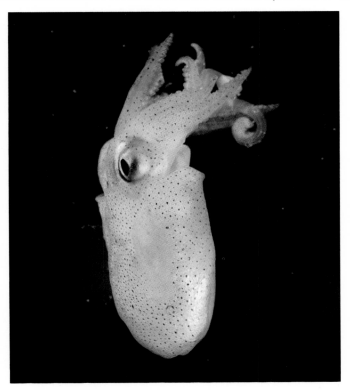

ABOVE **Cuttlefishes of the short-bodied genus *Sepiola* emit light by means of photobacteria—luminous bacteria that live in glands on either side of the ink** sac. **When attacked, sepiolids eject thousands of photobacteria with their defensive ink, dazzling their enemies with clouds of light.**

MOLLUSKS
CLASSIFICATION: 19

Cephalopods (2)

The order Teuthoidea is the second order in the cephalopod subclass Coleoidea, and contains all the true squids, of which there are probably over 300 species. They are divided into two suborders and 25 families. The suborder Myopsida contains four families: the Loliginidae contains all the common squids, such as the common squid, *Loligo vulgaris*; the Pickfordiateuthidae, which includes the Caribbean pygmy squid, *Pickfordiateuthis pulchella*; the Lepidoteuthidae with just a single species, the scaled squid, *Lepidoteuthis grimaldi*; and the Architeuthidae whose members include the giant squid, *Architeuthis dux*, of the Atlantic Ocean, which may grow to over 60 ft. long.

The second suborder of squids is the Oegopsida. Its 23 families include the Lycoteuthidae (containing the jeweled squid, *Lycoteuthis diadema*; the Enoploteuthidae (with the Atlantic hook-tentacled squid, *Abraliopsis atlantica*; the Octopodoteuthidae (including the tentacle-less squid, *Octopoteuthis sicula*; the Histioteuthidae, which has the Mediterranean odd-eyed squid, *Histioteuthis bonnellii*; the Ommastrephidae (flying squids); and the Cranchiidae, which contains the stalk-eyed squid, *Bathothauma lyrommas*, of the southern Atlantic Ocean.

The third grouping in the cephalopod subclass Coleoidea is the order Vampyromorpha, which has just one species, the vampire squid, *Vampyroteuthis infernalis*, of tropical and subtropical seas.

than 4.7-5 in. in length—turns bright red to demonstrate to females his readiness to mate. The male squid takes the initiative during mating, grasping the female from below or from the side, while his specially adapted leg, or hectocotylus, places spermatophores in the female's reproductive opening.

After mating, the entire loliginid shoal sinks slowly to the seabed, where the females lay their eggs. The eggs link together in long strings of about 100 each. Every female lays 20 or so strings, attaching the eggs' sticky surfaces to seaweed or rocks on the seabed. The young squids hatch approximately three weeks later, softening the eggshells with enzyme secretions and breaking through the weakened sections with their beak-like mouthparts.

The smallest squids

The smallest squid species belong to the family Pickfordiateuthidae: for example, the Caribbean pygmy squid, *Pickfordiateuthis pulchella*,—an inhabitant of Florida's coastline—seldom grows to more than 0.8 in. in length.

ABOVE Large populations of Caribbean reef squids, *Sepioteuthis sepioidea*, inhabit the shallow, tropical waters above the Atlantic's coral beds. Although most squids reach no more than 31 in. in length, some deep-water species grow to huge sizes. For example, on November 30, 1861, the French gunboat *Alecton* reputedly discovered a squid measuring over 75 ft. in length. Unfortunately, the *Alecton* harpooned the squid to death, destroying all evidence in support of its claim. The largest squid on official record measured 65 ft. 7 in. from the tip of its mantle to the end of its tentacles; it probably weighed over a ton.

The family Lepidoteuthidae contains the single squid species *Lepidoteuthis grimaldi*—the only cephalopod to have a body covering of scales. Until the 1980s, the only evidence of the species' existence was the rear part of a single specimen's body, vomited up by a mortally wounded sperm whale near the Azores.

Giant invertebrates

The teuthoidean suborder Oegopsida embraces 23 families of squids. One, the Architeuthidae, contains

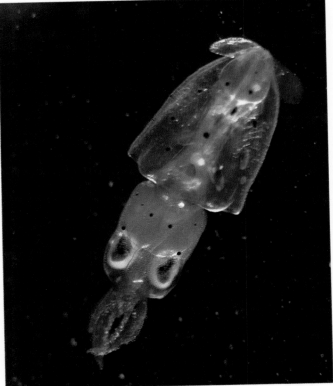

over 20 species, including the largest of all invertebrate animals. The most common Atlantic species is the giant *Architeuthis dux*, which may reach lengths of more than 60 ft. and weigh over a ton. The average architeuthid, however, measures between 20 and 45 ft. and weighs approximately 660 lbs.

The jeweled squid

The family Lycoteuthidae contains several species of small squids, which measure, on average, about 4 in. in length. Its most famous species is the jeweled squid, *Lycoteuthis diadema,*—an inhabitant of the southern Atlantic—whose "jewels" consist of 22 luminous organs concentrated mainly around its eyes and on the lower half of its body. The squid possesses additional, concealed, luminous organs within its mantle cavity. It is one of the few mollusks to have light-emitting organs on its tentacles. Some of the "jewels" on the animal's transparent body shine with bright red radiance, others with a bright blue light.

Moonlight mollusks

Squids of the two genera *Abralia* and *Abraliopsis,* within the family Enoploteuthidae, utilize moonlight as a means of camouflage. Like many cephalopods, enoploteuthid squids risk detection by predators when they enter well-lit open water. To minimize the risk of attack, the squids remain at depths of at least 2000 ft. during daylight hours. Under cover of darkness, however, they rise to between 150 and 350 ft. below the water's surface. If the moon illuminates their outlines, they emit a soft light that blends with the moonlight, thereby breaking up their bodies' outlines. Enoploteuthid squids can adjust the colors and strengths of their luminosity to suit prevailing light conditions.

Hooked tentacles

The Atlantic hook-tentacled squid, *Abraliopsis atlantica*, lives in the deepest waters of the tropical and subtropical Atlantic; its arms and tentacles bear huge, backward-pointing hooks that resemble the claws of birds of prey. When hunting, the squid extends its tentacles and ensnares its prey in its hooks, preventing any chance of escape. The Atlantic hook-tentacled squid evolved its special means of prey capture in order to cope with the scarcity of prey in its deep water habitat.

Squids of the family Octopodoteuthidae lose their two tentacles when they reach adulthood. Their bodies

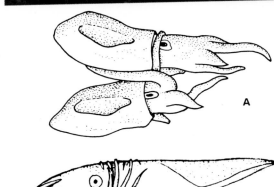

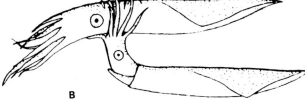

TOP Newly hatched squids usually measure about 0.2 in. in length. The two green blobs above the creature's arms are its half-formed eyes.
ABOVE During mating, the male squid uses his hectocotylan arm to insert a spermatophore into the female's reproductive opening (A). Common cuttlefish of the genus *Sepia* mate in a similar fashion (B).
PAGES 2864-2865 The ocean squid, *Onychia caribbaea,* steers through the water with its well-developed hind fins.

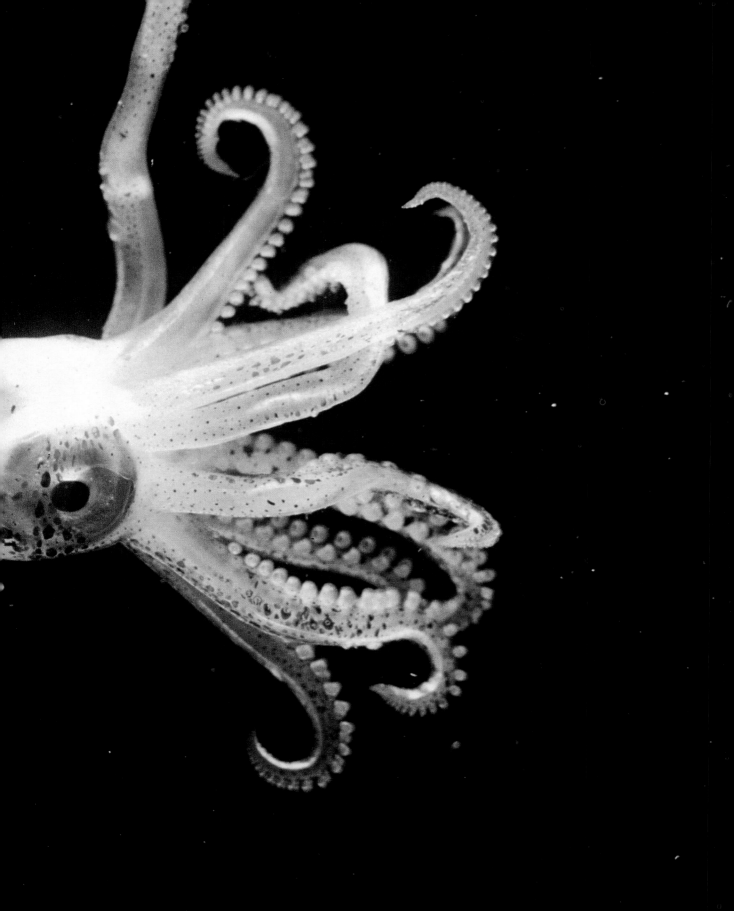

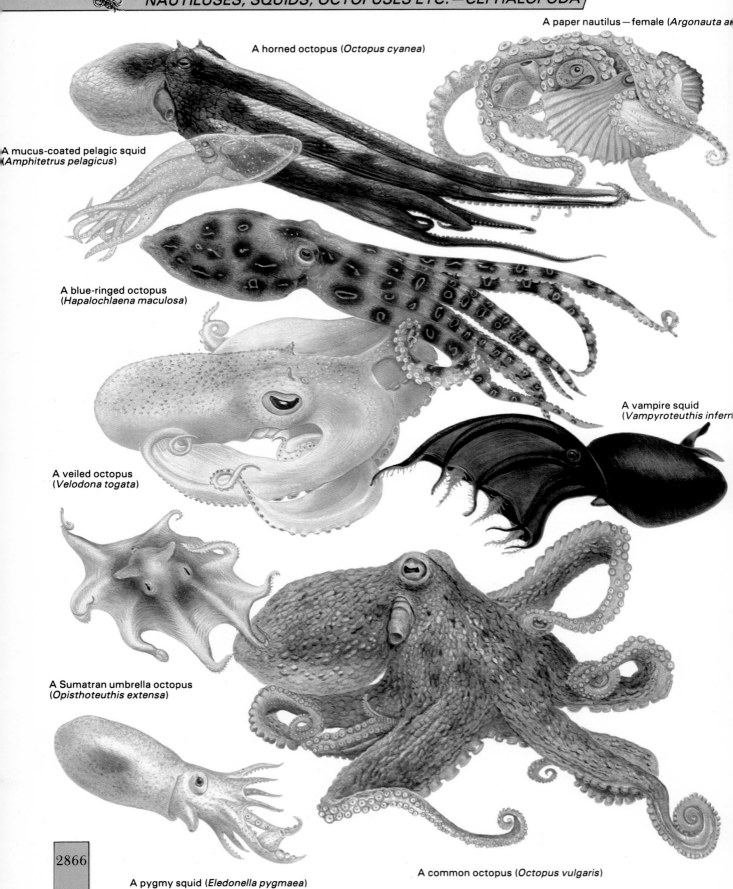

A horned octopus (*Octopus cyanea*)

A paper nautilus—female (*Argonauta a*

A mucus-coated pelagic squid
(*Amphitetrus pelagicus*)

A blue-ringed octopus
(*Hapalochlaena maculosa*)

A veiled octopus
(*Velodona togata*)

A vampire squid
(*Vampyroteuthis infern*

A Sumatran umbrella octopus
(*Opisthoteuthis extensa*)

A pygmy squid (*Eledonella pygmaea*)

A common octopus (*Octopus vulgaris*)

bear fins that comprise as much as 70 percent of the mantle length. The tentacle-less squid *Octopoteuthis sicula* inhabits the Mediterranean and the Indian Ocean.

Odd-eyed squids

Squids of the family Histioteuthidae inhabit all regions of the world. Their eyes show different types of development: the right eyes are large, while the left eyes are smaller, but more sensitive to light. The arrangement of a histioteuthid's eyes causes the large, right eye to look upward and receive light from the surface, while the left eye points forward to pick up light emitted by other marine animals. Odd-eyed squids of the species *Histioteuthis heteropsis* and *H. corona* inhabit the Indo-Pacific area, while *H. meleagroteuthis* lives in the Mediterranean. The Mediterranean odd-eyed squid *H. bonnellii* has a membrane that joins the lower lengths of its arms together, forming a web-like structure for catching prey.

Flying squids

Members of the squid family Ommastrephidae inhabit most of the world's seas. They are known as flying squids, or arrow squids, since they have the ability to leap through the water's surface. Well-known species are the American *Ommasthrephes bartramii* and *Ornithoteuthis volatilis*, a Japanese species that has the power to leap clear out of the water.

Flying squids usually feed communally, hunting shoals of fishes in large groups. When hunting, they swim tail-first (with their arms and tentacles streaming out behind them), at depths of 15-25 ft., rushing up to the surface in attempts to grab their elusive prey. Squids will chase fishes through various depths and even seize their victims in midair, spinning their bodies around in order to make use of their arms.

Plankton feeders

Squids of the family Chiroteuthidae have well-developed tentacles covered with adhesive "buttons" of flesh for catching plankton. One such species, *Chiroteuthis picteti*, has tentacles that grow to greater lengths than its body; it inhabits the Indo-Pacific area. The Mediterranean species *Chiroteuthis veranyi*—a similar chiroteuthid squid—does not exceed 6 in.

Although most members of the order Teuthidea are competent swimmers—rivaling fast fishes and whales

ABOVE The boreal squid, *Alloteuthis subulata*, inhabits the North Sea between the Shetland Islands and southern Norway. It is prey to a wide range of predators, including humans, who value it as a source of protein.

in speed—members of the teuthid family Cranchiidae do not swim, but allow themselves to be carried by water currents, holding themselves vertically with their heads pointing downward. The cranchiid's mantle cavity contains a sac filled with an ammonia-based liquid that is lighter than seawater—the liquid regulates the body's weight so that it equals that of the surrounding water and thereby prevents the squid from sinking. Cranchiids are further distinguished by their stalked eyes and absent tentacles: the tentacles disappeared through evolution, since they were not required for the squids' diet of plankton. The southern Altantic species *Bathothauma lyromma* is typical of the order Cranchiidae, except for its backward-looking eyes.

The vampire squid

The coleoid order Vampyromorpha contains the single species *Vampyroteuthis infernalis*, or vampire squid—a creature that resembles, in parts, both squid and octopus. Members of the species prey on small fishes and seldom exceed 12 in. in length.

ABOVE For only a few days each year, squids of the family Loliginidae gather together in mating shoals of tens of thousands of individuals. During mating, the male squids grasp the females from below or from the side.

The vampire squid has eight arms and—in place of tentacles—the vestigial (diminished due to lack of use) remains of what were once two additional arms. A membrane joins all the arms along their lengths as far as the tips. The membrane's interior surface is black, while the outside has a reddish black coloration. The species owes its vampire-like appearance to its two large, red eyes and two large, luminous organs near its fins—the luminous organs have lids that allow them to close.

Octopuses

Octopuses within the order Octopoda (the last order in the class Cephalopoda) have eight arms and derive their name from the Greek *octo* meaning "eight" and *pous* meaning "foot." They have eight arms that are joined at their bases by a web and surround a beaked mouth. Octopuses differ from the related squids and cuttlefishes in that they lack two long tentacles, and their suckers, which run the entire length of their arms, are not strengthened by the horny rings seen in the suckers of squids.

The order Octopoda is divided into two suborders: the Incirrata, which includes the common octopus, and the Cirrata, which includes the deepwater eyeless octopus. Like the vampire squid, cirratan octopuses have two rows of tendrils alongside the suckers on their arms.

Deep-sea octopuses

Only five specimens of the deepwater eyeless octopus, *Cirrothauma murrayi*, have ever been caught, although the species has often been filmed by cameras situated on the seabed. It normally swims with its head pointing downward, propelling itself through the water by contracting the large web that almost reaches to the tips of its arms. Besides the suckers on the undersides of its arms, it has rows of filaments that are thought to be used for catching food particles. Its transparent body has the texture of a jellyfish.

The umbrella octopuses of the genus *Opisthoteuthis* have flattened bodies—an adaptation to a life spent exclusively on the seabed. They are well camouflaged and only the large, bulging pairs of eyes on their backs are visible when the octopuses are lying on the seabed.

Octopuses belonging to the suborder Incirrata have suckers on their eight arms, but lack tendrils. They also lack shells, although the common octopus has the remnants of one. The suborder Incirrata is divided into nine families, including the Bolitaenidae, the Octopodidae, the Ocythoidae and the Argonautidae.

The common octopus is a predator that feeds mostly on crustaceans. It usually hides camouflaged among vegetation or rocks, ambushing its victims as they pass by. It brings its prey as close as possible to its mouth and immobilizes it with a poisonous liquid that it secretes from its salivary glands. Although the surrounding seawater dilutes the poison, it remains strong enough to paralyze the octopus' prey, which, after a brief but violent struggle, becomes still. The common octopus then carries it into its lair and slowly eats it. The octopus uses its tentacles to remove every piece of meat from the crustacean's shell, leaving the exoskeleton untouched. The common octopus does not always wait for its prey to pass by; sometimes it entices the prey into its lair. While remaining hidden, the octopus puts one wriggling tentacle out. Small crabs and other crustaceans that are attracted to this strange wriggling object are caught by the suckers on the octopus' tentacles.

Two Australian species of octopus, the blue-ringed octopus, *Haplochlaena lupulata*, and the species *H. maculosa*, secrete a highly potent poison that can kill prey or other animals in the vicinity without direct contact being made. These octopuses have been known to bite and kill humans. Unlike other octopuses that camouflage themselves to avoid their predators,

MOLLUSKS CLASSIFICATION: 20

Cephalopods (3)

The fourth and final cephalopod order in the subclass Coleoidea is that of the octopuses, Octopoda. It is divided into two suborders, 12 families and some 200 species. The suborder Cirrata contains the deepwater eyeless octopus, *Cirrothauma murrayi*, and the umbrella octopuses (genus *Opisthoteuthis*). The second suborder, Incirrata, is divided into some 170 species and nine families. These include the Bolitaenidae (containing the pygmy squid, *Eledonella pygmaea*); the Octopodidae, which contains the common octopus, *Octopus vulgaris*, the blue-ringed octopus, *Hapolochlaena lupulata*, the giant Pacific octopus, *O. dofleini*, the white-spotted octopus, *O. macropus*, the small-horned octopus, *O. salutii*, and the musk octopus, *Eledone moschata*; the Ocythoidae, containing the pelagic paper nautilus, *Ocythoe tuberculata*, of Mediterranean, Atlantic and Pacific waters; and the Argonautidae (genus *Argonauta*, such as the paper nautilus, *Argonauta argo*, and the lesser-ribbed paper nautilus, *A. hians*.

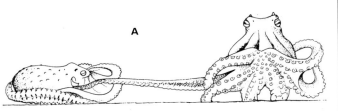

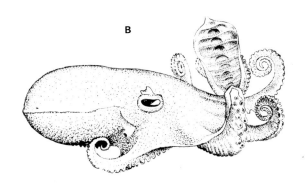

such as moray eels, crabs and sea perch, these species display aposematic, or warning, colors. They have large, bluish circles on their backs and arms that serve to warn other animals that they are dangerous.

Changing color

Octopuses change color to blend in with their surroundings, although color change is also associated with their emotional state. When attacking its prey, the common octopus continually changes color. When injured or frightened, it changes to white, and when it is angry, for example when it is taken out of the water, it turns bright red. When fighting, the attacking octopus is a reddish brown color, while the animal on the defensive pales in color, taking on a darker color when it counterattacks.

Simple courtship

An octopus will only tolerate the presence of another member of the same species near it during courtship and mating. Although elaborate color

TOP The giant Pacific octopus, *Octopus dolfeini*, inhabits the waters off the Californian coastline. Unlike cuttlefishes and squids, octopuses do not have teeth, hooks or hard rings on their suckers. The suckers usually originate near the mouth and run down most of the arm's length in pairs.
ABOVE The male octopus possesses a hectocotylus—a third arm adapted for transferring sperm to the female's reproductive opening (A). The hectocotylus' tip spreads into a wide, spatula-shaped area that supports the spermatophore during mating (B). The male first caresses the female at arm's length, before inserting his "spatula" into her mantle cavity.

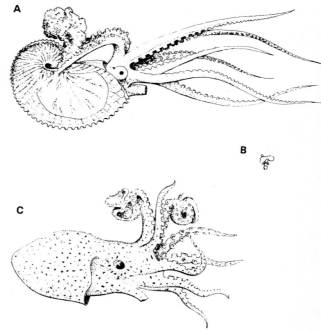

ABOVE The female paper nautilus, *Argonauta argo*, secretes a shell from special glands on her legs; the shell protects the nautilus' eggs until they hatch. Nautiluses live at depths of between 350 and 1600 ft.

ABOVE RIGHT The drawings demonstrate the difference in size between the female paper nautilus (A) and the male (B). Without her egg-protecting shell, the female paper nautilus resembles most octopus species (C).

FAR RIGHT An octopus' lair — usually a crevice between rocks — lies in the middle of its territory. The octopus is highly defensive of its territory, and will often defend it to the death, rather than relinquish it to another member of its species.

changes take place during courtship, they do not perform a courtship ritual. The female is only fertilized once in her life. After a successful mating she lays thousands of eggs, each in an oval capsule, in long strings. She attaches them by short stalks to the roof of her lair. While the eggs are incubating, the female never leaves them unattended. She often cleans both her lair and the eggs with her arms, or blows water over them using her funnel.

The musk octopus

The musk octopus derives its name from the musk-like odor that its body releases, even after it has dried out completely. It is widespread in the Mediterranean, where large quantities are often caught in nets that are dragged along the muddy seabed. The musk octopus is less sedentary and more sociable than the common octopus, and eats only dead animals. It occurs along the Atlantic coasts of Europe.

Paper nautiluses

The families Argonautidae and Ocythoidae contain only a few species that have certain interesting features. The pelagic paper nautilus of the family Ocythoidae is a widespread species that occurs in the Mediterranean Sea and in the Pacific and Atlantic oceans.

The genus *Argonauta* of the family Argonautidae contains the paper nautilus, the lesser paper nautilus and the granulated paper nautilus, all of which occur in tropical seas, while the paper nautilus also inhabits the Mediterranean. Male and female paper nautiluses vary greatly in size; males measure only 0.8-1.2 in. in length, while females can be up to 8 in. long.

The female paper nautilus broods her eggs in an unusual pouch. From two modified arms she secretes a large, thin, shell-like case. The pseudo-shell is not connected to the nautilus. The female holds it with her two upper arms and sits in it, protecting her eggs.